D0146825

Recent Titles from Quorum Books

Interpersonal Communication for Technically Trained Managers:
A Guide to Skills and Techniques
Dale E. Jackson

Improved Business Planning Using Competitive Intelligence
Carolyn M. Vella and John J. McGonagle, Jr.

Retail Marketing Strategy: Planning, Implementation, and Control
A. Coskun Samli

Venturing Abroad: Innovation by U.S. Multinationals
Frank Clayton Schuller

Microcomputers, Corporate Planning, and Decision Support Systems
The WEFA Group, David J. Gianturco, and Nariman Behravesh, editors

The Investment Side of Corporate Cash Management
Robert T. March

A Practical Approach to International Operations
Michael Gendron

Exceptional Entrepreneurial Women: Strategies for Success
Russel R. Taylor

Collective Bargaining and Impasse Resolution in the Public Sector
David A. Dilts and William J. Walsh

New Directions in MIS Management: A Guide for the 1990s
Robert J. Thierauf

The Labor Lawyer's Guide to the Rights and Responsibilities
of Employee Whistleblowers
Stephen M. Kohn and Michael D. Kohn

Strategic Organization Planning: Downsizing for Survival
David C. Dougherty

Joint Venture Partner Selection: Strategies for Developed Countries
J. Michael Geringer

Sustainable Corporate Growth

Sustainable Corporate Growth

A Model and Management Planning Tool

John J. Clark
Thomas C. Chiang
and
Gerard T. Olson

Q

Quorum Books

New York • Westport, Connecticut • London

Library of Congress Cataloging-in-Publication Data

Clark, John J.
    Sustainable corporate growth : a model and management planning
tool / John J. Clark, Thomas C. Chiang, and Gerard T. Olson.
        p. cm.
    Bibliography: p.
    Includes index.
    ISBN 0-89930-238-6 (lib. bdg. : alk. paper)
    1. Corporations—Growth. 2. Corporations—Finance. 3. Budget in
business. I. Chiang, Thomas C. II. Olson, Gerard T. III. Title.
HD2746.C56   1989
658.4'06—dc 19   88-6755

British Library Cataloguing in Publication Data is available.

Library of Congress Catalog Card Number: 88-6755

ISBN: 0-89930-238-6

First published in 1989 by Quorum Books

Greenwood Press, Inc.
88 Post Road West, Westport, Connecticut 06881

Printed in the United States of America

∞

The paper used in this book complies with the
Permanent Paper Standard issued by the National
Information Standards Organization (Z39.48-1984).

10   9   8   7   6   5   4   3   2   1

Copyright Acknowledgments

The authors and publisher gratefully acknowledge permission to use the following:

V. Govindarajan and John K. Shank, "Cash Sufficiency: The Missing Link in Strategic Planning." Reprinted with permission from *Corporate Accounting.* Copyright © Winter 1984, Warren, Gorham, & Lamont Inc., 210 South St., Boston, MA, 02111. All rights reserved.

Charles W. Kyd, "Managing the Financial Demand of Growth," *Management Accounting,* December 1981.

Michael J. Gombola and J. Edward Ketz, "A Note on Cash Flow and Classification Patterns of Financial Ratios," *Accounting Review,* January 1983. Permission granted by the authors and the American Accounting Association.

Robert C. Higgins, "How Much Growth Can a Firm Afford?" *Financial Management,* Fall 1987. Permission granted by the author and the Financial Management Association.

Dana Johnson, "The Behavior of Financial Structure and Sustainable Growth in an Inflationary Environment," *Financial Management,* Autumn 1981. Permission granted by the author and the Financial Management Association.

Evsey D. Domar, "Expansion and Employment," *American Economic Review,* vol. XXXVII, no. 1, March 1947. With permission of the American Economic Association.

Robert C. Higgins and Roger A. Kerin, "Managing the Growth-Financial Policy Nexus in Retailing," *Journal of Retailing,* vol. 59, no. 3, Fall 1983.

CONTENTS

EXHIBITS

PREFACE

This book is about growth and particularly about the management of growth in the business firm. Economists have long struggled with the problem in the macroeconomy. They early recognized that growth implied change, and change, some measure of instability. A few economists diagnosed business cycles as primarily caused by fluctuations in the rate of economic growth. Others averred that a consistently positive rate of growth could potentially generate as many economic and sociological dislocations as a persistently negative rate of growth. Out of these conundrums evolved the quest to define a growth rate that would promote economic stability at a tolerable level of unemployment. Because the perspective was that of macroeconomics, the economists' solutions did not address the issue of structural unemployment as old industries declined and new ones rose to dominate the industrial landscape. Dealing with comprehensive variables, the economists could broadly define equilibrium as the point where total savings and investment balanced to yield a growth rate that assured a specified level of employment. If the growth rate actually resulting was not compatible with the employment goal, then fiscal and monetary policies could provide the needed stimuli.

Nonetheless, despite the difference in the level of planning, the body of economic growth theory has much to contribute to business enterprise in managing expansion (or contraction) to assure the survivability of the firm. Similar to the macroplanner, the firm monitors growth in sales to avoid materiel and personnel bottlenecks that are damaging to its reputation. Sales growth, too, must be compatible with the criteria for managing the financial structure of the firm. Apropos of the financial structure, the resources on

hand or available have to underwrite both current sales and the requirements of future sales. The latter necessitates expenditures on which
there is no immediate return. Thus to maintain internal balance, the firm
has to correlate two budgets: the working capital budget relating to current
sales and the capital budget relating to future sales. Accordingly, the firm
achieves equilibrium when the funds available for investment equal the
funds required for investment, a position comparable to the macro-
equilibrium of savings and investment. Finally, as with the macroproblem,
this equilibrium can occur at different growth rates, but there is only one
that may be considered optimal.

It is useful to note that growth problems complicate the structuring of
business combinations. The type of consideration paid to affect a merger
reshapes, in most instances, the financial structure of the reorganized entity. In turn, the revised financial structure impacts the growth rate options
of management. If the affordable growth rate post-combination is less
than the pre-combination level, the combination may have to revise its
financial structure should enhanced growth be an objective of the merger.
The number of mergers subsequently undergoing financial restructuring
would suggest that too often a careful analysis of the terms of combination
in relation to post-merger performance had not been made.

To the preceding comments we must add a word of caution. Neither for
the economist dealing with the wealth creation issues of society nor for the
manager striving to provide a product or service is the calculation of a
desirable growth rate an exercise in statics. Both live in a dynamic environment buffeted by forces beyond their immediate control. And there is
always the factor of time. Variables do not move with the precision anticipated in mathematical derivations. Leads and lags appear and impose a
need for flexibility in decision making. Thus, for the economist and the
manager, the estimation of an optimal rate of growth is a bench mark of
what feasibility can be accomplished, not a prescription of what must be
accomplished. As events unfold, the actual growth rate may trend to a
higher or lower level. It then behooves the decision maker to take correc-
tive action, if that is necessary to maintain internal balance.

In conclusion, the growth models discussed in this book are illustrated, to
the extent possible, by the use of corporate data taken from SEC 10K reports
and annual financial statements. For this "digging" and analysis we are in-
debted to many graduate students of Drexel University's College of Business
and Administration and in particular to Robert Gold of FMC Corporation;
Amelia Maurizio, Assistant to the Vice-President for Academic Affairs at
Drexel; as well as Sallie Anderson, Jan Jaksina, Don Kutch, and Zaher Zan-
tout (American University of Beirut). For the judgements involved in modeling the data the authors bear the burden of responsibility.

PART I

CONCEPTUAL BASIS OF FIRM GROWTH ANALYSIS

1

MACROECONOMICS AND SUSTAINABLE GROWTH

The history of economic thought attests to the discipline's preoccupation with growth and stabilization. That the two goals might be fundamentally at odds was a paradox eventually bridged by the exposition of models that allowed for balanced growth through an equilibrium of key variables. Although the models are aesthetically pleasing to their authors, the persistence of the conundrum in practice testifies that a final solution has not been reached, if indeed it can be. After all, growth is endemically disruptive, and stabilization implies continuity in social and economic relationships.

Classical economists tended to think in terms of long-term growth of a self-limiting character. The law of diminishing returns is per se a kind of growth model. Smith and Ricardo believed that only in a growing economy could wages be kept above the sustainable level. But the Reverend Malthus direly predicted a natural propensity of the population to increase and press upon the means of subsistence, causing famine, wars, and social disruption. In the fatalistic and pessimistic pronouncements of the early English Classicalists, we see the hint at least that too much growth in a factor of production can be as destructive as no growth. Growth for the sake of growth is not a viable policy, as amply demonstrated by the experience of society and individual business units.

Classical economics also contained the germs of present-day growth models. Smith separated aggregate demand into consumer and investment goods components, while the French economist J. B. Say, more optimistically inclined, argued that supply equals demand *ex ante* and that a higher rate of savings will subsequently generate a greater aggregate output. Disequilibrium could occur in the economy if the internal proportions of aggregate output differed from consumer preferences. However, the latter were short-term, self-correcting frictions (Sowell 1974).

Nonetheless, the instabilities of the business cycle continued to plague a century and a half of economic progress, and Classical economic theory was found wanting—in its diagnosis of events. In the long run, as Keynes observed, equilibrium is achieved when savings equaled investment. However, the equality could take place at less than full employment. If so, Keynes viewed fiscal policy as the engine to thrust the economy. He made deficit financing—a perennially attractive policy to governments—respectable and broke with the traditional laissez-faire policy by assigning government an active role in economic stabilization.

The Keynesian equilibrium between savings and investment can take place at full employment or less than full employment. In achieving and maintaining full employment, investment (I) is the crucial variable through its effect on national income (Y). But it is not total investment (I) that holds the key to higher levels of national income. It is rather the increment investment (ΔI). Domar observes:

If investment today, however large, is equal to that of yesterday, national income of today will just equal and not be any larger than that of yesterday. All this . . . is stressed here to underline the lack of symmetry between the effects of investment on productive capacity and national income. (Domar 1947)

Domar illustrates the relations by:

$$\Delta Y = \Delta I \times 1/(\alpha) \tag{1.1}$$

where

ΔY = the change in national income;
ΔI = the change in investment;
α = marginal propensity to save;
$1/\alpha$ = the multiplier effect of investment.

Since annual increase in potential capacity is equal to $I\sigma$ (where σ represents the rate of increase in capacity) and national income equals its productive capacity at full employment, what is the rate of growth in income and capacity that will maintain this position? For Domar, it is

$$\Delta I \times 1/(\alpha) = I\sigma, \tag{1.2}$$

which yields

$$\Delta I/I = \alpha\sigma. \tag{1.3}$$

The left side denotes the annual percentage growth of investment. This must equal $\alpha\sigma$ to sustain full employment. Domar states:

To summarize, the maintenance of a continuous state of full employment requires that *investment and income grow at a constant annual percentage (or compound interest) rate* equal to the product of marginal propensity to save and the average (to put it briefly) productivity of investment.

This result can be made clearer by a numerical example. Let $\sigma = 25$ percent per year, $\alpha = 12$ percent, and $Y = 150$ billions per year. If full employment is to be maintained, an amount equal to $150 \times (12/100)$ should be invested. This will raise productivity by the amount invested times σ, i.e., by $150 \times (12/100) \times (25/100)$ and national income will have to rise by the same annual amount. But the relative rise in income will equal the absolute increase divided by the income itself, i.e.,

$$(150 \times \frac{12}{100} \times \frac{25}{100}) \times \frac{1}{150} = \frac{12}{100} \times \frac{25}{100}$$

$$= \alpha\sigma = 3\%.$$

This brief survey of macroeconomic equilibrium theory is intended to show that concept of balanced growth is not a novel one and its application to the business is a logical extension of a long-standing search for stability. The business firms are in equilibrium, as we shall demonstrate in the following chapters, when the Funds Required for Investment (FRI) equal the Funds Available for Investment (FAI) at a given growth rate in sales.

MODERN ECONOMIC GROWTH THEORY

At the macro level the theory of economic growth concerns the long-term trend or the potential growth path of the economy. Assuming that monetary and fiscal policies can be effectively used to keep the economy near full capacity, the theorists then concentrate on the full-employment path. Because output production depends on inputs such as capital, labor, land, technology, and entrepreneurship, the growth of output in turn depends on the growth of these inputs. Given the endowed land, the economists then focus on the accumulation of capital and the incrementation of the labor force, as well as the factors that can possibly influence these inputs for promoting production.

The growth rate of the labor force is usually assumed to be exogenously determined; the output growth is carried on by the growth of capital and the technical progress. The technical advancement is essentially brought out by research and development, which is an investment in human capital, while the capital increment is achieved by business physical investment. Thus the investments play a crucial role in the growth of the economy. The question is how are the investment projects financed? Obviously, one major source of the funds is the contribution of savings from the business sector, which holds financial assets. The financial intermediaries transfer the funds between the lenders (households) and the borrowers (investors). It is likely that the economy does not have sufficient funds to finance its investments projects. This is especially true for the economy when the saving propensity is low. One possible solution is to obtain funds from the external source by borrowing capital from foreign countries. However, this scheme may impede the long-run growth, owing to the continual payment of interest for the external borrowing. The commitment of interest payments in the later periods represents that part of future income that will have to be drained from the economy. This will reduce the funds available for further investment opportunity. This scheme can be justifiable only if its return exceeds the cost of interest.

To see the dynamics of economic growth, we assume that the economy starts with an endowment of output at time t. Assume that the household sector, based on intertemporal choice, is willing to enlarge the future consumption set by sacrificing current consumption through a well-specified consumption function. In a well-developed financial system this can be achieved by purchasing financial assets. The specific form of financial assets that the asset-holders would like to absorb into their portfolio depends on the required rate of return and the preference toward risk. In this respect, the funds are supplied by the household sector or through the financial intermediaries.

On the other hand, the entrepreneurs are willing to borrow the funds to engage in physical investments, motivated by the possiblity of earning a profit large enough to cover the cost of capital and to reward the risk taking. In the aggregate sense, the investment is equal to the saving. If a discrepancy should exist, the difference is assumed to be eliminated by an appropriate monetary or fiscal policy.

The business investments thus add new capital to the inherited capital stock of the economy. The enlarged capital stock, passed on to the next period, $t + 1$, then combines with the larger labor force in $t + 1$ to produce an increased level of output through the production function. This process will continue to be repeated. That is, the economy will not consume all the output and will engage in savings and investments, and so on. Now, the questions for the growth model are whether or not this process will naturally settle down to a stable growth path, which is the optimal path for the economy. The answers are provided by the neoclassical analysis. The source of instability embodied in a model such as Harrod and Domar's stems from the rigidities of the production function, which assumes a constant output capital ratio and a constant capital-labor ratio. This assumption, together with the constant saving ratio and the fixed coefficient of labor growth rate, leaves no freedom for the economy to move toward equilibrium once the system deviates from the initial equilibrium. In particular, the equilibrium condition of the Harrod-Domar model is derived by assuming that both capital and labor will be fully employed as the economy grows. Thus, if the natural rate (labor force growth rate) exceeds the warranted rate (the output growth rate for capital fully employed), there will be an excessive labor force, thus creating unemployment. On the other hand, if the growth rate of capital exceeds that of the labor force, this will bid down the productivity of redundant capital and the profit rate to zero, discouraging the investment. In either case, the state of the economy violates the initial full employment condition, and the growth path tends to move away from equilibrium.

Recognizing the rigidity of the fixed combination of capital and labor in the production process and the likelihood of creating an unstable growth path, neoclassical economists alter the production function by permitting the substitution of capital and labor in the production mode. With this modification they show that the equilibrium is expected to be restored by means of an appropriate adjustment in the capital-labor ratio.

Because many possible combinations of the capital-labor ratio (k) may be used in production, an equilibrium level of k should be chosen to achieve a target growth rate. The target growth rate path should be consistent with the golden rule path, the equilibrium path that maximizes per capita consumption over all time, once the economy attains that path. This path is achieved when the capital-labor ratio settles at the level where the profit rate is equal to the natural growth rate.

One should be aware that the economy at a given point of time may fall below the golden rule path. However, in the longer-time horizon, the economy is advised to move to that path. To this end the government may use an appropriate policy, say a tax instrument, to stimulate saving. In this way the current generation would have to sacrifice current consumption for the benefit of future generations. Apparently the costs to move the economy to the golden rule path should be relatively small as compared with the long-run benefits from attaining it. Based on this principle, the turnpike theorem suggests that the economy should spend most of its time staying on the turnpike (the optimal path) if the longer-time horizon is permitted.

Turnpike theorists also observe that a time preference exists between current and future incomes and consumption. Thus it is necessary to discount future incomes and consumption to their present value with an appropriate social discount rate. It follows that with a long-planning horizon, the economy should set the saving rate at the point where the profit rate, after subtracting the social discount rate, is equal to the natural rate of growth. With this condition the economy is able to settle at the golden rule path. What we should emphasize here is the concept of the optimum rather than that of the maximum. It is not wise to pursue a maximum growth by setting a maximum saving rate. A high saving rate results in sacrificing the consumption of the current generation, although it will benefit future generations. On the other hand, a low saving rate or a high consumption rate (especially with an exhausted natural resource) will inevitably cost the economy, since it will take a long time to reach the golden rule path. Apparently the selfish current generation would impede the social welfare of future generations. It is clear by now that the economy should be operated on the optimal growth path for all the times that balance both costs and benefits over intergenerations (Branson 1979).

THE GROWTH OF THE CORPORATION

It is argued that one of the objectives of the firm is to maximize its growth. This growth may be in terms of profits, the volume of sale, the size of the enterprise, or the rate of total productive assets. However, the firm also has several subgoals to be fulfilled that may limit its growth. As pointed out by Galbraith (1967) and Herendeen (1975), the firm first must pay an acceptable rate of dividends to the stockholders and then it has to promote a high level of technical competence; finally, the firm must have sufficient internal funds available for expansion.

As in the macrogrowth model, the source of internal funds for a firm is the business savings. When the planned investment spending exceeds these savings, the additional financing must come from external funds. Thus the firm's growth depends not only on the profit rate of its assets, but also on its ability to obtain additional funds and the risk associated with increased borrowing and the rising costs of maintaining the firm's rate of return on assets. From the accounting relation the firm can calculate its profit rate on the basis of sales, the prices of goods sold, and the various outlays. These microvariables are thought to be highly correlated with the fluctuations of macrovariables such as the gross national product (GNP) and general price movements. The firm's financial ability, especially in the future, depends on the cost of funds, which can be manipulated by the Federal Reserve Board's monetary policy. Thus it is important to examine the relations (and the channels) between the macroeconomic and microeconomic variables for the firm, especially the impacts of macrodisturbances on corporate growth.

MACROFLUCTUATIONS AND CORPORATE GROWTH

The impacts of macroeconomic variables on the decision making of a corporation are complex. Instead of going through a formal and tedious modeling process, we focus on a few key linkages between these two sets of variables. The key macrovariables with which we are most concerned are the GNP, the inflation rate (π), the interest rate (r), and public policies (both monetary and fiscal).

GNP Fluctuation and Corporate Growth

The effect of GNP on sales runs through the channel of the demand for product. An increase in the GNP, according to the standard Keynesian theory, will create a higher demand for consumption, which promotes the sale of products. A higher level of sales brings about a higher profit rate. This will provide new funds for acquiring additional capital goods for business expansion. Because the service of new capital will provide a stream of output extending into future periods, it is important to see whether there is sufficient demand in the future time. It follows that the information about whether an increase in the product demand is permanent or not becomes a crucial factor. Sometimes this factor depends on whether or not the economic expansion measured by the increase in the GNP is able to last a relatively long period of time. Although the current GNP, or current sales, is an important source of loanable funds for growth, expectations of future sales, which in turn form the expectations of future incomes, are more important to the firm for projecting the funds for current and future growth.

The correlation coefficient between the firm's sales and GNP fluctuations reflects the risk factor that arises from the business cycle. When the business cycle is in the upswing, the sales level in general is higher than average. The firm thus is able to accumulate more funds than in the ordinary case. As a result, the sustainable growth rate is expected to be higher. On the other hand, the firms will have less sales in the downswing of the cycle, resulting in a lower sustainable growth rate. Of course, the slowdown of the growth rate under this perspective can also be attributable to pessimistic expectations.

Inflation and Sustainable Growth

The nominal sales growth can come from either an increase in physical volume or an increase in prices. It is important in an inflationary period to differentiate the real sustainable growth rate, g_r^*, from the nominal sustainable growth rate, g^*. The difference between these two rates is the growth rate of the selling price for the product (Higgins 1981). In the absence of taxes and given a particular financial structure, it can be argued that uniform inflation has no effect on real sustainable growth. In practice, although the selling price, the wage rate, and other input costs are sensitive to general price movements, these variables do not necessarily display the same speed of adjustment. The firm may find that inflation is not neutral and has a significant effect on production, sales, profits, and the growth rate.

It is recognized that the historical cost of the depreciation and inventory accounting in the inflationary period will have to adjust; the real after-tax profits vary inversely with the inflation rate (Higgins 1981). Also, evidence shows that the debt-equity ratio is positively related to the rate of inflation. Johnson (1981) indicates that some firms, in order to avoid a decrease in the real sustainable growth rate in the presence of inflation, have to raise their debt-equity ratio. Moreover, when inflation is volatile, the firm has to adjust its financial structure to meet the goal of sustainable growth. Thus the existence of inflation forces a firm to choose between increased leverage or reduced real sustainable growth.

Interest Rates, Public Policy, and
Sustainable Growth

The influence of the interest rate on a firm's growth is due to its effect on the costs of borrowing. Because the growth of firms may be financed by funds from an external source, a higher interest rate means a high cost of funds, which would decrease the growth rate. As in the case of inflation, volatile movements of the interest rate will cause variability in the debt-equity ratio, creating instability in the firm's financial structure.

In practice, the firm has no ability to control interest rates, which are the results of the market forces of supply and demand, market expectations, the fiscal policy, and the Federal Reserve's monetary policy.

When the federal government runs into a deficit, this deficit must be financed by issuing debts or by alternative means (such as an increase in taxes). In order to attract the public to hold government securities, the government has to offer a higher return than the competing instruments provided by the business sector, crowding out the funds demanded by the private sector. This phenomenon has been called the crowding-out effect, in a sense that the government investments replace the private investments (Branson 1979; Dornbusch and Fischer 1981). If the debts are financed through the channel of monetization, the economy may appear to have an excessive amount of funds. The impact on interest rates is equivalent to the case of an expansionary monetary policy. The theory predicts that an excessive growth of the money supply will bid down the interest rates in the short run because of the liquidity effect.

In the long run, however, especially in the case of full employment, the interest rates turn higher because of anticipation of inflationary pressures from the excessive expansion in the money supply. Empirical evidence shows that the growth of the money supply and interest rates are positively correlated. The precise impacts of an expansionary monetary policy on the firm's financial structure and growth are less clear, depending on how the expectations are formed and what is the correct time to operate on the markets. An anticipated excessive growth of money supply is likely to produce higher expectations of the inflation rate and in turn a higher future interest rate. Accordingly, the firm will have to adjust its financial structure and/or its sustainable growth rate.

SUMMARY

This chapter surveys macroeconomic growth theory and the component variables as a background for our principal interest, sustainable growth in the business firm. We have seen that firm growth draws on these broader conceptions of how the economy grows and how the economy affects the behavior of the firm. We now focus our interest on the firm.

REFERENCES

Branson, William H. *Macroeconomic Theory and Policy*. New York: Harper & Row, 1979.

Domar, Evsey D. "Expansion and Employment," *The American Economic Review* (March 1947), pp. 34–55.

Dornbusch, Rudiger, and Stanley Fischer. *Macro-Economics*. New York: McGraw-Hill, 1981.

Galbraith, John K. *The New Industrial State*. Boston, Mass.: Houghton-Mifflin, 1967.

Herendeen, James B. *The Economics of the Corporate Economy*. New York: Dunellen, 1975.

Higgins, Robert C. "How Much Growth Can a Firm Afford?" *Financial Management*, Fall 1977, pp. 7–16.

_____ . "Sustainable Growth Under Inflation," *Financial Management*, Autumn 1981, pp. 36–40.

Johnson, Dana J. "The Behavior of Financial Structure and Sustainable Growth in an Inflationary Environment," *Financial Management*, Autumn 1981, pp. 30–35.

Sowell, Thomas. *Classical Economics Reconsidered*. Princeton, N.J.: Princeton University Press, 1974.

2

FIRM SUSTAINABLE GROWTH

A goal of the strategic planning process is the effective management of the firm's growth. The growth objectives can be described in terms of market share or overall growth in sales. However stated, the growth objectives should take into consideration the factors beyond and within the firm's control.

Factors beyond the firm's control include macroeconomic factors. There are two categories of macroeconomic forces that may affect the firm. First, the national environment, which includes the country's level of gross national product (GNP), interest rates, and inflation rate, the efficiency of its financial system, the degree of foreign competition, and the stability of the political environment, can have a profound influence on the growth in the firm's markets during the planning period. Because the firm is unable to control or influence these factors, the decision makers are relegated to forecasting their effects.

Second, for multinational firms, the international environment can affect the growth rates of its markets. Forces whose effects management must estimate include exchange rates, trade barriers, cultural differences, and, perhaps most important, the political environment.

The macroeconomic environment affects the growth of the markets in which the firm operates, whereas the microeconomic environment can affect not only the growth of the markets, but also each firm's market share. The structure of the markets is perhaps the most important microeconomic factor influencing the growth in the firm's market share and the growth of the markets in which it operates. In the economics literature market structures are characterized as either perfectly competitive, monopolistically competitive, oligopolistic, or monopolistic. An understanding of the market structure in which the firm is operating is a necessary input in setting realistic and attainable growth targets.

The internal environment may also affect the firm's growth rate. The firm must have the managerial and labor talent capable of absorbing the growth. If not, the wealth position of the owners may be greatly deteriorated. Other interrelated internal factors that influence growth include the firm's current size, capacity, and production process.

A firm's strategic plan should take into consideration the aforementioned factors in setting growth targets for the planning period. In this chapter we describe planning models that incorporate the macroeconomic and microeconomic factors and the internal environment in setting the firm's sales growth and market share goals. In chapters 3 and 4 we present sustainable growth models that incorporate the firm's internal operating and financial constraints to determine a feasible growth for the planning period. The two growth rates must be contrasted to determine their simultaneous attainability.

SOURCES OF FIRM GROWTH

A firm's sales growth can be decomposed into two parts: the growth resulting from the growth in the markets in which the firm sells its products and the growth that is achieved as a result of an increased market share. The source of the sales growth, market growth, or share growth may influence the firm's operating and financial targets as well as its stock price relative to other firms in the industry.

Varadarajan (1983) developed a strategic planning model that determined the annual growth in sales required during the planning period for a forecasted market growth and targeted market share. The Varadarajan model makes the following assumptions:

1. The size of the market is beyond the influence of firms within the market.
2. The market growth rate is constant throughout the planning period.
3. The firm is operating in one market.
4. Growth rates and market shares are stated in terms of volume.

The first assumption will be addressed later in the discussion of market structures. It will be demonstrated that the second and third assumptions can be readily relaxed to allow for a more realistic and comprehensive planning tool without altering the basic implications of the model. For our purpose, we can define growth rates and market shares in terms of dollars instead of volume. Thus our version of the fourth assumption in the Varadarajan model assumes that "growth rates and market shares are stated in terms of dollars."

To demonstrate the Varadarajan model we define,

g = growth rate in sales during the planning period.
s_t = targeted market share to be attained by period t.
s_o = current market share.
G = constant market growth during the planning period.
t = planning period.
g^* = total sales growth over the planning period.

Given the assumptions above, the relation between market share and growth can be depicted by the following equation:

$$s_t / s_o = (1 + g)^t / (1 + G)^t \qquad (2.1)$$

Equation 2.1 can be applied by focusing on either side of the equality. If the firm emphasizes market share targets for the planning period, the left-hand side of the equation would be set in the strategic plan. For the firm with a goal of increased market share, $s_t > s_o$, it is evident that the firm must grow over the planning period at a rate greater than the growth of the market, $g > G$. If the goal is market share maintenance, $s_t = s_o$, the firm must grow at the same rate as the market, $g = G$.

When the strategic plan focuses on growth targets, the right-hand side of the equation would be set in the strategic plan. The impact on market share would be determined by the relation between the firm's growth and the growth in the market. If the firm can achieve a growth during the planning period that is greater than the growth in the market, $g > G$, the firm will experience an increased market share, $s_t > s_o$. If however, the firm is unable to keep pace with the growth in the market, $g < G$, during the planning period, its market share will decline, $s_t < s_o$.

Solving equation 2.1 for g results in the following equation, the annual growth in sales that a firm must attain during the planning period t for a target market share and forecasted growth of the market:

$$g = [(s_t / s_o)^{1/t} (1 + G)] - 1 \qquad (2.2)$$

The firm with a current market share of 10 percent, a target market share of 15 percent, a forecasted market growth rate of 5 percent, and a planning period of five years will have to grow during the period at an annual rate of 13.9 percent.

$$g = [(.15 / .10)^{1/5} (1 + .05)] - 1$$

$$g = .139 = 13.9\%$$

Exhibit 2.1 depicts the annual growth rate in sales required for various market shares objectives and planning horizons. The exhibit is constructed assuming that the market in which the firm is operating will grow at a constant

Exhibit 2.1
Annual Growth Rate for a Target Market Share, Assumed Market Growth = 5.00 Percent

planning period in years

St/So	1	2	3	4	5	6	7
1.10	15.5%	10.1%	8.4%	7.5%	7.0%	6.7%	6.4%
1.20	26.0%	15.0%	11.6%	9.9%	8.9%	8.2%	7.8%
1.30	36.5%	19.7%	14.6%	12.1%	10.7%	9.7%	9.0%
1.40	47.0%	24.2%	17.5%	14.2%	12.3%	11.1%	10.2%
1.50	57.5%	28.6%	20.2%	16.2%	13.9%	12.3%	11.3%
1.60	68.0%	32.8%	22.8%	18.1%	15.3%	13.6%	12.3%
1.70	78.5%	36.9%	25.3%	19.9%	16.8%	14.7%	13.3%
1.80	89.0%	40.9%	27.7%	21.6%	18.1%	15.8%	14.2%
1.90	99.5%	44.7%	30.0%	23.3%	19.4%	16.9%	15.1%
2.00	110.0%	48.5%	32.3%	24.9%	20.6%	17.9%	15.9%

percent throughout the planning period. The first column, S_t / S_o, depicts the ratio of the target market share at the end of the planning period t to the current market share. The entries under each of the various planning periods represent the annual growth rates in sales required to attain the targeted market share. For Exhibit 2.1 the ratio of the market shares is equal to

$$S_t / S_o = .15 / .10 = 1.50.$$

Thus, the appropriate row for the first column is 1.50. Moving down the column with the heading of five years, our assumed planning period, and across the 1.50 row we find the entry 13.9 percent, the same result derived earlier. It should be noted that the entries of Exhibit 2.1 are based on the assumption that the market will grow at a constant rate of 5 percent throughout the planning period.

It is evident from inspection of equation 2.2 that the variables that affect the annual growth rate include the targeted market share by the end of the planning period (S_t), the current market share (S_o), the forecasted growth of the market (G), and the planning horizon (t). The current market share is beyond the control of the strategic planner; it is treated as a given for planning purposes. The other variables, however, must be addressed by the strategic planner.

The relation between the annual growth rate and the planning horizon can be demonstrated by Exhibits 2.1 and 2.2. For a given ratio of market shares, S_t / S_o, and an assumed constant market growth of 5 percent, we observe from inspection of Exhibit 2.1 that as the planning horizon, t, increases, the smaller the required annual growth to meet the targeted market share.

Exhibit 2.2 presents the relation between required annual growth rates and planning horizons for an assumed market growth of 5 percent ($G = 5\%$), a current market share of 10 percent ($S_o = 10\%$), and varying targeted market shares, S_t. We see graphically that for a given target market share, the required annual growth rate dramatically declines and then flattens out as the planning horizon increases. In addition, as the targeted market share, S_t, increases from 15 percent to 17 percent to 20 percent, the annual required growth rate increases. The amount of the required increase in the growth rate necessary to attain the targeted market share depends on the planning horizon. Notice in Exhibit 2.2 that for a short planning horizon, the difference in the required growth rates is larger than for longer planning periods.

Exhibit 2.3 demonstrates the relation between required annual growth rates and various forecasted market growth rates. The exhibit is based on a current market share of 10 percent and a planning horizon of five years. We see from the exhibit that as the forecasted growth in the market increases, the required annual growth rate increases for a given targeted market share. Notice that the vertical intercept is positive, indicating that the firm that wants to increase its market share must grow at a faster rate than the growth in the market. Also, the amount of the increase in the market share influences the amount by which the annual growth rate must exceed the market growth rate. In addition, the difference between required annual growth rates for different target market shares increases as the forecasted growth in the market increases.

Exhibit 2.4 demonstrates the relation between required annual growth rates and various targeted market shares. The exhibit is based on a current market share of 10 percent and a planning horizon of five years. It is evident that as the firm increases its targeted market share, a higher annual growth rate will be required. Affecting the annual growth rate will be the growth of the market. Notice that the vertical intercepts correspond to the forecasted growth rates of the market, since the firm is assumed to have a current market share of 10 percent. In other words, the vertical intercept denotes the annual growth required to maintain market share (i.e., the growth of the market). As the targeted market share increases, the difference in the required annual growth rates increases for the various market growth rates. This is reflected by observing that the difference in required annual growth rates for a market share of 10 percent is less than the difference in growth rates for a market share of 45 percent.

Exhibit 2.2
Annual Growth Rate and Planning Period

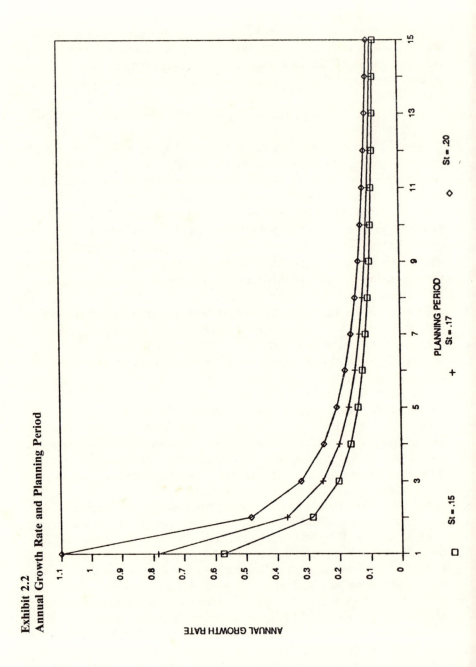

Exhibit 2.3
Annual Growth Rate and Market Growth

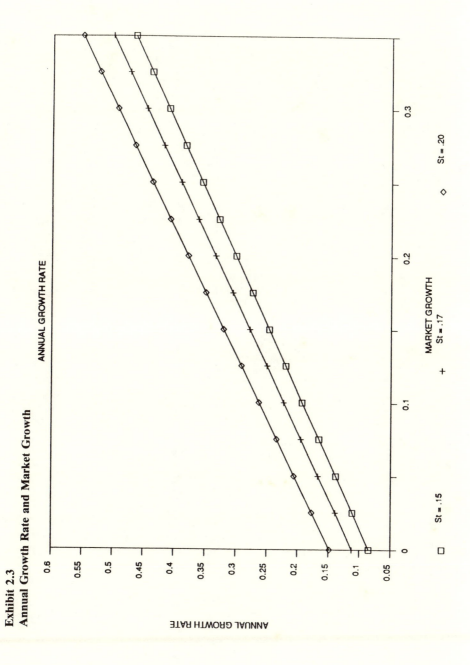

ANNUAL GROWTH RATE

Exhibit 2.4
Annual Growth Rate and Target Market Share

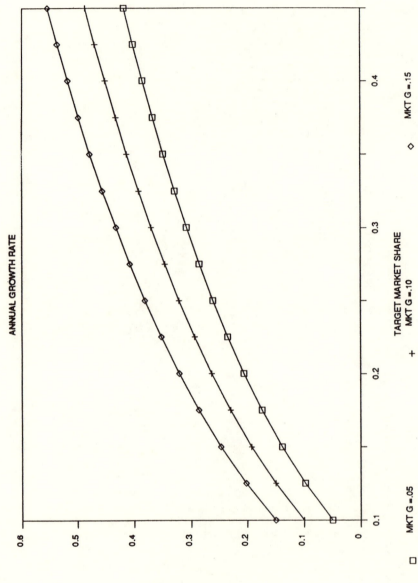

ANNUAL GROWTH RATE

TARGET MARKET SHARE

□ MKT G =.05   + MKT G =.10   ◇ MKT G =.15

To obtain another perspective on the relation between the growth requirements to attain a target market share, Varadarajan used the following:

$$g^* = (S_t / S_o)(1 + G)^t - 1. \tag{2.3}$$

The term g^* refers to the total growth in sales required over the planning period to achieve the desired target market share. If we assume that the firm currently has a 10 percent market share but wants to increase the share to 15 percent in four years, and the forecasted growth of the market is 5 percent, the total growth in sales required by the end of year 4 is 82.3 percent.

$$g^* = (.15 / .10)(1 + .05)^4 - 1$$

$$g^* = .823 = 82.3\%$$

In other words, the firm sales must be 82.3 percent higher than the current level in order to achieve the target market share, given a planning horizon of four years and a forecasted growth in the market of 5 percent.

Exhibit 2.5 presents the total percentage of increase in sales required to achieve a target market share for a specific planning period. The exhibit is based on a forecasted constant market growth of 5 percent and is thus only valid for this market growth. For the example above, the ratio of the target market share to the current share is 1.5.

$$S_t / S_o = .15 / .10 = 1.5$$

Thus we move across the 1.5 row of the first column and down column 4, since we assumed a four-year planning period. At the intersection of the row and column we observe the value 82.3 percent, the value calculated above. Other entries of Exhibit 2.5 can be similarly interpreted.

NONCONSTANT MARKET GROWTH

The models developed by Varadarajan must be modified for the firm that anticipates that the market growth will not be constant throughout the planning period, and for firms that operate in more than one market. For the firm that expects the market growth to vary throughout the planning period, we can use an adjusted version of equation 2.2. We can define G_i as the expected market growth during period i. Equation 2.4 allows for the more realistic assumption that the growth in the market is not a constant, but is related to changing macroeconomic events.

$$g = (S_t / S_o)^{1/t} [(1 + G_1)(1 + G_2) \ldots (1 + G_t)]^{1/t} - 1 \tag{2.4}$$

Exhibit 2.5
Total Growth Required over Planning Period for a Target Market Share,
Assumed Market Growth = 5.00 Percent

planning   period   in   years

St/So	1	2	3	4	5	6	7
1.10	15.5%	21.3%	27.3%	33.7%	40.4%	47.4%	54.8%
1.20	26.0%	32.3%	38.9%	45.9%	53.2%	60.8%	68.9%
1.30	36.5%	43.3%	50.5%	58.0%	65.9%	74.2%	82.9%
1.40	47.0%	54.4%	62.1%	70.2%	78.7%	87.6%	97.0%
1.50	57.5%	65.4%	73.6%	82.3%	91.4%	101.0%	111.1%
1.60	68.0%	76.4%	85.2%	94.5%	104.2%	114.4%	125.1%
1.70	78.5%	87.4%	96.8%	106.6%	117.0%	127.8%	139.2%
1.80	89.0%	98.5%	108.4%	118.8%	129.7%	141.2%	153.3%
1.90	99.5%	109.5%	119.9%	130.9%	142.5%	154.6%	167.3%
2.00	110.0%	120.5%	131.5%	143.1%	155.3%	168.0%	181.4%

Suppose the firm anticipates that the economy will grow next year but will enter a recession in year 2. Most likely the market in which the firm is operating will not, in this scenario, grow at a constant rate. Thus equation 2.2 may not be appropriate. Suppose the firm, after analyzing macroeconomic events, anticipates that the market will grow by 8 percent during year 1, 5 percent during year 2, and 4 percent during year 3. If the current market share is 10 percent and the target market share is 15 percent and the planning period three years, the required annual growth rate is 20.9 percent.

$$g = (.15 / .10)^{1/3} [(1 + .08)(1 + .05)(1 + .04)]^{1/3} - 1$$

$$g = .209 = 20.9\%$$

We used equation 2.3 to determine the total percentage of increase in sales over the planning period to achieve the target market share under the assumption that the market growth was constant. To relax this assumption, we can use the following equation:

$$g = (S_t / S_o)(1 + G_1)(1 + G_2) \ldots (1 + G_t) - 1. \tag{2.5}$$

Assuming the same values for the variables as in the preceding example, the total increase in sales required over the three-year period to attain the market share objective is 76.9 percent.

$$g = (.15 / .10)(1 + .08)(1 + .05)(1 + .04) - 1$$

$$g = .769 = 76.9\%$$

Thus the firm must grow by 76.9 percent by the end of the third year in order to reach the target market share of 15 percent if the market grows at a rate of 8 percent during year 1, 5 percent during year 2, and 4 percent during year 3.

MULTIPLE PRODUCT LINES

The previous models assumed, for ease of analysis, that the firm was operating in only one market. The extension for the firm operating in several markets with different growth rates is straightforward. To determine the average required annual growth in total sales to attain the target market shares for each of the firm's product lines, we can use the following equation:

$$g = (W_1)g_1 + (W_2)g_2 + \ldots + (W_n)g_n, \tag{2.6}$$

where W_i refers to the proportion of the current period's sales for market i to the firm's current total sales; g_i refers to the required growth in market i using equation 2.2 or 2.4; $i = 1, 2, \ldots, n$; n refers to the number of markets in which the firm is operating. If the firm is operating in three markets and the current period's sales in market 1 is \$1,000, in market 2 \$2,000, and in market 3 \$7,000, and if the required annual growth rates are 12 percent, 15 percent, and 18 percent for the three markets, the annual growth in total sales necessary to meet the target market shares is 16.8 percent.

$$g = (1000/10000).12 + (2000/10000).15 + (7000/10000).18$$

$$g = .168 = 16.8\%$$

ROLE OF MARKET STRUCTURE

It has been demonstrated that a firm can achieve a growth in sales owing to two sources: growth in the market in which its products are sold and growth owing to an increased market share. Depending on the structure of the markets in which the firm operates, these two sources of growth may have different implications for the firm's operating and financial targets.

As stated earlier, the macroeconomic environment will influence the growth of the markets in which the firm is operating. The principal microeconomic factor that affects the growth of the firm is the structure of its markets. Market structures have been characterized as perfectly competitive, monopolistically competitive, oligopolistic, and monopolistic. The market structure in which the firm is operating will influence the amount of attainable growth and, consequently, should be incorporated into the planning process.

A perfectly competitive market is one in which there is a large number of buyers and sellers. Characteristics of perfectly competitive markets include that the firm is capable of selling all its products at a given price and that it is such a small portion of the entire market for these goods that its actions will have no influence on any of the other firms. Thus the reactions of rival competitors need not be taken into consideration when deriving the strategic plan. For the firm that operates in a perfectly competitive market a target growth rate for the planning period may be determined without including the impact of growth in volume on the selling price of the product or the reactions of its competitors. The limiting factors on the growth of the firm in this environment include financial and operating constraints. Both of these factors are incorporated in the models of sustainable growth and do not directly enter in the setting of the growth objectives described in this chapter. As will be evident later, however, they can indirectly enter the models of this chapter.

Unfortunately most firms do not operate in perfectly competitive markets. In imperfectly competitive markets the amount that the firm can sell in the marketplace is constrained by the size of the market and by the action and reactions of its rivals.

A monopolistically competitive market is one in which a relatively large number of firms, although fewer than in the perfectly competitive market, sell similar but not identical products. Price and nonprice competition exist in this market structure. Because they are not identical, advertising is an important variable in identifying real or imagined differences in the products. Thus, in setting market share objectives, the firm should include assumptions concerning not only the effectiveness of its own planned advertising campaign and pricing policies, but also the reaction of its rivals.

The consideration of the reaction of rivals is most important for firms operating in oligopolistic markets. An oligopolistic market is one in which only a few firms exist, each of which has a significant share of the market. In an oligopolistic market the setting of growth objectives different from the forecasted growth of the market should incorporate some anticipated response from the powerful rivals.

Firms that operate in a monopolistic market do not have to consider their competitors. A monopolistic market is characterized as one in which there exists one seller for a product with no close substitutes. Because the size of the firm is the size of the market, the issue of a target market share is not relevant. However, the growth of the market is an important part of the firm's planning process. Most firms that operate in monopolistic markets are regulated by some governmental unit, and consequently the growth of the market may be beyond their control.

INTERRELATED GOALS

In setting objectives for the planning horizon the firm should take into consideration the mutual feasibility of the objectives. Growth or market share objectives must be contrasted to the other objectives of the firm. Although several studies (see Schoeffler, Buzzell, and Heany 1974; Buzzell, Gale, and Sultan 1975) have found a significant positive relation between market share and profitability, market share or growth objectives may cause significant problems for the firm.

The decision concerning a target market share or growth objective over the planning period should take into consideration the effects on operating performance, the financial requirements, and the accompanying risk factors. There are numerous examples of firms that were able to achieve a significant growth rate but that ultimately went bankrupt. One way to incorporate these factors is to use the growth rates determined from the models in this chapter and contrast them to the sustainable growth rates derived from the models in Chapters 3 and 4. If the two growth rates are incompatible, the firm must change one or more of its objectves. The result will be a strategic plan with mutually consistent objectives.

REFERENCES

Bloom, P., and P. Kotler. "Strategies for High Market Share Companies," *Harvard Business Review*, November/December 1975, pp. 63–72.

Buzzell, R., B. Gale, and R. Sultan. "Market Share—A Key to Profitability," *Harvard Business Review*, January/February 1975, pp. 97–106.

Donaldson, Gordon. "Financial Goals and Strategic Consequences," *Harvard Business Review*, May/June 1985, pp. 57–66.

Fruhan, William. "Pyrrhic Victories in Fight for Market Share," *Harvard Business Review*, September/October 1972, pp. 100–107.

Rue, L., and T. Clark. "Dangers Inherent in Growth Objectives," *Managerial Planning*, May/June 1975, pp. 24–28.

Schoeffler, S., R. Buzzell, and D. Heany. "Impact of Strategic Planning on Profit Performance." *Harvard Business Review*, March/April 1974, pp. 137–145.

Varadarajan, Poondi. "The Sustainable Growth Model: A Tool for Evaluating the Financial Feasibility of Market Share Strategies." *Strategic Management Journal*, Vol. 4, 1983, pp. 353–367.

3

SUSTAINABLE GROWTH: FIRM AGGREGATE MODELS

In the context of managing growth, the initial question of an appropriate growth rate over a defined time frame takes the form: What rate of growth is sustainable vis-a-vis the financial profile of the firm, the productivity of factor inputs, and the dividend payout policy? Stated differently, if the productivity of factor inputs is held constant, what percentage of increase in sales can be maintained without necessitating a change in financial policy? If sales grow at a higher rate, the firm can exercise a combination of options to finance the increment in total sales: increase debt, reduce dividend payout, or issue equity securities. Each option alters established financial policies. On the other hand, if the productivity of factor inputs could be increased, improved operating performance would generate higher profit margins that, at a constant dividend payout ratio, would favorably affect retained earnings. Thus, while the models presented in this introductory chapter have primarily a financial orientation, they incorporate an important, underlying technological component.*

However, management must recognize the distinction between sustainable and optimal growth. The two can coincide but may diverge. The objective of management is to maximize the market value of the common stock. This is achieved when the financial structure minimizes the weighted average cost of capital. The common shareholders at this point receive a return commensurate with the risk of their investment. Under these conditions the sustainable rate of growth consistent with the maintenance of the minimum cost of capital would be the optimal sustainable growth rate.

---

*As we delve deeper into the topic, we shall have to broaden and recast our concept of sustainable growth.

However, the sustainable growth rate may be the product of a sub-optimal financial structure. In this event a revised financial policy might minimize the cost of capital and concurrently optimize sustainable growth, and the risk-return trade-off is beyond the scope of our current inquiry. A full discussion of this complex problem is undertaken in Chapter 6, Optimal Sustainable Growth.

THE HIGGINS MODEL

In 1977 and 1981 Robert C. Higgins demonstrated that the financial policies of many corporations may be at variance with their growth objective (Higgins 1977b, 1983). As a guide for setting compatible financial policies and growth objectives, Higgins developed a formula to calculate a rate of sustainable growth. In deriving his formula Higgins made the following assumptions:

1. Book depreciation is adequate to recapture the value of existing assets;
2. Profit margin (P) on new sales (S_1) corresponds to that on existing sales (S_o); hence the change in sales (ΔS) equals $S_1 - S_o$;
3. The firm has an established financial structure (L) without the sale of new common stock. The financial structure is the total of all debt and equity financing current and long-term assets;
4. The firm has an established dividend payout rate (D); thus the target retention ratio is ($1 - D$);
5. New fixed assets (F) at book value represent a stated proportion of the change in physical volume of output (real estate);
6. New current assets (C) are a stated proportion of sales in nominal dollars;
7. Sales at the beginning of the period are represented by (S_o) and the projected sales during the period by (S_1);
8. T denotes the ratio of total assets to net sales, and the ratio is constant for new and existing sales;
9. Firm will rely on retained earnings for equity financing, and new common stock will not be issued.

Based on these assumptions, Higgins describes the derivation of the basic formula:

P and T are the same for new sales as for existing sales, the new assets required to support increased sales are forecast to be $\Delta S(T)$. . . . On the other side of the balance sheet, total profits for the year are expected to be $(S + \Delta S)P$ and additions to retained earnings to be $(S + \Delta S)P(1 - D)$ . . . because every \$1 added to retained earnings enables the company to borrow \$L$ without increasing its debt to equity ratio . . . new borrowings should equal $(S + \Delta S)P(E - D)L$. (Higgins 1977a)

Because assets must equal liabilities plus equity, additions to assets must be covered by an increase in retained earnings and new debt. Setting the two quantities equal and solving for $\Delta S/S_o$ yields the following equation:

$$g^* = \frac{\Delta S}{S_o} = \frac{P(1 - D)(1 + L)}{T - [P(1 - D)(1 + L)]} . \tag{3.1}$$

Appendix 3.1 presents the consolidated statements of the Burroughs Corporation for 1980 and 1981. These form the basic data to illustrate the calculations of sustainable growth under conditions of stable prices, rising and falling prices, and with and without the imposition of a corporate income tax. Exhibit 3.1 puts the Burroughs data on a pre-tax basis, and Exhibit 3.2 lists the post-tax data. Both exhibits display the relevant variables in the models discussed.

Case 1. Higgins Model: Stable Prices and No Corporate Income Tax

Taking the data from Exhibit 3.1 and using equation 3.1,

$$g^* = \frac{.0746(1 - .426)(1 + 1.036)}{1.304 - [.0746(1 - .426)(1 + 1.036)]}$$

$$= \frac{.0871823}{1.2168177}$$

$$= .0716478 \text{ or } 7.16\% \text{ (rounded)}.$$

Unless the actual growth rate (g) equals the sustainable growth rate (g^*), the firm will have to reassess its financial policies. Thus, if $g > g^*$, the company may have excess capital relative to investment needs and may increase dividends, reduce leverage, or increase liquid assets (Higgins 1977a).

Case 2. Higgins Model: Rising Prices and No Corporate Income Tax

Equation 3.1 can be modified to allow for price increases or decreases. This yields the following equation:

$$g^* = \frac{\Delta S}{S_o} = \frac{[(1 + J)P(1 - D)(1 + L) - JC}{[(1 + J)C + F] - [(1 + J)P(1 - D)(1 + L)]} . \tag{3.2}$$

Taking the data from Exhibit 3.1, a 9 percent rise (J), we have

$$g^* = \frac{[(1 + .9).0746(1 - .426)(1 + 1.036)] - (.09)(.676)}{[(1 + .09).676 + .446] - [(1 + .09).07641(1 - .426)(1 + 1.036)]}$$

$$= \frac{.0341887}{1.0855184}$$

$$= 0.031952 \text{ or } 3.15\% \text{ (rounded)}.$$

Exhibit 3.1
Burroughs Corporation Consolidated Income Statement, 1981 Dollars before Taxes
(Thousands of Dollars)

Total Revenues		$3,405,428
Less		
Operating Cost		3,006,224
Earnings Before Interest and Taxes		$ 399,204
Less		
Interest Expense		145,078
Earnings Before Taxes		$ 254,126
Shares Outstanding	=	41,641,000
Dividends Per Share	=	$2.60
Net-Income Per Share (EPS)	=	$6.103
Profit Margin (P)	=	.0746
Dividend Payout Ratio (D)	=	.426
Retention Ratio (1-D)	=	.574
Total Assets/Sales (T)	=	1.304
Financial Structure (L) = Total Debt/Equity	=	1.036
Current Assets/Current Sales (C)	=	.676
Fixed Assets/Sales (F)	=	.446
Price Trend (J)	=	+ .09/-.09
Net-Working Capital/Sales (W)	=	.279801
Long Term Debt to Equity (LL)	=	.3689508

Exhibit 3.2

Burroughs Corporation Consolidated Income Statement, 1981 Dollars after Taxes (Thousands of Dollars)

Total Revenues	$ 3,405,428
Less	
Operating Cost	3,006,224
Earnings Before Interest and Taxes	$ 399,204
Less	
Interest Expense	145,078
Earnings Before Taxes	$ 254,126
Less	
Taxes (58.6%)	105,200
Earnings After Taxes	$ 148,926
Less	
Dividends	$ 108,540
Addition to Retained Earnings	$ 40,386
Dividends Per Share	$2.60
Net-income Per Share (EPS)	$3.58
Average Shares Outstanding	41,641,000
Profit Margin (P)	.0437
Dividend Payout Ratio (D)	.729
Retention Ratio (1-D)	.271
Total Assets/Sales (T)	1.304
Financial Structure (L) = Total Debt/Equity	1.306
Current Assets/Current Sales (C)	.676
Fixed Assets/Sales (F)	.446
Price Trend (J)	+ .09/-.09
Net-Working Capital/Sales (W)	.279801
Long Term Debt to Equity (LL)	.3689508

Case 3. Higgins Model: Declining Prices and No Corporate Income Tax

Using equation 3.2 and the data from Exhibit 3.1, we have

$$g^* = \frac{[(1 + .09).0746(1 - .426)(1 + 1.036)] - (.09)(.676)}{[(1 + .09).676 + .446] - [(1 + .09).0746(1 - .426)(1 + 1.036)]}$$

$$= \frac{.1401759}{0.9818243}$$

$$= 0.1427708 \text{ or } 14.28\% \text{ (rounded)}.$$

Although we cannot fully discuss the impact of price changes on sustainable growth without taking into account the tax factor, it is obvious that the effect of price increases or decreases on sustainable growth in a particular company must depend on (a) the degree that price variations affect specific revenue and expense items; (b) the mix of fixed and variable costs; and (c) whether the annual depreciation is sufficient to maintain the replacement value of existing assets. Based on his research on U.S. manufacturing in 1974, Higgins concluded that

roughly speaking, the real sustainable growth rate declines by 2.2% for every 5 percentage point increase in the inflation rate. With approximate 10% inflation rate in 1974, real sustainable growth falls from an inflation-free 10.5% to 6.1%. For comparison, the actual real growth in manufacturing sales in 1974 was 3.8 percent, while figures for the prior two years were 8.2% and 8.4%. (Higgins 1981)

Descending from the macroview to the individual firm, the effects of price level changes are really indeterminate. For example, if, for a particular company at a given quantity of output, revenues rose faster than costs, then the following scenario might unfold:

- An improved profit margin (P)
- Assuming higher interest rates, an increase in the cost of capital
- Depreciation charges inadequate to cover the cost of replacement assets
- Debt repayment in cheaper real dollars (L)
- Pressure to raise dividend payouts (D)
- Higher inventory investment costs
- A rachet effect to higher tax brackets
- A search for takeover targets that, if acquired, might reduce the effective rate

Conversely, if the upward price push affected outflows more than inflows, the following might occur:

- A lower profit margin (*P*) and perhaps negative earnings
- Assuming rising interest rates, a higher cost of capital
- Depreciation charges based on book value inadequate to cover replacement costs of equipment
- Debt repayment in cheaper dollars (*L*)
- Lower value of common stock owing to lower profit margins and higher interest rates
- Slower or negative growth in retained earnings (1 − *D*)
- A drop to lower tax brackets and/or accumulation of losses
- A search for takeover targets that might yield economies of scale

The reader can easily outline similar sequences of events to cover the phenomenon of the falling price level. Two conclusions are readily apparent, however: (1) a computer model of the firm would be necessary to forecast the impact of rising or falling price levels on the *nominal* sustainable growth of the firm; (2) the computer model, with equal ease, could adjust for price changes and project *real* sustainable growth of the firm.

Case 4. Higgins Model: Stable Prices; After Taxes

Using the data from Exhibit 3.2 and equation 3.1, we have

$$g^* = \frac{P(1 - D)(1 + L)}{T - [P(1 - D)(1 + L)]} \tag{3.1}$$

$$= \frac{.0437(1 - .729)(1 + 1.036)}{1.304 - [.0437(1 - .729)(1 + 1.036)]}$$

$$= .0188389 \text{ or } 1.88\% \text{ (rounded)}.$$

Case 5. Higgins Model: Rising Prices; After Taxes

Combining the data from Exhibit 3.2 with equation 3.2, we have

$$g^* = \frac{[(1 + J)P(1 - D)(1 + L) - JC}{[(1 + J)C + F] - [(1 + J)P(1 - D)(1 + L)]} \tag{3.2}$$

$$= \frac{[(1 + .09).0437(1 - .729)(1 + 1.036)] - (.09)(.676)}{[(1 + .09).676 + .446] - [(1 + .09).0437(1 - .729)(1 + 1.036)]}$$

$$= \frac{-.0845502}{1.1565583}$$

$$= -0.073105 \text{ or } -7.31\% \text{ (rounded)}.$$

Case 6. Higgins Model: Falling Prices; After Taxes

In this case, a 9 percent decline in price is inserted into equation 3.2:

$$g^* = \frac{[(1 - .09).0437(1 - .729)(1 + 1.036)] - (-.09)(.676)}{[(1 - .09).676 + .446] - [(1 - .09).0437(1 - .729)(1 + 1.036)]}$$

$$= \frac{.0827617}{1.0392185}$$

$$= 0.0796576 \text{ or } 7.96\% \text{ (rounded).}$$

The effect of the imposition of a corporate income tax is consistent at all price levels. Sustainable growth is sharply reduced by the tax bite.

THE JOHNSON MODEL

Johnson (1981) qualified the original Higgins model and the presumption of a constant *financial* structure. The former hinged the discussion on the rate of sustainable growth using a constant *capital* structure [long-term debt to equity (L_L)]. Based on Higgins' assumptions, Johnson shows that total uses of funds are composed of the change in total nominal *current* assets, $[(S + \Delta S)(1 + J) - S]C$ plus *new nominal fixed assets*, $(\Delta S)F$. Sources of funds equal the increase in nominal debt plus retained earnings, $(S + \Delta S)(1 + J)P(1 - D)(1 + L)$. However, Johnson, by focusing on capital structure (long-term debt to equity), allows working capital to float with nominal sales. Thus, under the Johnson model, new sources of funds include changes in net working capital plus increases in long-term debt required to sustain a constant ratio with the additions to retained earnings. The revised real sustainable rate of growth thus takes the following form:

$$g_R = \frac{\Delta S}{S_0} = \frac{Y(1 + J) - WJ}{F - [(1 + J)Y] + [W(1 + J)]}, \tag{3.3}$$

where $Y = P(1 - D)(1 + L_L)$ and $W =$ the ratio of nominal net working capital to nominal sales.

Case 1. Johnson Model: Stable Prices; No Taxes

Using the data from Exhibit 3.1 and equation 3.3, we have

$$Y = .0746(1 - .426)(1 + .3689508)$$

$$= .0589619.$$

Then the real sustainable growth (g_R) under the Johnson methodology becomes

$$g_R = \frac{.0589313(1 + 0) - (0)(.279801)}{.446 - [(1 + 0).0589313] + [.279801(1 + 0)]}$$

$$= \frac{.0589313}{.6668697}$$

$$= .8837 \text{ or } 8.84\% \text{ (rounded).}$$

This compares with a sustainable growth rate of 7.16 percent under the Higgins model.

Case 2. Johnson Model: Rising Prices; No Taxes

Inserting the 9 percent price increase into equation 3.3., we have

$$g_R = \frac{.0589313(1 + .09) - (.09)(.279801)}{.446 - [(1 + .09).0589313] + [.279801(1 + .09)]}$$

$$= \frac{.0390531}{.6867479}$$

$$= .0568667 \text{ or } 5.69\% \text{ (rounded).}$$

Note that Y, once calculated, is a constant.

Case 3. Johnson Model: Falling Prices; No Taxes

Inserting the 9 percent decrease into equation 3.3, we have

$$g_R = \frac{.0589313(1 - .09) - (.09)(.279801)}{.446 - [(1 - .09).0589313] + [.279801(1 + .09)]}$$

$$= \frac{.0536554 + .0251821}{.446 - 0536553 + .2546189}$$

$$= \frac{.0788374}{.6469636}$$

$$= .1218576 \text{ or } 12.1\% \text{ (rounded).}$$

Case 4. Johnson Model: Stable Prices; After Taxes

With the introduction of the corporate income tax, Y must be recalculated

$$Y = .0437(1 - .729)(1 + .3689508)$$

$$= .016212.$$

Then, from Exhibit 3.2 and equation 3.3,

$$g_R = \frac{.016212(1 + 0) - (0)(.279801)}{.446 - [(1 + 0).016212] + [.279801(1 + 0)]}$$

$$= \frac{.016212}{.709586}$$

$$= .0228471 \text{ or } 2.28\% \text{ (rounded)}.$$

Case 5. Johnson Model: Rising Prices; After Taxes

Introducing an upward trend in prices of 9 percent into equation 3.3 downgrades sustainable growth:

$$g_R = \frac{.016212(1 + .09) - (.09)(.279801)}{.446 - [(1 + .09).016212] + [.279801(1 + .09)]}$$

$$= \frac{-.007511}{.733312}$$

$$= -.0102425 \text{ or } -1.02\% \text{ (rounded)}.$$

Case 6. Johnson Model: Declining Prices; After Taxes

Once again tax effects and declining prices can combine to affect positively sustainable growth. Assuming a downward trend in prices of 9 percent,

$$g_R = \frac{.016212(1 - .09) - (-.09)(.279801)}{.446 - [(1 - .09).016212] + [.279801(1 + .09)]}$$

$$= \frac{.0399349}{.685866}$$

$$= .0582257 \text{ or } 5.82\% \text{ (rounded)}.$$

SUMMARY AND COMPARISON

The following table presents a comparison of the Burroughs' results, using the Higgins and Johnson models.

	Higgins Model (g^*)	Johnson Model (g_R)
Before Taxes		
Stable prices	7.16%	8.84%
Rising prices	3.15%	5.69%
Declining prices	14.28%	12.19%
After Taxes		
Stable prices	1.88%	2.28%
Rising prices	−7.31%	−1.02%
Delining prices	7.96%	5.82%

The reader will recall that the essential difference between the models lies in the assumption of a constant financial structure by Higgins and a constant capital structure by Johnson. The latter allows for the effects of period price changes on current assets and current liabilities. Thus in a period of rising prices, with a constant capital structure, the sustainable growth is higher than that attainable when the firm adheres to an established financial structure.

On the other hand, in both cases (a target financial structure and a target capital structure) the sustainable growth rate is lower under rising prices than under conditions of price stability. The reason for this phenomenon lies in the historical cost financial statements used to describe financial or capital structures and to set target ratios. It follows that in the face of persistent inflation, management can maintain a stable capital structure over time only by using a constant dollar debt-equity ratio or one based on market values.

Similar reasoning explains the behavior of sustainable growth in periods of declining prices. In both models sustainable growth exceeds that obtainable under conditions of stable prices, but the sustainable growth rate from the Higgins model exceeds that of the Johnson model. Again, the phenomenon is attributable to the price effects on net working capital incorporated in the Johnson model.

Both the Higgins and Johnson models escape the problem of optimal sustainable growth by implicitly assuming that the firm has achieved an optimal financial or capital structure.

PLANNING MODE

To this point we have used the Higgins and Johnson models to identify a sustainable rate of growth based on the financial/capital resources of the firm. If the actual growth rate exceeded the sustainable growth rate (or was less than the sustainable growth), then the situation suggested changes in the financial and/or capital structures.

However, as with any equation, the models can be used from either side of the equality. The firm could set up a target rate of growth and then solve for the financial or capital structure compatible with that rate. For example, in 1983 IBM had an actual rate of growth of 15 percent. Its profit margin (P) equaled .137; $D = .41$; and $T = .937$. What financial structure would support the actual growth rate? Using the Higgins model,

$$g^* = \frac{P(1 - D)(1 + L)}{T - [P(1 - D)(1 + L)]} \tag{3.1}$$

Given the value of P, D, T, and g^*, we can solve $(1 + L)$:

$$1 + L = \frac{g^* T}{P(1 - D)(1 + g^*)} .$$

Then,

$$L = \frac{g^* T}{P(1 - D)(1 + g^*)} - 1,$$

and, substituting the actual figures into above equation yields:

$$L = \frac{(.15)(.937)}{(.137)(1 - .41)(1 + .15)} - 1$$

$$= 51.2\%.$$

The debt-equity ratio consistent with the targeted growth rate is therefore 51.2 percent.

Similarly, a firm can test the compatibility of other variables, such as dividend payout, total assets to sales, profit margin, and so forth, with any given target rate of growth. Also, the manager can perform a sensitivity analysis on each of the variables in the equation to develop a series of values for each variable compatible with specific growth rates. With a range of values for each variable, management can then devise the most appropriate combination or identify the crucial variable to the achievement of the target rate. These procedures will be illustrated in subsequent chapters.

However, sustainable growth is not a surrogate for detailed financial analysis. It is a valuable appendage to traditional financing analysis that reinforces management's ability to plan and control the operations of the enterprise. In this role it offers a set of interrelated advantages.

1. Adhering to the stated assumptions of the Higgins and Johnson models, the concept enhances management's capability to monitor the contribution of internal operations to retained earnings.

2. As a corollary, it concentrates attention on key financial ratios that measure internal performance, such as asset turnover, operating margin, and return on assets.

3. Sustainable growth can be calculated at the firm level or disaggregated by department or division. It can thus be used to set performance goals by organizational unit or by function (marketing, procurement, manpower resources, and production).

4. Calculation of a sustainable rate of growth based on a stipulated financial structure establishes a parameter useful in market analysis and forecasting.

5. The projection of a sustainable rate of growth is an equally significant input in short-term budgeting: cash management and working capital management (Chapter 8). The total sales for the next period, based on a sustainable growth rate, can be segmented by the month or quarter with due allowance for seasonal variations. From these data, monthly or quarterly cash flows can be projected to determine points of excess inflows

for investment in marketable securities or short-term borrowings. Similarly, from the sales data pro-forma estimates of receivables, inventories, and other current assets can be derived to assist working capital management.

6. In the longer term, company acceptance of a sustainable rate of growth is a factor in the formulation of the capital budget (Chapter 9). Whether net present value, internal rate of return, payback, or average return is the criterion for project acceptance or rejection, the relation between the capital budget and the sustainable rate of growth cannot be ignored. The capital budget affects future operating margins and the risk-return posture of the firm. Capital budgets have to be financed and, hopefully, as the component projects come on line, make their contribution to retained earnings.

7. It follows that capital budgeting links closely to the management of the firm's financial stucture—to the identification of debt-equity ratio that *minimizes* the company's cost of financing. In turn this financial structure is the basis for calculating optimal sustainable growth.

8. Finally, the concept is a constitutent of the firm's information system between different levels of management. An understanding of the concept allows supervisory managers to relate their function to the firm's growth rate, profitability, and, ultimately, the value of the common stock.

In summary, sustainable growth is a comprehensive tool in corporate planning and control, in short- and long-term budgeting, in management of the financial structure, and in the elaboration of a flow of information to facilitate the achievement of company objectives.

However, there are certain caveats attached to the calculation and use of the sustainable growth by management.

1. A single-period calculation of sustainable growth is of minimum value. Rather, the calculation should cover an extended time frame—perhaps ten fiscal periods—to allow for the analysis of trends in the sustainable growth rate and in the component variables.

2. The disparity between actual and sustainable growth should be examined with a view to ascertaining the causes and bringing the two measures into harmony. As with all financial models used by management, the basic formulas have to be honed to fit the experience of the firm.

3. Business cycles affect firms and industries differently. Some firms and industries exhibit wider variations than the general economy; others fluctuate within a narrow range. It behooves management to review the influence of cyclical fluctuations on the firm's sustainable growth rate. For example, in firms subject to wide variations in performance, the usefulness of the sustainable rate of growth concept is limited. For firms characterized by narrow variations in performance, the variables in the calculation can be averaged to obtain a viable figure. Alternatively, a sustainable rate of growth could be calculated for different states of the economy, and probabilities assigned to each scenario. Planning might then proceed on a best case, worst case, and most likely case basis. Analyses of this type, on the other hand, presuppose an adequate display of historical data.

4. It is well to recall that retained earnings are affected by variables other than the firm's profit margin and retention ratio. Adjustments relating to prior accounting periods and asset write-offs come readily to mind. Increases in deferred taxes, the capitalization of financial leases, and other accruals affect the financial structure, and hence the sustainable growth rate. Employee stock purchase plans, depending on the provisions of the arrangement, may increase the equity base of the enterprise. These firm-specific items have to be factored into the basic formulas of sustainable growth.

SELF-SUSTAINING GROWTH

In their survey of 108 retailing companies in five industries over the period 1972–1980, Higgins and Kevin (1983) demonstrated that

the actual growth rate in sales, g, exceeded the sustainable growth rate for every industry in every year except two, and for the combined sample in every year . . . actual growth rate for the combined sample was 12.1 percent, while sustainable growth was only 7.8 percent.

As to how these firms financed the excess sales, Higgins and Kevin (1983) note:

By far the single most important reason that sample retailers were able to grow faster than their sustainable growth rates was increased use of financial leverage. In every industry studied, the assets-to-equity ratio inexorably rises over the decade. The combined firms' ratio is representative: A increased from 2.09 in 1972 to a high of 2.79 in 1980, a 33 percent rise despite the increase in equity from new stock sales.

The period from 1970 to 1980 was one of significant inflation. The consumer price index increased from 116.3 in 1970 to 246.8 in 1980. At the macro level inflation increases nominal interest rates with adverse effects on profit margins (P) and sustainable growth (g^*); accelerates nominal sales growth, which tends to increase the disparity between actual growth (g) and sustainable growth (g^*); and by increasing the nominal value of the firm's nonmonetary assets, T tends to create added debt capacity (Higgins and Kevin 1983).

At the macro level the preceding rationale is an attractive explanation, but at the micro or firm level the argument primarily rests on hindsight. The Higgins and Johnson models are essentially static conceptions; that is, sustainable growth is calculated at the start of a fiscal period and compared with the actual growth rate by the end of that period. The resulting tale of how the two statistics are balanced is mainly historical and devoid of the dynamic adjustments that accompany ongoing operations.

For example, using the Johnson model (equation 3.3) with the data taken from Exhibit 3.3, Burroughs had a sustainable growth calculated at

Exhibit 3.3
Burroughs Corporation Consolidated Income Statement, 1980 Dollars after Taxes
(Thousands of Dollars)

Total Revenues	$2,902,356
Less	
Operating Cost	2,686,611
Earnings Before Interest and Taxes	$ 215,745
Less	
Interest Expense	81,373
Earnings Before Taxes	$ 134,372
Less	
Taxes (39%)	52,400
Earnings After Taxes	$ 81,972
Less	
Dividends	107,501
Addition (Decrease) in Retained Earnings	($ 25,529)

Net-Income Per Share (EPS)	=	$1.99
Dividends Per Share	=	$2.60
Profit Margin (P)	=	.0282
Dividend Payout Ratio (D)	=	1.3065
Retention Ratio (1-D)	=	- .3065
Total Assets/Sales (T)	=	1.3281
Total Debt/Equity (L)	=	.8140
Long Term Debt to Equity (LL)	=	.1753
Current Assets/Current Sales (C)	=	.7010
Net-Working Capital/Sales (W)	=	.2643
Fixed Assets/Sales (F)	=	.4645
Price Trend (J)	=	+ .09

Exhibit 3.4
Johnson Model—Self-sustaining Growth

Equation 3:

$$Y = P(1 - D)(1 + LL)$$

$$= .0282 \ (1 - 1.3065)(1 + .1753)$$

$$= (- .0086433)(1.1753)$$

$$= - .0102 \ \text{(rounded)}$$

$$g_R = \frac{Y(1+J) - WJ}{F - [(1+J)Y] + [W(1+J)]}$$

$$= \frac{- .0102 \ (1+.09) - (.2643)(.09)}{.4645 - [(1+.09) - .0102] + [.2643 \ (1+.09)]}$$

$$= \frac{- .01118 - .023787}{.4645 - [1.0798] + [.288087]}$$

$$= \frac{- .034967}{- .327213}$$

$$= .1068631 \ \text{or} \ 10.69 \ \text{(rounded)}$$

Actual Growth (g) 1980 to 1981

$$\frac{\Delta S}{S_0} = \frac{\$ \ 503,072}{\$ \ 2,902,356} = .17333 \ \text{or} \ 17.33\% \ \text{(rounded)}$$

the end of fiscal 1980 of 10.69 percent (Exhibit 3.4) The actual growth for the ensuing period (1981) was 17.33 percent. How did Burroughs cover the disparity? Cash (including noncash book charges, current assets, and current liabilities) provided $732,582,000, of which $548,504,000 was used for capital additions, leaving net cash provided by operations of $184,078,000. Financing and investment activities (including business combinations and dividend payouts) resulted in a net cash draw down of $187,468,000 and an ultimate drop in cash and short-term investments of $3,390,000 (Appendix 3.1).

In the Burroughs case current operations contributed disproportionately to financing the difference between sustainable growth and actual growth. This suggests that sustainable growth is not per se a limit on actual growth (confirmed by the Higgins–Kevin study) or rigidly constrained by the limits of a target financial or capital structure. It is also a product of the firm's current operations profile, that is, the composition of current assets and liabilities and their turnover rates. The need is for a disaggregated, dynamic model of the firm that permits the analyst to forecast the behavior of financial statement variables over the planning period. The issue is not resolved by the insertion of a single variable, profit margin (*P*), to capture the contribution of current operations to the financing of growth.

SUMMARY

The Higgins and Johnson models are aggregate representatives of firm growth potential and, *if the stated assumptions are adhered to*, set the upper limit to the growth in sales. What is needed for managerial purposes is a disaggregated firm model that will facilitate forecasting of financial statement variables and give due weight to those instances when current sales can make an ongoing contribution to financing actual growth above the sustainable level. This is the subject matter of Chapter 5.

In addition to the constraints imposed by their assumptions, the Higgins and Johnson models suffer the deficiencies of accounting numbers that reflect historical costs and are the product of a notable number of options available to management. These create inconsistencies in valuation between firms and, over time, within firms. In this respect the Burroughs experience suggests that we might improve the analyses by shifting to a cash flow basis for the calculation of sustainable growth.

Finally, the models discussed here also rest on the hidden assumption that all assets are sales productive in each fiscal period. In many industries, especially the capital-intensive type, the reality is otherwise.

REFERENCES

Clark, John J. *Business Merger and Acquisitions Strategies.* Englewood Cliffs, N.J.: Prentice-Hall, 1985.

Clark, John, J., Margaret T. Clark, and Andrew Verzilli. "Strategic Planning and Sustainable Growth," *The Columbia Journal of World Business.* Fall 1985, pp. 47–51.

Fruhan, William E. "How Fast Should a Company Grow?" *Harvard Business Review*, January/February 1984, pp. 84–93.

Govindarajan, V., and John K. Shank. "Cash Sufficiency: The Missing Link in Strategic Planning," *Corporate Accounting*, Winter 1984, pp. 23–31.

Higgins, Robert. "Sustainable Growth: New Tool in Bank Lending," *The Journal of Commercial Lending*, June 1977a, pp. 48–58.

———. "How Much Growth Can a Firm Afford?" *Financial Management.* Fall 1977b, pp. 7–15.

———. "Sustainable Growth Under Inflation," *Financial Management*, Fall 1981, pp. 36–40.

Higgins, Robert C., and Roger A. Kevin. "Managing the Growth-Financial Policy Nexus in Retailing," *Journal of Retailing*, Fall 1983, pp. 19–47.

Johnson, Dana. "The Behavior of Financial Structure and Sustainable Growth in an Inflationary Environment," *Financial Management*, Autumn 1981, pp. 30–35.

APPENDIX 3.1
CONSOLIDATED FINANCIAL STATEMENTS,
BURROUGHS CORPORATION, 1980–1981

Income Statement

	1981	1980	Increase (+) Decrease (−) Over 1980
Total Revenues	$3,405,428	$2,902,356	+$503,072
Less			
Operating Cost	3,006,224	2,686,611	+ 319,613
Earnings Before Interest and Taxes	$ 339,204	$ 215,745	+$183,459
Less			
Interest Expense	145,078	81,373	63,705
Earnings Before Taxes	$ 254,126	$ 134,372	$119,754
Less			
Taxes (58.6%) (39%)	105,200	52,400	52,800
Earnings After Taxes	$ 148,926	$ 81,972	$ 66,954
Less			
Dividends	$ 108,540	107,501	1,039
Addition to Retained Earnings	$ 40,386	($ 25,529)	$ 65,915

Appendix 3.1 (continued)

Balance Sheet

			Increase (+) Decrease (−)
Current Assets	1981	1980	Over 1980
Cash	$ 9,065	$ 23,370	−$ 14,305
Short Term Investments	46,028	35,113	+ 10,915
Accounts and Notes Receivable, net	1,052,433	906,637	+ 145,796
Inventories			
Finished Equipment, supplies and accessories	691,455	554,939	+ 136,516
Work in Process	383,477	417,068	− 33,591
Prepaid taxes and other	119,878	96,834	+ 23,044
Total Current Assets	$2,302,306	$2,033,961	$ 268,345
Long-Term Receivables, net	$ 385,730	$ 349,366	+$ 36,364
Rental Equipment and Related Inventories	$1,628,777	$1,524,500	+$104,277
Less			
Accumulated Depreciation	716,624	693,532	+ 23,092
Net	$ 912,153	$ 830,968	+$ 81,185
Properties	$1,059,950	$ 920,259	+$139,691
Less			
Accumulated Depreciation	453,772	402,878	+ 50,894
Net	$ 606,178	$ 517,381	+$ 88,797
Other Assets	$ 233,033	$ 123,018	+$110,015
Total Assets	$4,439,400	$3,854,694	+$548,706

	1981	1980	Increase (+) Decrease (−) Over 1980
Current Liabilities			
Notes Payable	$ 397,442	$ 513,910	−$116,468
Current Maturities of Long Term Debt	31,343	106,548	− 75,205
Accounts Payable	397,104	270,641	+ 126,463
Accrued Payrolls & Commissions	163,752	107,922	+ 55,830
Accrued Taxes other than income Taxes	69,408	66,379	+ 3,029
Customers' Deposits & Prepayments	154,893	155,685	− 793
Dividends Payable	27,681	26,982	+ 699
Estimated Income Taxes	110,531	18,800	91,731
Total Current Liabilities	$1,352,154	$1,266,867	+$ 85,287
Long-Term Liabilities			
Deferred Income Taxes	$ 102,829	$ 90,346	+$ 12,483
Long Term Debt	$ 804,341	$ 372,455	+$431,886
Stockholders' Equity			
Common Stock ($5 par)	$ 210,317	$ 207,756	+$ 2,561
Paid-in Capital	448,144	436,041	+ 12,103
Retained Earnings	1,522,030	1,481,644	+ 40,386
Treasury Stock (41,000 shares at Cost)	(415)	(415)	0
Total Equity	$2,180,076	$2,215,026	+$ 55,050
Total Liabilities and Equity	$4,439,400	$3,854,694	+$584,706

Source: Burroughs 1981 Annual Report

4

OTHER FIRM AGGREGATE
MODELS AND CASH
FLOW ANALYSIS

This chapter presents alternative calculations of sustainable growth, including those based on accrual accounting values and those based on cash flows. The features of each approach are delineated and the usefulness of the models as instruments of management control are assessed.

The accounting-based models, essentially similar to the Higgins and Johnson models, are described in articles by Charles W. Kyd (1981, 1986). The cash flow models are derived from several sources, as cited in the text. The results from these versions will be compared with those obtained using the Higgins and Johnson models. Concluding comments address the questions of reconciling differences.

SUSTAINABLE GROWTH: ACCOUNTING NUMBERS

Exhibit 4.1 presents the illustrative data used in the explanation of the accounting models. These data are taken from the Annual Report 1986 of Ameritech (American Information Technologies Corporation). Ameritech is the parent of five Bell companies and several other communication-related subsidiaries (Annual Report 1986).

Balanced growth, referred to by Higgins and Johnson as sustainable growth, is termed affordable growth by Kyd. He defines the affordable growth rate (g^*) as "the annual percentage increase in sales which a firm can maintain while keeping its capital structure in balance" and that "is equal to the annual percentage increase in a firm's stockholders' equity section of its balance sheet" (Kyd 1981).

Exhibit 4.1
Ameritech Data, 1985

EBIT (Earnings Before Interest and Taxes)	$2,319.3 (millions)
EAT (Earnings After Taxes)	$1,077.7 (millions)
ROE (Return on Equity)	.147
EPS (Earnings Per Share)	$7.35
Dividends Per Share	$4.40
Number of Shares	$146.7 (millions)
Dividend Payout Ratio	.5986
Retention Ratio (1-D)	.4014
Leverage (L) = Debt/Equity	1.436
Return on Assets (ROA)	.05938
Tax RAte (T)	.4320122
Marginal Cost of Debt Capital (K_{dmc})	.5935817

(Approximated as a weighted average cost of existing debt capital)

Earnings on Assets EOA =

    EBIT for 1985/Total Assets at End of 1984   .131516

Earnings on Assets (EOA') =

    EBIT for 1985/Total Assets at end of 1985   .1277935

Note: See Appendix 4.1 for the pertinent financial statements of Ameritech.

AFFORDABLE GROWTH: BASIC MODEL

The basic model or growth equation is derived as follows:

$$g^* = \frac{\text{Earnings after dividends}}{\text{Beginning stockholders' equity}}$$

$$= \frac{\text{Earnings after dividends}}{\text{Earnings}}$$

$$= \frac{\text{Earnings after dividends}}{\text{Beginning stockholders' equity}}$$

$$= \text{Earnings retention ratio} \times \text{ROE}$$

$$= bR, \tag{4.1}$$

where

b = Earnings retention ratio $(1 - D)$, and

R = Return on equity (Kyd 1986).

Applying the Ameritech data, we have

g^* = 0.4014 × .147

= 0.0590058 or 5.9% (rounded).

The projected 1986 affordable growth rate (AGR) for Ameritech is thus calculated from the year-end financial statements of the previous period (1985). The actual growth (g) in sales for Ameritech in 1986 was as follows:

1986 revenues	$9,362,100,000
1985 revenues	$9,021,100,000
Increase in revenues	$ 341,000,000

$$g = \frac{\$341}{\$9,021.1} = 0.0378002 \text{ or } 3.78\%$$

The AGR of Ameritech exceeds the actual growth rate. Disparity between affordable or sustainable growth rates and the actual growth rate is not an uncommon phenomenon. These plus or minus variations are essentially attributable to two factors: (1) the dynamic nature of the growth process (the actual growth rate in the following period is, to some degree, self-financing) and (2) the assumptions of the growth models. However, the gap between actual and sustainable growth rates must be analyzed if affordable or sustainable growth concepts are to serve as viable tools of management control. We shall return to the topic in Chapter 9.

The basic AGR model depends on three assumptions:

1. Assets grow at the same rate as sales.
2. Debt increases at the same rate as equity.
3. Earnings after taxes is the only source of additions to equity.

Realistically, all these assumptions are dubious at best. Assets must grow at the same rate as sales only if the analysis commences with the firm operating at capacity. If at the end of the previous period the firm had excess capacity and inventories, sales could increase without a comparable increase in assets. For example, Ameritech revenues increased 3.78 percent in 1986 compared with an increase in assets of 3.25 percent. Similarly, debt need not increase at the same rate as equity, and there are other sources of additions or substractions from equity (write-offs, adjustments to retained earnings relating to prior periods, issuance of common stock, etc.). Finally, the basic model has small value as a tool of management planning and control.

AFFORDABLE GROWTH: STRATEGIC EQUATION

Initially used by Hewlett-Packard in the 1950s, the Strategic Equation represents an expansion of the basic model. The AGR is now measured by

$g^* =$ Earnings retention ratio $\times$ Leverage $\times$ Net profit margin
$\times$ Asset turnover.

Translating the equation into the symbols used in the Higgins model (Chapter 3, equation 3.1), we have

$$g^* = (1 - D) \times (1 + L) \times P \times T \qquad (4.2)$$

Because the product of the profit margin (P) and asset turnover (T) equals the return on assets (ROA), we may substitute ROA in equation 4.2. Thus

$$g^* = (1 - D) \times (1 + L) \times \text{ROA}. \qquad (4.3)$$

Inserting the Ameritech Data from Exhibit 4.1, we have

$$g^* = .0414 \times (1 + 1.436) \times 0.5938$$

$$= 0.0580623 \text{ or } 5.81\% \text{ (rounded)}.$$

The Strategic Equation facilitates the use of AGR in management planning and control. For example, using sensitivity analysis, management may identify a series of AGR rates and determine the appropriate financial structure dividend policy, degree of financial leverage, and so on for each AGR rate. Conversely, it might assume certain values for leverage and retention ratios and proceed to establish a compatible growth rate and target ROA necessary to achieve the desired rate of growth. The latter would assist the articulation of marketing and production strategies.

Although the Strategic Equation constitutes a significant improvement over the basic AGR formulation, its advantages are limited by the failure to explicitly treat tax and interest charges. Kyd (1981) notes:

It was said that ROA is the overall measure of operating performance. It is an appropriate measure when one wishes to take a broad view of a firm's performance. It is an inappropriate measure when one wishes to understand and evaluate internal operations in any detail because both interest and taxes, which are included in the numerator, tend to complicate the analysis of the other aspects of performance.

AFFORDABLE GROWTH: FINANCIAL PLANNING EQUATION

As the term connotes, the Financial Planning Equation is primarily designed to assess the impact of different degrees of financial leverage on affordable growth, to evaluate the risk of reliance on long-term debt capital, and to identify a possible optimal debt structure. The AGR is expressed by

$$g^* = (1 - D) \times (1 - T) \times (\text{EOA} + L \times (\text{EOA} - i)), \qquad (4.4)$$

where

$1 - D$ = Earnings retention ratio;

$1 - T$ = Effective tax rate;

EOA = Earnings before interest and taxes = (EBIT)/Total assets at the *beginning* of the period;

i = Average *before* tax cost of debt.

AGR, therefore, is a composite of two rates: (1) the before interest and tax return on firm assets as a result of operating performance and (2) the net benefit to equity from the use of debt. The composite of these two rates is reduced by two earning retention ratios: after dividends and after taxes.

Applying the Ameritech data to calculate the AGR at the end of 1985, we have

$$g^* = (1 - .5986) \times (1 - .4320122) \times (.131516 + 1.436)$$

$$\times (.131516 - .0594459)$$

$$= .4014 \times .5679878 \times (.131516 + 1.436 \times 0.720701)$$

$$= .2279903 \times (.131516 + .1034926)$$

$$= 0.0535817 \text{ or } 5.34\% \text{ (rounded)}.$$

The Financial Planning Equation demonstrates that the use of debt capital is warranted only if the cost of debt capital is significantly less than the return on assets before interest and taxes; and that AGR will consistently rise with successive increments in leverage, albeit subject to the commensurate increase in financial risk manifested in the greater volatility of earnings after taxes. The equation also allows management to evaluate the advantages and disadvantages of short-term, intermediate, and long-term debt by disaggregating the last term in the equation:

$$\frac{\text{Debt A}}{\text{Equity}} \times (\text{EOA} - \text{Interest rate A})$$

$$\frac{\text{Debt B}}{\text{Equity}} \times (\text{EOA} - \text{Interest rate B})$$

and so on, where Debt A + Debt B = total debt.

DUPONT EQUATION

The Financial Planning Equation represented the firm's operating performance (EOA) as earnings before interest and taxes (EBIT) divided by total assets. Exhibit 4.2 relates this measure of performance to the cost and asset centers that constitute measure. "The figure, in other words, outlines

Exhibit 4.2
DuPont Equation Detail

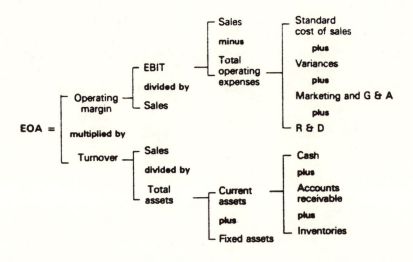

Source: Kyd (1981).

a framework which management can use to translate its overall growth and profitability objectives into objectives for departments and individuals at all levels of the firm" (Kyd 1981). The balance sheet data used in the Du-Pont Equation normally come from the present balance, not that at the end of the previous period—in this case Ameritech's total assets at the end of 1985. Recall that the Financial Planning Equation used the EBIT for 1985 in relation to the total assets at the end of 1984. By using current balance sheet data, management can establish both asset growth and earnings performance ratios for month-to-month reporting.

Comparing the two versions of EOA, we have

$$\text{EOA} = \frac{\text{EBIT for 1985}}{\text{Total assets at end of 1985}} = \frac{\$2,319.3}{\$17,635.1}$$

$$= .131516,$$

and the modified EOA

$$\text{EOA}' = \frac{\text{EBIT for 1985}}{\text{Total assets for 1985}} = \frac{\$2,319.3}{\$18,148.8} = .1277935.$$

The relation between the two measures thus becomes

$$\text{EOA}' = \frac{\text{EOA}}{1 + g^*}$$

Then

$$.1277935 = \frac{.131516}{1 + g^*}$$

and

$$g^* = .0291294 \text{ or } 2.91\% \text{ (rounded)}.$$

Because the numerator (EBIT) is the same for both equations (EOA and EOA'), the affordable sustainable growth (g^*) reflects the contribution of internal operations to the increase in total assets. EBIT measures the productivity of the firm's operating assets and constitutes a pool of income for the payment of interest, taxes, and dividends and the contribution to retained earnings. It focuses attention on key operating ratios such as

$$\text{Asset turnover} \times \text{Operating margin} = \text{EOA}$$

$$\frac{\text{Sales}}{\text{Total assets}} \times \frac{\text{EBIT}}{\text{Sales}} \times \frac{\text{EBIT}}{\text{Total assets}}$$

Using the 1985 data of Ameritech to illustrate the relation, we have

Asset turnover

$$\frac{\text{Sales}}{\text{Total assets}} = \frac{\$9,021.1}{\$18,148.8} = 0.490631$$

Operating Margin: Times

$$\frac{\text{EBIT}}{\text{Sales}} = \frac{\$2,319.3}{\$9.021.1} = 0.2570972$$

EOA   Equals

$$\frac{\text{EBIT}}{\text{Total assets}} = \frac{\$2,319.3}{\$18,148.8} = 0.1277935$$

Each of these key ratios can be disaggregated by department and/or division and by composition of total assets: current assets (cash, receivables, inventories), fixed assets, and so on to set performance goals for internal operations in relation to sustainable affordable growth.

The DuPont Equation calculates the firm's ability to grow through internal performance. Obviously management's ability to grow by retained earnings is constrained by several factors. A high operating margin does not necessarily produce commensurate increases in cash flow. If the firm consumes more cash than it generates, management will have to sell stock, reduce dividends, or resort to debt issues to raise the cash essential to maintain a desired growth rate. The nature of the industry—whether it is capital or labor intensive—and the mix of fixed and variable costs inhibit management's control over the operating margin. Capital-intensive firms will usually exhibit low asset turnover and high operating margins; firms with lower per capital fixed investment generally enjoy a higher asset turnover but lower operating margins. Competitive forces within the industry make it difficult for a firm to consistently improve on the ratios typical of its industry. Finally, the level of research and development (R&D) expenditure necessary to maintain the firm's market share affects the timing of cash flows. Cash outlays on R&D detract from cash flow in the short term and limit capacity to support sales growth by internal financing.

CASH FLOW MODELS (g_c^*)

The Higgins, Johnson, and Kyd models measure sustainable/affordable growth based on accrual accounting information. Accural accounting statements constitute an amalgam of values taken at different price levels and embody varying degrees of liquidity. Thus, in the models examined, the sustainable/affordable growth rate is determined by the historical values of the account distribution to take place at a price level that may be higher or lower than the average implicit in the distribution. The historical values of the balance sheet, for example, cycle through the income and expense statement, affecting the key variable in the growth models, that is, the profit margin (P). Moreover, the accretion in retained earnings ($P[1 - D]$) may be impounded in nonliquid assets or assets not currently producing income and not immediately available to finance growth in sales. Conversely, the growth calculation may be understated by charges against income that do not represent cash payments.

The growth models discussed above primarily rely on ratios of profitability—profit margins, sales to assets, return on assets, and so forth—which record sales or revenues (cash inflows, receivables, and accrued incomes) less operating and financial expenses (cash outflows, payables, and accrued expenses). It is the objective of cash flow analysis to adjust the conventional statements to show the cash available for investment (cash from operations, cash from net debt and equity transactions, the change in working capital) and the cash required for investment (cash outlays for plant and equipment, merger acquisitions, dividends, etc.). The bottom line, therefore, is the change in cash and temporary investments. Thus cash flow analysis does not abandon the traditional accounting information system. Rather, it builds on the information in the balance sheet and income statements to picture another aspect of the firm's situation, the statement of changes in financial position.

On the other hand, it is not appropriate simply to add back accruals and non-cash charges and call the product "cash flow." A too-common practice among practitioners is to add back depreciation expense to net income (EAT) to secure the firm's "cash flow." Gombola and Ketz (1983b) stress that financial analysts "employing net-income plus depreciation should be warned that this measure is not a measure of cash flow, but rather a measure of profitability." They distinguish between working capital from operations and cash flow from operations. Exhibit 4.3 shows the Gombola–Ketz adjustments to secure cash flow from operations.

We should take special note of depreciation and other accrued charges among the adjustments to convert conventional accounting statements to a cash flow basis. The accruals constitute tax deductions and thereby create tax savings. Nonetheless, depreciation is added back to earnings after taxes (EAT) without regard to tax effects. The rationale underlying the procedure can be illustrated by assuming a firm that keeps its books on a cash basis and has $20,000 in sales, a tax rate of 40 percent, and adds $10,000 to a cash fund for the replacement of fixed assets. The calculation on a cash basis is:

Profit and Loss Statement

Sales	$20,000
Depreciation	0
Earnings before taxes	$20,000
Taxes ($20,000 × .40)	(8,000)
Earnings after taxes	$12,000

Exhibit 4.3
Computation of Cash Flow

I - <u>Working Capital from Operations (WCO)</u> - WCO is equal to net income plus or minus the following items:

Additions

---

1. Depreciation expense, depletion expense, amortization of intangibles, and deferred charges.

2. Amortization of discount on bonds payable.

3. Amortization of premium on bond investments.

4. Additions to deferred investment tax credits.

5. Increase in deferred income taxes payable.

6. Pro-rate share of reported losses in excess of cash dividends recognized from unconsolidated stock investments under the equity method.

7. Minority interest in consolidated subsidiaries net income.

8. Losses from non-operating items.

Subtractions

---

1. Amortization of deferred credits.

2. Amortization of premium on bonds payable.

3. Amortization of discount on bond investments.

4. Amortization of deferred income taxes payable.

5. Decrease in deferred income taxes payable.

6. Pro-rate share of reported income in excess of cash dividends recognized from unconsolidated stock investment under the equity method.

7. Minority interest in consolidated subsidiaries net loss.

8. Gains from non-operating items.

II - <u>Cash Flow from Operations (CFO)</u> - CFO is equal to WCO plus or minus the following:

Exhibit 4.3 (Continued)

Additions

---

1. Decrease in trade accounts and notes receivable.

2. Decrease in inventory.

3. Decrease in prepaid expenses.

4. Increase in trade accounts and notes payable.

5. Increase in accrued liabilities.

Subtractions

---

1. Increase in trade accounts and notes receivable.

2. Increase in inventory.

3. Increase in prepaid expenses.

4. Decrease in trade accounts and notes payable.

5. Decrease in accrued liabilities.

Source: Gombola and Ketz (1983a).

Cash Flow

Inflows	$20,000
Outflows (tax payments)	(8,000)
Addition to cash or temporary investments	$12,000

On the cash basis, the firm does not pick up in the current period the tax savings on depreciation ($10,000 × .40) that would increase the addition to cash and temporary investments by $4,000.

Now assume that the same firm converts to accrual accounting. The calculation follows:

Profit and Loss Statement

Sales	$20,000
Depreciation	10,000
Earnings before taxes	$10,000
Taxes ($10,000 × .40)	(4,000)
Earnings after taxes	$ 6,000

Cash Flow

Inflows	$20,000
Outflows	(4,000)
Addition to cash or temporary investments	$16,000

or

Earnings after taxes	$ 6,000
Plus	
Depreciation	(10,000)
Addition to cash or temporary investment	$16,000

The same reasoning applies to other expenses that do not involve cash outlays (depletion, amortization of intangible assets, and deferred charges). By adding total depreciation to EAT we automatically adjust for the cash flow from the tax savings.

It should be obvious that to project sustainable/affordable growth from the statement of changes in financial position requires a model of greater complexity and a knowledgeable financial analyst to make the judgment calls on the content and calculations of the component variables. The complexity of the models and requisite experienced judgment of the analyst are traceable to the marked diversity between industries and firms within the same industry (Gombola and Ketz 1983a).

Casting the notion of sustainable growth in a cash flow context also broadens the question raised by the sustainable growth models of Higgins, Johnson, and Kyd. These accounting-based models asked the question "What rate of growth in sales can be maintained over the following period without the need to alter the existing financial (or capital) structure?" The models were also subject to a plethora of restrictive assumptions that detracted from their contribution to management planning. By contrast, the cash flow models *explicitly* ask the question "What is the sustainable growth rate in sales that can be maintained from resources required to finance the working capital and capital budgets of the firm?" The latter represent a draw down on financial resources (outflows) that may not be offset by inflows in the next period.

The accounting growth models are derived from the basic accounting equation: assets = liabilities + equity. The cash flow approach states that the firm is in equilibrium when the funds available for investment (FAI) = funds required for investment (FRI). FRI links directly to the working and capital budgets of the firm (Govindarajan and Shank 1984).

GOVINDARAJAN-SHANK MODEL

Govindarajan and Shank (1984) speak to the "maximum growth in sales that a firm can sustain" and advocate that statistic as an important element in cash sufficiency planning. Exhibit 4.4 presents their model illustrated with the data of a hypothetical company. The firm is in equilibrium with a sales growth rate of 20 percent. At this rate, cash "generated from operations plus the debt the internal funds are assumed to support just equals the funds required to support the incremental sales and to maintain the existing productive capacity (Govindarajan and Shank 1984)."

However, because of the nature of the utility business, the application of the model to Ameritech requires interpretation of the nine variables listed in Exhibit 4.4.

Exhibit 4.5 presents Ameritech's Statement of Changes in Financial Position, and Exhibit 4.6, the variables in the Govindarajan-Shank model defined to conform to the accepted practices and traditions of the communications industry. Exhibit 4.7 calculates Ameritech's cash sustainable growth using the Govindarajan-Shank model.

Typical of financial models, the Govindarajan-Shank model is not without caveats. Note the following.

1. The format assumes that to support each dollar of extra sales an extra investment in plant and equipment would be required. This would be a valid assumption only if the company were operating at capacity. If the company were operating at less than capacity, the extra investment in plant and equipment would be zero.

Exhibit 4.4

Computation of Sustainable Growth Rate for Hypothetical Company

Computation of Sustainable Growth Rate for a Hypothetical Company

Consider the following facts for a hypothetical company:

1. To support each $1 of extra sales, the extra investment in plant and equipment is $.50.

2. To support each $1 of extra sales, the extra investment in working capital is $.15.

3. For each $1 of sales, $.02 must be reinvested to maintain the productive capacity of the existing plant and equipment.

4. Profit before interest and taxes is 18 percent of sales.

5. Interest expense is 2 percent of sales.

6. Depreciation expense (a noncash charge) is 4.4 percent of sales.

7. The income tax rate is 50 percent, including federal, state, and local taxes.

8. The dividend payout is 40 percent of earnings after taxes.

9. Each $1 of retained cash from operations is supplemented with $.40 of borrowed funds[1].

1
Funds provided by operations = 16% x (1 - 50%) x (1 - 40%)

+ 4.4%

= 9.2% of sales

Funds available for investment = 9.2% x (1 + sales growth rate)

x (1 + 40%)

Funds required to be invested = (Sales growth rate x 50%)

+ (Sales growth rate x 15%)

+ ([1 + Sales growth rate] x 2%)

Exhibit 4.4 (Continued)

Since funds available for investment have to equal funds required to be invested for the hypothetical firm to be in equilibrium, algebraic derivation shows that the maximum sustainable sales growth will be 20 percent. The following illustrates this solution:

Funds available for investment = Funds required to be invested

$$9.2\% \times (1 + 20\%) \times (1 + 40\%) = (20\% \times 50\%) + (20\% \times 15\%) +$$

$$(1 + 20\%) \times 2\%$$

$$15.4\% = 15.4\%[2]$$

[1]The term "funds" refers to cash and temporary investments. "Temporary investments" denote short term, highly liquid investments of minimal risk of loss in principle, i.e. Treasury Bills, quality commercial paper.

[2]The Govindarajan and Shank (G & S) model described in Exhibit 4.4 makes nine assumptions concerning the relationship among various profit and loss and balance sheet accounts. For example, G & S state "To support each $1 of extra sales, the extra investment in plant and equipment is $.50." However, the realities of business allow few such certainties, except in the form of averages calculated over five or ten periods. Therefore, without averaging, the model's projection of sustainable growth can manifest wide swings in the volatility of the results. The model will be especially sensitive to leads and lags in the receipt and disbursement of funds.

Source: Govindarajan and Shank (1984).

Exhibit 4.5
American Information Technologies Corporation,
Consolidated Statement of Changes in Financial Position (Dollars in Millions)

Funds from Operations	1986	1985	1984
Net Income	1,138.4	1,077.7	990.6
Add Non Cash Expenses:			
Depreciation	1.664.5	1,602.7	1,347.3
Deferred Income Taxes-Net	215.3	202.3	263.8
Investment Tax Credit-Net	(14.5)	45.8	41.8
Deduct Income not Providing Funds			
Interest During Construction	42.0	44.2	30.6
working Capital from Operations	2,961.7	2,884.3	2,612.9
External Financing-Source (Uses)			
Issuance(Repurchase) Common Stock	(297.6)	(68.0)	96.6
Issuance of Long & Intermediate			
Debt	573.7	35.0	34.1
Increase (Decrease) in S/T			
Borrowings-Net	138.1	(58.3)	0.0
	414.2	(91.3)	130.7
Retirement of Long & intermediate			
Debt	(709.4)	(218.8)	(186.2)
	(295.2)	(310.1)	(55.5)

Exhibit 4.5 (Continued)

	1986	1985	1984
Uses of funds			
Construction Activity	2,076.3	1,991.3	1,746.6
Dividends	691.3	644.8	585.8
Acquisitions		217.5	
Other-Net	(95.9)	(4.5)	(108.9)
	2,671.7	2,849.1	2,223.5
Changes in Working Capital (Excluding Cash and Temporary Cash Investments, Debt Maturing in One Year, and Income Taxes Deferred For One Year)			
Receivables-Net	5.2	0.5	(171.8)
Material and Supplies	38.6	(53.1)	(65.0)
Other Current Assets-Net	5.0	(26.3)	(42.9)
Accounts Payable	60.2	104.3	29.6
Accrued Payroll	(9.6)	26.7	(0.6)
Accrued Taxes	110.0	0.4	(72.4)
Advance Billing and Customer's Deposits	12.2	9.7	1.1
Dividends Payable	18.1	13.6	147.1
Accrued Interest	(18.8)	(10.8)	(19.8)
	220.9	65.0	(155.1)
Increase (Decrease) in Cash and Temporary Cash Investments	215.7	(209.9)	178.8

Note: At the time of publication, the Financial Accounting Standards Board issued a release, FASB-95, that renders the Statement of Changes in Financial Position nominally obsolete. FASB-95 prescribes a new format under which the bottom line is Cash and Temporary Investments, as stated in the current balance sheet, in contrast to the old bottom line of Changes in Cash and Temporary Investments. The innovation, undertaken to assist investors, does not affect the models presented in the text. The required data for the models are clearly identified under the new format.
Source: Annual Report, Ameritech (1986).

Exhibit 4.6

Govindarajan and Shank Model—Ameritech Data, 1985 and 1986

(Dollars in Millions)

F = Fixed Asset Investment Rate (Construction Activity + Capitalized Interest + Acquisitions/Net Sales) =

$\underline{1985}$ = ($1,991.3 + $44.2 + $217.5 + $4.5)/$9,021.1 =

$2,248.5/$9,021.1 = 0.2492489

$\underline{1986}$ = ($2,076.3 + $42.0 + $95.9)/$9,362.1 =

$2,022.4/$9,362.1 = 0.2160199

Note: Capitalized Interest ($44.2 and $42.0) taken from Notes

to Consolidated Statements.

W = Change in Working Capital/Change in Net-Sales[1]:

$\underline{1985}$ = $144.9/$674.3 = 0.2148895

1986 = $436.3/$341 = 1.2803519

M = Maintenance Expense/Net-Sales:

$\underline{1985}$ = $1,646.9/$9,021.1 = 0.1825608

$\underline{1986}$ = $1,664.5/$9,362.1 = 0.1777913

P = EBIT/Net Sales:

$\underline{1985}$ = $2,319.3/$9,021.1 = 0.2570972

$\underline{1986}$ = $2,458.2/$9,362.1 = 0.2625692

i = Interest Expense/Net Sales:

$\underline{1985}$ = $421.9/$9,021.1 = 0.0467681

1986 = $390.4/$9,362.1 = 0.0417000

D_p = Depreciation Expense/Net Sales:

$\underline{1985}$ = $1,602.7/$9,021.1 = 0.1776612

$\underline{1986}$ = $1,664.5/$9,362.1 = 0.1777913

T = Income Tax Rate = Tax Expense/EBT:

$\underline{1985}$ = $819.7/$1,897.4 = 0.4320122

$\underline{1986}$ = $929.4/$2,067.8 = 0.4494849

D = Dividend Rate = Dividends/EAT =

$\underline{1985}$ = $644.8/$1,077.7 = 0.5983112

$\underline{1986}$ = $691.3/$1,138.2 = 0.6072557

Exhibit 4.6 (Continued)

```
R  = Debt Supplement to Internally Generated Funds =

     Change in Long and Intermediate Debt²/Cash Retained by
     Company³ where Cash Retained by Company = Working Capital
     Provided by Operations + Change in Working Capital⁴ -
     Dividends

     1985 = ($281.7)/$2,304.5 = -0.1222390

     1986 = ($21)/$2,491.3 = -0.0084293
```

Notes:
[1]Change in Working Capital includes Cash and Temporary Cash Investments.
[2]Taken from Balance Sheets of cited years.
[3]Taken from Statement of Changes in Financial Condition, Exhibit 4.5.
[4]Change in Working Capital excludes Cash and Temporary Cash Investment.

2. If an extra investment in plant and equipment is required to service additional dollars of sales, it may not be possible to acquire the addition to fixed assets in time to service the next period's sales. This would place a constraint on sustainable growth outside the parameters of the model, a common problem in capital budgeting.

3. The model establishes linear relations between sales and other variables such as maintenance, EBIT, depreciation, working capital, and interest expense. Actually these relations are not constant from period to period or from one sales level to another. In other words, the relations need not be linear. We know, for example, that in many industries, up to some point, average variable cost will decrease as sales increase and turn upward, forming a U-shaped curve.

These troubles, of course, can be mitigated by constructing pro-forma financial statements for the next period and from these estimating the component values required by the model.

4. The model, as interpreted for the Ameritech situation, is sensitive to changes in the firm's cash or debt position that are not reflected in *sales-generating* fixed asset purchases or acquisitions. As noted in *#2* above, the event lies outside the parameters of the model. The issue is discussed in Chapter 9. A similar situation arises when a firm accumulates excess cash and temporary investments from internal operations and/or debt not intended for operational employment. Defense against takeover moves represents a case in point.

Exhibits 4.8, 4.9, and 4.10 use Campbell Soup data for 1981 and 1982 to measure cash sustainable growth by the Govindarajan–Shank model.

Exhibit 4.7
Govindarajan and Shank Model—Solution Using Ameritech Data

I - Funds Provided by Operations (FPO) =

$\quad$ (P - i) x (1 - T) x (1 - D) + Dp

$\quad$ <u>1985</u>

$\quad$ (0.2570972 - 0.0467681) x (1 - 0.4320122) x

$\quad$ (1 - 0.5983112) + 0.1776612

$\quad$ = 0.2103162 x 0.5679878 x 0.4016888 + 0.177612 =

$\quad$ = 0.2255965

$\quad$ <u>1986</u>

$\quad$ (0.2625692 - 0.0417000) x (1 - 0.4494849) x

$\quad$ (1 - 0.6072557) + 0.1777913

$\quad$ = 0.2208692 x 0.5505151 x 0.3927443 + 0.1777913 =

$\quad$ = 0.2255457

II- Funds Available for Investment (FAI) =

$\quad$ FPO x (1 + gc*) x (1 + R)

$\quad$ <u>1985</u>

$\quad$ 0.2255965 x (1 + gc*) x (1 + 0.1222390)

$\quad\quad$ <u>1986</u>

$\quad\quad$ 0.2255457 x (1 + gc*) x (1 + 0.0084293)

III - Funds Required for Investment (FRI) =

$\quad$ (gc* + F) + (gc* + W) + ([1 + gc*] x M)

$\quad\quad$ <u>1985</u>

$\quad\quad$ = (gc* x 0.2492489) + (gc* x (-0.2148895)) + ([1 + gc*] x 0.1825608)

$\quad\quad$ <u>1986</u>

$\quad\quad$ = (gc* x 0.2160199) + (gc* x 1.2803519) + ([1 + gc*] x

$\quad\quad\quad$ 0.177913)

66

Exhibit 4.7 (Continued)

IV - Funds Available for Investment (FAI) = Funds Required for Investment

(FRI) =

FPO x (1 + gc) x (1 + R) = (gc x F) + (gc x W) + ([1 + gc] x M)

Solving for sustainable growth by cash flow (gc) =

$$gc* = \frac{FPO + (FPO \times R) - M}{(F + W + M - FPO) - (FPO \times R)}$$

1985

$$gc* = \frac{0.2255965 + (0.2255965 \times (-0.1222390)) - 0.1825608}{\begin{array}{l}0.2492489 + (-0.2148895) + 0.1825608 - 0.2255965) \\ - (0.2255965 \times 0.1222390)\end{array}}$$

$$= \frac{0.01544617}{-0.0086763 - (-0.0275766)}$$

$$= \frac{0.0154461}{0.0189003}$$

= 0.8172409 or 81.72% (rounded)

1986

$$gc* = \frac{0.2255457 + (0.2255457 \times (-0.0084293)) - 0.1777913}{\begin{array}{l}(0.2160199 + 1.2803519 + 0.1777913 - 0.2255457) - \\ (0.2255457 \times (-0.0084293)\end{array}}$$

$$= \frac{0.0458533}{1.4486174 - (- 0.0019011)}$$

$$= \frac{0.0458533}{1.4467163}$$

= 0.0316947 or 3.17% (rounded)

67

Exhibit 4.8
Campbell Soup Company, Consolidated Statements of Changes in Financial Position
(Dollars in Millions)

	1982	1981	1980
Cash provided by:			
Operations			
Net Earnings	$149,613	$129,717	$121,655
Items not requiring the use of funds			
Depreciation and Amortization	87,990	79,418	69,716
Other, principally deferred taxes	8,951	6,481	5,211
(Increase)Decrease in Operating			
Working Capital(see below)	61,139	23,200	(69,215)
Effect of translation adjustments			
on Working Capital	(6,603)		
Cash provided by operations	301,630	238,816	127,367
Borrowings			
Long-term debt incurred	112,624	36,114	109,855
Long-term debt repaid	(28,273)	(23,406)	(8,274)
Increase(decrease) in short-term			
debt	(31,183)	(3,877)	79,289
Cash provided by borrowings	53,168	8,831	180,237
	354,798	247,647	308,237
Cash used for:			
Plant assets			
Purchased	147,574	135,402	97,391
Acquired	28,354	19,873	58,405
Sold	(11,208)	(13,268)	(13,806)
	164,720	142,007	141,990
Goodwill and other assets	12,312	49,470	65,503
Dividends	67,709	66,298	61,479
Treasury stock transactions,net	361	21,061	1,578
Other, net	13,359	(13,130)	(19,828)
	258,461	265,706	254,722

Exhibit 4.8 (Continued)

Increase(decrease) in cash and temporary investments	$96,337	$(18,059)	$53,515
	=======	=========	=======
(Increase)decrease in operating working capital:			
(Increase)decrease in accounts receivable	2,175	(11,555)	(32,692)
(Increase)decrease in inventories	13,809	16,819	86,883
(Increase)decrease in prepaid expenses	4,195	(6,821)	(7,800)
Increase(decrease) in payable to suppliers and others	32,395	16,411	22,773
Increase(decrease) in accrued liabilities	8,565	8,346	35,387
	$61,139	$23,200	$(69,215)
	=======	=======	========

Note: In 1982, the Company adopted the cash flow concept of the Statement of Changes in Financial Position. The 1981 and 1980 Statements have been reclassified to conform with the concept. The accompanying Summary of Significant Accounting Policies and Notes are an integral part of the financial statements.

Source: Annual Reports 1981 and 1982, Campbell Soup Company; Appendix 4.2.

—

Exhibit 4.9
Govindarajan and Shank Model—Campbell Soup Company, 1981-1982
(Dollars in Millions)

F = Fixed Asset Investment Rate (Net Fixed Assets Purchased + Capitalized Interest + Acquisitions/Net Sales):

    1981 = ($135,402 + $1,712 + $19,873 + $13,268)/$2,797,663

       = 0.051371

    1982 = ($147,574 + $8,693 + $28,354 + $11,208)/$2,944,779

       = 0.0588791

W = Change in Working Capital/Change in Net Sales[1]:

    1981 = $5,141/$237,094 = 0.0216833

    1982 = $157,476/$147,116 = 1.0704206

M = Maintenance Expense/Net Sales:

    1981 = $90,484/$2,797,663 = 0.0323427

    1982 = $93,722/$2,933,779 = 0.0318264

P = EBIT/Net Sales:

    1981 = $274,669/$2,797,663 = 0.098178

    1982 = $298,802/$2,933,779 = 0.1014683

i = Interest Expense/Net Sales:

    1981 = $30,302/$2,797,663 = 0.0108311

    1982 = $21,939/$2,944,779 = 0.0074501

Exhibit 4.9 (Continued)

D_p = Depreciation Expense/Net Sales:

<u>1981</u> = $79,418/$2,797,663 = 0.0283872

<u>1982</u> = $87,990/$2,944,779 = 0.02988

T = Income Tax Rate = Tax Expense/EBT:

<u>1981</u> = $114,650/$244,367 = 0.4691713

<u>1982</u> = $127,250/$276,863 = 0.4596135

D = Dividend Rate = Dividends/EAT:

1981 = $66,298/$129,717 = 0.5110972

1982 = $67,709/$149,613 = 0.4525609

R = Debt Supplement to Internally Generated Funds = Change in Long and Intermediate Debt /Cash Retained By Company(2, 3)

where Cash Retained by Company = Working Capital Provided by Operations + Change in Working Capital(4) - Dividends

1981 = $12,708/($215,616 + $23,200 - $66,298)

= $12,708/$172,518 = 0.0736618

1982 = $85,573/($240,491 + $61,139 - $67,709)

= $85,573/$233,921 = 0.36582

Notes:
[1]Change in Working Capital includes Cash and Temporary Cash Investments.
[2]Taken from Balance Sheets of cited years.
[3]Taken from Statement of Changes in Financial Condition, Exhibit 4.8.
[4]Change in Working Capital excludes Cash and Temporary Investments.

Exhibit 4.10
Govindarajan and Shank Model—Solution Using Campbell Soup Data

I - Funds Provided by Operations(FPO) = $(P - 1)$ x $(1 - T)$ x

$(1 - D) + D_p$ =

1981

= $(0.098178 - 0.0108311)$ x $(1 - 0.4691713)$ x $(1 - 0.5110972)$

+ 0.0283872

= (0.0873469) x (0.5308287) x (0.4889028) + 0.0283872

= 0.0510557

1982

= $(0.1014683 - 0.0074501)$ x $(1 - 0.4596135)$ x

$(1 - 0.4525609)$ + 0.02988

= (0.0940182) x (0.5403865) x (0.5474391) + (0.02988)

= 0.0576932

II - Funds Available for Investment(FAI):

= FPO x $(1 + g_c)$ x $(1 + R)$

1981

= 0.0510557 x $(1 + g_c)$ x $(1 + 0.36582)$

1982

= 0.0510557 x $(1 + g_c)$ x $(1 + 0.36582)$

III - Funds Required for Investment(FRI):

= $(g*_c$ x F$)$ + $(g*_c$ x W$)$ + $([1 + g*_c]$ x M$)$

1981

= $(g*_c$ x 0.051371$)$ + $(g*_c$ x 0.0216833$)$ + $([1 + g*_c]$ x

$0.0323427)$

1982

= $(g*_c$ x 0.0588791$)$ + $(g*_c$ x 1.0704206$)$ + $([1 + g*_c]$ x

$0.0318264)$

IV - Funds Available for Investment (FAI) = Funds Required for

Investment(FRI):

= FPO x $(1 + g*_c)$ x $(1 + R)$ = $(g*_c$ x F$)$ + $(g*_c$ x W$)$ +

$([1 + g*_c]$ x M$)$

72

Exhibit 4.10 (Continued)

Solving for sustainable growth by cash flow $(g*c)$ =

$$g*c = \frac{FPO + (FPO \times R) - M}{(F + W + M - FPO) - (FPO \times R)}$$

<u>1981</u>

$g*_c = \dfrac{0.0510557 + (0.0510557 \times 0.098178) - 0.0323427}{(0.051371 + 0.0216833 + 0.0323427 - 0.0510557) -}$
$(0.0510557 \times 0.98178)$

$\quad = \dfrac{0.0237205}{(0.0543413) - (0.0050125)}$

$\quad = \dfrac{0.0237255}{0.0493288}$

$\quad = 0.4809664$ or 48.1%(rounded)

<u>1982</u>

$g*_c = \dfrac{0.0576932 + (0.0576932 \times 0.36582) - 0.0318264}{(0.0588791 + 1.0704206 + 0.0318264 - 0.0576932) -}$
$(0.0576932 \times 0.36582)$

$\quad = \dfrac{0.0469721}{1.1034329 - 0.0211053}$

$\quad = \dfrac{0.0469721}{1.0823276}$

$\quad = 0.0433991$ or 4.34% (rounded)

SUMMARY

It will be helpful at this point to recapitulate the growth rates projected by the different models for Ameritech and the Campbell Soup Company:

Ameritech	g^* (%)
Higgins (after tax)	
1985 (end-of-year calculation)	6.16
1986 (end-of-year calculation)	6.22
Johnson (after tax)	
1985 (end-of-year calculation)	4.86
1986 (end-of-year calculation)	4.84
Kyd models (after tax)	
Basic—1985 (end-of-year calculation)	5.90
Strategic—1985 (end-of-year calculation)	5.81
Financial Planning—1985 (end-of-year calculation)	5.34
DuPont	
1985 (end-of-year calculation)	2.91
Govindarajan-Shank (after tax)	
1985 (end-of-year calculation)	81.72
1986 (end-of-year calculation)	3.17
Actual 1985-1986	3.80
Campbell Soup Company	
Higgins (after tax)	
1981	6.75
1982	8.41
Johnson (after tax)	
1981	6.93
1982	8.72
Govindarajan-Shank	
1981	48.1
1982	4.34
Actual	
1981–1982	9.26
1982–1983	5.26

Some observations are in order. The Govindarajan–Shank model is extremely sensitive to changes in the cash or debt position that are not applied to fixed asset purchases or acquisitions. These changes affect the debt supplement to internally generated funds (R) and can skew the results significantly if an increase in debt results in an increase in cash. Both Campbell and Ameritech exhibited substantial variations in R. For Campbell, R increased from 0.0736618 in 1981 to 0.36582 in 1982, while the change in cash and temporary investments jumped from $(18,059) in 1981 to $96,337 in 1982; for Ameritech, R increased from -0.1222390 in 1985 to -0.0084293 in 1986, and the change in cash and temporary investments rose from $(209.9) in 1985 to $215.7 in 1986. In all cases funds provided by operations were remarkably stable.

The Ameritech case, as noted above, suggests the need to divide assets into operational and nonoperational categories. Firms expend funds for many purposes not directly or immediately associated with net sales. These include capital investments that require long periods of construction before they become operational, R&D expenditures, developing defensive positions against possible takeover moves, accumulating reserves against unfavorable economic conditions, and so forth. Chapter 9 illustrates a methodology for adopting the Govindarajan–Shank model to account for nonoperational expenditures. By failing to allow for nonoperational investments, the models overstate the assets available to support current sales.

In 1985 the sustainable growth projections were generally higher than the actual growth for Ameritech (except for the Govindarajan–Shank model). In 1981 the sustainable growth of Campbell's was generally lower than the actual growth and in 1982 generally higher (except for the Govindarajan–Shank model). The literature, although hardly voluminous, suggests that actual growth trends exceed sustainable growth. The Higgins and Kevin (1983) study attributes this in the retailing industry to increased financial leveraging. However, one would intuitively expect a disparity to result from the self-financing of growth as the firm moves dynamically through the next period. Similarly, the business cycle would seem to have a role. As the economy moves from prosperity to recession, it would seem reasonable to expect that sustainable growth would exceed actual growth. Then, as the recession erodes profits and retained earnings, sustainable growth would decline. In the upswing of the cycle it would seem natural for actual growth to exceed sustainable growth. However, much more empirical research is required to validate these intuitive generalizations.

We may now turn our attention to another cash version of sustainable growth.

OLSON MODEL

The Olson model is cast in direct dollar values for cash flow (with two exceptions), rather than in ratios anchoring the variables to net sales, earnings before interest and taxes (EBIT), earnings before taxes (EBT), or earnings after taxes (EAT). The disadvantage of the latter approach is twofold. First, the variables in the statement of changes in financial condition may not correlate directly with the designated base value. Leads and lags complicate the adjustment of the variables. There exists an intricate web of variances and covariances among the variables in the statement. Second, the size of the account values and the degree of correlation with the denominators selected is at least partially subject to management decision and budget process controls, that is, the interlocking of operating, liquidity, and capital budgets. In short, ratios are not cast in stone from period to period, and reflect, within limits, the changing objectives and nuances in firm planning.

Exhibit 4.11 presents the significant account variables in the model using Ameritech data from Exhibit 4.5. Appendix 4.1 contains the derivation of the Olson model.

In final form, the model is expressed

$$g_c^*{}_{1986} = \frac{F + D + O_u - E + i - S_E}{(P - W)S_O} = \frac{P}{P - W} \tag{4.5}$$

$$g_c^*{}_{1986} = \frac{\$2,076.3 + \$691.3 + (\$-95.9) - \$1,865.3 + \$42.0 - (\$-295.2)}{(0.121966 - (-0.152492))\,\$9,021.1}$$

$$- \frac{0.1215966}{0.1215966 - (-0.0152492)}$$

$$= \frac{\$1143.6}{0.1368458 \times \$9,021.1} - \frac{0.1215966}{0.1368452}$$

$$= .926372 - 0.8885704.$$

Exhibit 4.11
Olson Model—Ameritech Data, 1985–1986 (Dollars in Millions)

F = Addition to Plant and Equipment = \$2,076.3

D = Dividends Paid = \$691.3

O_u = Other Use of Funds = (\$95.9)

E = Expenses Not Requiring Current Outlays (Depreciation, Deferred Income Taxes, Investment Tax Credits) = \$1,664.5 + \$215.3 + (\$14.5) = \$1,865.3

i = Income Not Currently Providing Cash = \$42

S_E = External Sources of Funds = (\$295.2)

P = Profit Margin = \$1,138.4/\$9,362.1 = 0.1215966

W = Cash and Temporary Investments(Increase or Decrease) = Changes in Working Capital/Change in Sales =

($215.7 - $220.9)/($9.362.1 - $9,021.1) = ($5.2)/$341 = 0.0152492

S = Net Sales = 1986: \$9,362.1; 1985: \$9,021.1

$\triangle S$ = Change in Sales = S_{1986} -S_{1985} = \$9,361.1 - \$9,021.1 = \$341

Then

$$g_c^*{}_{1986} = 0.0377968 \text{ or } 3.78\% \text{ (rounded)}.$$

The 3.78 percent growth rate computed on 1986 data exactly equals the actual growth rate in sales from 1985 to 1986.

$$(S_{1986} - S_{1985} = \frac{\$9,362.1 - \$9,021.1}{\$9,021.1} = \frac{\$341}{\$9,021.1} = 3.78\%)$$

The Olson model is also applied to the Campbell Soup Company for the 1981–1982 fiscal years. Exhibit 4.8 contains the appropriate data for g_c^* and Exhibit 4.12 displays the calculated variables.

$$g_c^*{}_{1986} = \frac{F + D + O_u - E + i - S_E}{(P - W)S_O} - \frac{P}{P - W} \tag{4.5}$$

$$g_c^*{}_{1982} = \frac{\$164,720 + \$67.709 + \$26.032 - \$96.941 + 0 - \$53.168}{(0.0508061 - 0.2804657)\ \$2,797,663}$$

$$- \frac{0.0508061}{0.0508061 - 0.2804657}$$

$$= \frac{\$108.352}{\$642,510.16} - \frac{0.0508061}{0.2296596}$$

$$= 0.525849 \text{ or } 5.26\% \text{ (rounded)}$$

The sustainable growth rate of 5.26 percent coincides with the actual growth in Campbell net sales from 1981 to 1982. From the 1982 data, therefore, *assuming the same pattern of cash flows*, we would project a sustainable growth for 1982–83 of 5.26 percent. The actual growth rate, however, could be higher if the cash flow from operations increased during the 1982–83 period, or if Campbell sought additional outside funding or reduced its dividend payout. Recall that we have mentioned that actual growth can exceed sustainable growth owing in part to the self-generating factor in the actual growth rate, that is, the contribution of current operations to cash flow as the firm moves dynamically through the next fiscal period.

In addition, the analyst using the Olson model can plug in an estimate of each variable to obtain a sustainable growth rate for the next period. If the actual growth rate (g) were then to exceed the sustainable (g_c^*), the discrepancy could be analyzed in terms of forecast error, the self-generating factor in the actual growth rate, or new financing by the firm.

The Campbell calculation again illustrates the need for caution in applying cash flow models to different firms. The content and the positioning of the

Exhibit 4.12
Olson Model—Campbell Soup Company Data, 1981-1982
(Dollars in Millions)

1982

F = Additions to Plant and Equipment = $164,720

D = Dividends Paid = $67,709

O_u = Other Use of Funds = (Goodwill, Treasury

    Stock Transactions) $26,032

E = Expenses Not Requiring Current Outlays

    (Depreciation, Amortization, Deferred Taxes)= $96,941

i = Income Not Currently Providing Cash =   0

S_E = External Sources of Funds = $53,168

P = EAT/Sales = $149,613/$2,944,779 =   0.0508061

W = Cash and Temporary Investments (Increase or Decrease) -

    Changes in Working Capital/Change in Sales = ($96,337 -

    $55,076)/$147,116 = $41,261/$147,116 +   0.2804657[1]

S = Net Sales = 1982: $149,614; 1981: $129,717

ΔS = Change in Sales = S_{1982} - S_{1981} =
    $149,613 - $129,717 = $19,896

g = Actual Growth in Sales 1981 to 1982 =

    $147,116/$2,797,663 = 0.0525853 or 5.26%(rounded)

A = Effect of Translation Adjustment on

    Working Capital   ($6,063)

[1] Change in Working Capital ($61,139) adjusted for Translation
Adjustments on Working Capital ($6,063)

variables differ with each firm, although the overall schemata and objective of the statement of changes in financial position remain constant. The reader is also alerted—and this is true in the interpretation of all financial statements—that a truly precise estimate of the firm's cash flow can be accomplished only from inside the firm. The external picture presented in annual reports and 10 K's to SEC, is always proximate. This is not the product of disingenuousness, but of the added complexity of reports as the attempt is made to convey more detailed information.

The Govindarajan-Shank model uses the present to project the future. The Olson model uses the actual growth in sales and supporting cash resources to provide a bench mark for future planning.

REFERENCES

Annual Report of the American Information Technologies Corporation and Subsidiaries (Ameritech), 1986.

Annual Report of the Campbell Soup Company, 1981 and 1982.

Bradley, Gale T., and Ben Branch. "Cash Flow Analysis: More Important Than Ever," *Harvard Business Review*, July/August 1981, pp. 132–135.

Fruhan, William E. "How Fast Should a Company Grow?" *Harvard Business Review*, January/February 1984, pp. 84–93.

Gombola, Michael J., and J. Edward Ketz. "A Note on Cash Flow and Classification Patterns of Financial Ratios," *The Accounting Review*, January 1983a, pp. 105–114.

———. "A Caveat on Measuring Cash Flow and Solvency," *Financial Analysts Journal*, September/October 1983b, pp. 66–72.

Govindarajan V., and John K. Shank. "Cash Sufficiency: The Missing Link in Strategic Planning," *Corporate Accounting*, Winter 1984, pp. 23–31.

Higgins, Robert C., and Roger A. Kerin. "Managing the Growth-Financial Policy Nexus in Retailing," *Journal of Retailing*, Fall 1983, pp. 19–48.

Kyd, Charles W. "Managing the Financial Demands of Growth," *Management Accounting*, December 1981, pp. 33–41.

———. "Determining Sustainable Growth," *Lotus*, February 1986.

APPENDIX 4.1
CONSOLIDATED FINANCIAL STATEMENTS, AMERICAN INFORMATION TECHNOLOGIES CORPORATION AND SUBSIDIARIES (AMERITECH)

	1986	1985	1984
Total Revenues	$9,362.1	$9,021.1	$8,346.8
Costs and expenses Maintenance	1,656.1	1,646.9	1,587.9
Depreciation	1,664.5	1,602.7	1,347.3
Other operating expenses	2,922.4	2,763.0	2,546.5
Taxes other than income taxes	694.2	719.5	714.0
	6,937.2	6,732.1	6,195.7
Other income-net	33.3	30.3	61.5
Income before interest and income taxes	2,458.2	2,319.3	2,212.6
Interest expense	390.4	421.9	436.6
Income before income taxes	2,067.8	1,897.4	1,776.0
Income taxes	929.4	819.7	785.4
Net Income	$1,138.4	$1,077.7	$990.6
Earnings per share*	$7.87	$7.35	$6.78
Dividends per share*	$4.79	$4.40	$4.00
Average common shares outstanding (millions)	144.6	146.7	146.1

*Share and per share data reflect three-for-two stock split effective December 31, 1986.

	Dec. 31, 1986	Dec. 31, 1985
Current Assets		
Cash and temporary cash investments	$ 357.9	$ 142.2
Receivables less allowance for uncollectibles of $76.9 and $70.0, respectively	1,545.4	1,589.6
Material and supplies	173.8	212.4
Other	248.5	253.5
Total Current Assets	2,364.	2,197.7
Fixed Assets		
Property plant and equipment		
In service	22,393.3	20,956.6
Under construction	451.8	495.4
	22,845.1	21,452.0
Less accumulated depreciation	7,056.2	6,090.5
	15,788.9	15,361.5
Other assets and deferred charges	585.9	589.6
Total assets	$18,739.4	$18,148.8

Liabilities and Shareowners' Equity

Current Liabilities

Debt maturing within one year	$ 227.7	$ 227.6
Accounts payable	1,304.2	1,244.6
Accrued payroll	93.1	102.7
Accrued taxes	505.7	395.7
Income taxes deferred for one year	185.9	141.4
Advance billing & customers' deposits	204.5	192.3
Dividend payable	178.8	160.7
Accrued interest	96.4	115.2
	2,796.3	2,579.6
Long and intermediate term debt	4,496.6	4,517.6

Deferred credits

Accumulated deferred income taxes	2,805.3	2,572.4
Unamortized investment tax credits	921.4	935.9
Other	110.9	93.8
	3,837.5	3,602.1

Shareowners' Equity

Common stock	$ 146.9	$ 98.1
Proceeds in excess of par value	5,555.5	5,616.5
Reinvested earnings	2,250.0	1,802.9
Treasury stock, at cost	(343.4)	(68.0)
	7,609.0	7,449.5
Total Liabilities and Shareowners' Equity	$18,739.4	$18,148.8

APPENDIX 4.2
CONSOLIDATED FINANCIAL STATEMENTS, CAMPBELL SOUP COMPANY
CONSOLIDATED STATEMENT OF EARNINGS

	1982	1981	1980
	(52 weeks)	(52 weeks)	(53 weeks)
Net sales	$ 2,944,779	$ 2,797,663	$ 2,560,569
Costs and expenses			
Cost of products sold	2,221,341	2,172,806	1,976,754
Marketing and sales expenses	305,700	256,726	213,703
Administrative and research expenses	118,936	93,462	102,445
Interest - net	21,939	30,302	10,135
	2,667916	2,553,296	2,303,037
Earnings before taxes	276,916	244,367	257,532
Taxes on earnings	127,250	114,650	122,950
Earnings before prior year effect of change in accounting principle	149,613	129,717	134,582
Prior year effect of 1980 change to LIFO method of inventory accounting	(12,655)		
Net earnings	$149,613	$129,717	$121,655

Per share (based on average shares outstanding):

Earnings before prior year effect of change in accounting principle	4.64	4.00	4.08
Prior year effect of 1980 change to LIFO method of inventory accounting	(.39)		
Net earnings	4.64	4.00	3.69

	Aug. 1, 1982	Aug. 2, 1981
Current assets		
Cash	$22,588	$26,515
Temporary investments, at cost (approximates market)	178,960	78,696
Accounts receivable	214,271	216,446
Inventories	470,385	484,194
Prepaid expenses	35,297	39,492
	921,501	845,343
Other assets	128,640	122,513
Plant assets, net of depreciation	815,378	755,020
	$1,865,519	$1,722,876

Current liabilities

Notes payable	$93,603	$124,786
Payable to suppliers and others	253,772	221,377
Accrued payrolls, taxes, etc.	87,281	88,081
Accrued income taxes	52,218	42,853
	486,874	477,097
Long-term debt	236,160	150,587
Other liabilities	6,643	19,237
Deferred income taxes	80,080	75,445

Stockholders' equity

Capital stock	20,343	20,343
Capital surplus	35,184	35,122
Earnings retained	1,083,725	999,966
Capital stock in treasury, at cost	(55,282)	(54,921)
Cumulative translation adjustments	28,208	_____
	1,055,762	1,000,510
	$1,865,519	$1,722,876

APPENDIX 4.3
DERIVATION OF OLSON MODEL

Net Income = P (So + S)

Hence, $P (So + S) + E - I + SE = F + D + O_u + NWC$

Where, NWC denotes Net Working Capital

Then,

$P (So + S) + E - I + SE = F + D + O_u + WS$

Where,

$WS = NWC / S = (C_T - WC) / S$

and S represents Net Sales and ΔS the change in Net Sales

Then,

$S (P) + SoP + E - I + S = P - W \hat{} S$

and,

$(P - W) \hat{} S = (F + D + O_u - E + I - S_E) / So - P$

Therefore,

$$g^*_c = \frac{S}{So} = \frac{F + D + O_u - E + 1 - S_E}{(P - W)So} - \frac{P}{(P - W)}$$

F = Addition to Plant and Equipment

D = Dividends Paid

O_u = Other Use of Funds

E = Expenses Not Requiring Current Outlays

I = Income Not Currently Providing Cash

S_E = External Sources of Funds

P = Profit Margin = EAT / Net Sales

W = Cash and Temporary Investments

S = Net Sales at the End of Period t

So = Net Sales at the Beginning of Period t

NWC= Net Working Capital

C_T = Cash and Temporary Investment

5

DISAGGREGATED MODEL OF SUSTAINABLE GROWTH

The models presented in the previous chapters assume that certain key ratios are held constant throughout the planning period. If this is a reasonable approximation of the experiences of the firm, these models can be used in conjunction with its strategic plan. For many firms, however, the key ratios are not stable from period to period. In this chapter we present disaggregated models of sustainable growth that can be used when the ratios are subject to period-to-period fluctuations. The models can also be used to determine the interrelations among the firm's financial policy, dividend policy, asset management, operating performance, and growth. In this manner it can be ascertained whether the firm's financial and dividend policies, performance goals, and growth objectives are mutually feasible.

THE DISAGGREGATED MODEL

The assumptions used by some of the models of sustainable growth (Higgins 1977, 1981; Johnson 1981) were described in Chapter 3. These models may be of only limited use to financial managers because of their restrictive assumptions and the nature of a static formulation. As developed, a constant ratio between asset accounts and sales is implicitly assumed. The models also assume a constant profit margin throughout the planning period. Moreover, these models implicitly assume that the firm is operating in perfectly competitive markets. A characteristic of a perfectly competitive market is that the firm can sell all the products that it is capable of producing at a constant price without fear of any reaction from its competitors. Unfortunately most firms do not operate in this type of market.

In the Higgins model it was assumed that the firm maintained a constant financial structure. Johnson relaxed this assumption by reformulating the model with a constant capital structure, noting that "for a given increase in nominal sales the increase in nominal current liabilities . . . automatically arises from the corresponding purchases of material on credit, accrued labor charges, and drawing down lines of credit in the ordinary course of producing for this new nominal sales level" (Johnson 1981).

To the extent that these assumptions may not accurately reflect the environment of the firm, a disaggregated model may be more appropriate. The disaggregated models allow for the forecasting of sustainable growth and the calculation of pro forma variables, given the firm's targeted financial or capital structure. The models can be used to determine the required adjustments in financial policy variables when there is a deviation between the firm's actual growth and its sustainable growth.

To develop a dynamic model of sustainable growth we define,

x = long-term debt/equity.

y = total debt/equity.

e_0 = equity as of time period 0 or equity as of time period 0 plus new equity and other changes in equity during period 1.

m = profit margin as of time period 1.

d = dividend payout ratio.

s_0 = sales as of time period 0.

s_1 = sales as of time period 1.

c = cash as of time period 1.

r = accounts receivable as of time period 1.

i = inventory as of time period 1.

o_c = other current assets as of time period 1.

f = fixed assets as of time period 1.

o_f = other fixed assets as of time period 1.

a = accounts payable as of time period 1.

n = notes payable as of time period 1.

o_L = other liabilities as of time period 1.

L = long-term debt as of time period 1.

g^* = the firm's sustainable growth rate.

For analysis, the appropriate period, or time horizon, is either one-fourth or one year. This is when the firm's quarterly or annual performance reports and balance sheets are available and when planning for future periods can take into consideration the most current financial information.

SUSTAINABLE GROWTH WITH A TARGET
CAPITAL STRUCTURE

A firm's capital structure refers to its relative amounts of long-term debt and equity financing. One measure of the capital structure that is frequently used is the ratio of long-term debt to equity (x, using our notation). If an objective of the strategic plan is to achieve or maintain a target capital structure, the appropriate disaggregated sustainable growth model can be specified using equation 5.1. (For a derivation of the disaggregated models, the interested reader is referred to Appendix 5.1.)

$$g^* = \{[c + r + i + o_c + f + o_f - a - n - o_L - e_0(1 + x)]/$$

$$m(1 - d)(1 + x)s_0\} - 1 \qquad\qquad (5.1)$$

The firm's sustainable growth as specified by equation 5.1 can be interpreted as the expected growth rate in sales that the firm can achieve, given its forecasts of each of the balance sheet accounts, profit margin, financial structure, and dividend policy. A deviation of the actual growth rate from the sustainable growth rate may result from an unexpected change in one of the parameters on the right-hand side of the equation.

Exhibits 5.1 and 5.2 provide information for the Campbell Soup Company. If it is assumed that the firm could accurately forecast the size of its assets, profit margin, dividend payout, and capital structure, and changes in its equity account, its sustainable growth for 1983, using equation 5.1, is

$$g = \frac{(1991526) - (574657) - (1055762 + 216 + 548 - 2017)(1.2327)}{(.0501)(1 - .4249)(1 + .2327)(2955649)} - 1$$

$$= .1139 = 11.39\%.$$

The firm's actual growth rate in sales for 1983 can be determined by the following equation:

$$g = (s_1 - s_0) / s_0 \qquad\qquad (5.2)$$

$$= (\text{Sales}_{83} - \text{Sales}_{82}) / \text{Sales}_{82}$$

$$= (3292433 - 2955649) / 2955649$$

$$= .1139 = 11.39\%.$$

Because it was assumed that Campbell could accurately forecast the size of its assets, profit margin, dividend payout, and capital structure, and changes in its equity account, the firm's actual growth in sales and its sustainable growth were identical. When a deviation between a firm's sustainable growth, using equation 5.1, and the actual growth in sales occurs, it will be due to an error in forecasting the parameters on the right-hand side of the equation.

Exhibit 5.1
Campbell Soup Company, Consolidated Balance Sheet
(Dollars in Thousands)

	7/31/83	8/1/82	CHANGE
CASH AND EQUIVS.	$213079	$210548	$11531
ACCOUNTS RECEIVABLE	237271	214271	23000
INVENTORIES	456484	470385	-13901
OTHER CURRENT ASSETS	25265	35297	-10032
TOTAL CURRENT	$932099	$921501	$10598
NET FIXED ASSETS	889156	815378	73778
OTHER ASSETS	170271	128640	41631
TOTAL ASSETS	$1991256	$1865519	$126007
CURRENT LIABILITIES			
NOTES PAYABLE	$44624	$93603	$-48979
ACCOUNTS PAYABLE	255795	253772	2033
ACCRUALS	152781	139499	13282
DEFERRED INCOME TAXES	96947	80080	16867
MINORITY INTERESTS	15965	0	15965
OTHER LIABILITIES	8545	6643	1902
LONG TERM DEBT	267465	236160	31305
TOTAL LIABILITIES	$842122	$809757	$32365
STOCKHOLDERS EQUITY			
PAID IN COMMON	55743	55527	216
RETAINED EARNINGS	1178620	1083725	94895
TREASURY STOCK	-54734	-55282	548
CUM. TRANSLATION ADJ	-30225	-28208	-2017
TOTAL	$1149404	$1055762	$93642
TOTAL LIAB. AND EQUITY	$1991526	$1865519	$126007

Exhibit 5.2
Campbell Soup Company, Consolidated Statement of Earnings
(Dollars in Thousands)

	7/31/83	8/1/82	CHANGE
NET SALES	$3292433	$2955649	$336784
LESS			
OPERATING EXPENSES	2947121	2656847	290274
NET OPERATING INCOME	$345312	$298802	$46510
LESS			
NET INTEREST	39307	21939	17368
EARNINGS BEFORE TAXES	$306005	$276863	$29142
LESS			
TAXES	141000	127250	13750
NET INCOME	$165005	$149613	$15392
LESS			
DIVIDENDS	70110	67709	2401
ADDITION TO RETAINED EARN	$94895	$81904	$12991
capital structure	.2327	.2237	
financial structure	.7327	.7670	
profit margin	.0501	.0506	
dividend payout	.4249	.4526	

Source: Campbell Soup Company 1983 Annual Report.

SUSTAINABLE GROWTH WITH A TARGET FINANCIAL STRUCTURE

A firm's financial structure refers to the relative amounts of debt and equity that are used to finance the acquisition of its assets. A measure of the firm's financial structure is the ratio of *total* debt to equity. For some firms the objective is to achieve or maintain a target financial structure or ratio of total debt to equity.

If the objective of the strategic plan were to achieve a target financial structure, equation 5.1 must be modified. We can define y as the ratio of total debt to equity desired by the firm by the end of the next period. After making the necessary adjustments to equation 5.1, it can be shown that the disaggregated sustainable growth for the firm with a target financial structure is depicted by the following equation:

$$g^* = \{[(c + r + i + o_c + f + o_f) - e_0(1 + y)]/$$

$$(m(1 - d)(1 + y))s_0\} - 1. \tag{5.3}$$

The difference between equation 5.1 and equation 5.3 is that a more restrictive assumption—a target or constant financial structure—is imposed by the latter.

Equation 5.3 can also be used in a similar fashion as equation 5.1 to contrast the firm's sustainable growth with its actual growth. If it is assumed that Campbell could accurately forecast the size of its assets, profit margin, dividend payout, financial structure, and changes in its equity account, its sustainable growth for 1983, using equation 5.3, is

$$g = \frac{(1991526) - (1055762 + 216 + 548 - 2017)(1.7327)}{(.0501)(1 - .4249)(1.7327)(2955649)} - 1$$

$$= .1139 = 11.39\%.$$

Because the actual values of the parameters on the right-hand of equation 5.3 were used, Campbell's actual growth in sales was found. A deviation between the firm's actual growth and its sustainable growth will be due to a forecasting error in at least one of the parameters on the right-hand side of equation 5.3.

It can be readily demonstrated that equation 5.3 is a generalized version of the Higgins model of Chapter 3. According to Higgins' definition, a firm's sustainable growth rate in the absence of inflation is given by the following equation:

$$g^* = [m(1 - d)(1 + y)] / [t - m(1 - d)(1 + y)], \tag{5.4}$$

where t is the ratio of total assets to sales and y is the ratio of total debt to equity. Using the Campbell Soup Company data, the firm's sustainable growth rate using the Higgins model is 8.41 percent; that is,

$$g^* = [.0506(1 - .4526)(1 + .767)]/[.6312 - (.0506(1 - .4526)(1 + .767)]$$

$$= 8.41\%.$$

Because this result depends on a constant ratio of assets to sales and profit margin as well as a constant financial structure, equation 5.3 must be modified to reflect these restrictions. The term t in the Higgins model refers to the ratio of total assets to sales. Constraining this ratio to be constant for the next period,

$$t = (c + r + i + o_c + f + o_f) / s_1. \tag{5.5}$$

Constraining the ratio of total debt to equity, y, to be constant and assuming a constant profit margin, m, it can be shown that

$$g^* = [(e_0(1 + y)) / (t - m(1 - d)(1 + y))s_0] - 1. \tag{5.6}$$

Using the Campbell Soup Company data, the disaggregated model will provide the same results as the Higgins model:

$$g^* = \frac{(1055762)(1.767)}{(.6312 - (.0506)(1 - .4526)(1.767))2955649} - 1.$$

$$= 1.0841 - 1 = 8.41\%.$$

Thus the Higgins model is a special case of equation 5.3. However, the utility of using equation 5.3 when the firm has a target financial structure is that the restrictive assumptions of a constant profit margin, dividend payout, and ratio of assets to sales can be used but are not necessary. Because it is more realistic for most firms to experience period-to-period fluctuations in these variables, equation 5.3 provides a better measure of the firm's sustainable growth when the firm has a target financial structure.

APPLICATIONS

A firm's balance sheet and income statement items can be forecasted by such common methods as trend, regression, exponential smoothing, Box–Jenkins technique, and judgmental forecasting. The advantage of the disaggregated models, depicted by equations 5.1 and 5.3, is that the projected balance sheet and income statement data can be used to forecast the sustainable growth rate without imposing the restrictive assumptions of the other sustainable growth models. In addition, both equations allow for the case in which the firm currently has excess capacity or when the purchases of plant and equipment can be obtained only in fixed increments. The other sustainable growth models, however, do not allow for the use of these methods because of the assumption of a constant ratio of assets to sales. Consequenlty the disaggregated models provide a higher degree of flexibility because they incorporate information the manager may have at his disposal at the beginning of the planning period.

To demonstrate how the disaggregated model can be used with forecasting techniques such as those cited above, we can focus on next period's cash, c. For instance, we assume that next period's cash account is a linear function of sales. That is,

$$c = z_1 + z_2 s_1, \tag{5.7}$$

where z_1 and z_2 are estimated coefficients. Substituting equation 5.7 into equation 5.1 and solving for g^* yields

$$g^* = \frac{[z_1 + r + i + o_c + f + o_f - a - n - o_L - e(1 + y)]}{((1 + y) m (1 - d) - z_2)s_0} - 1. \qquad (5.8)$$

In this example we assumed that cash was a linear function of sales and demonstrated the required adjustments to the general expression. Comparable adjustments may be made for receivables, inventory, fixed assets, accounts payable, and notes payable through appropriate specifications. Assuming that the derived sustainable growth rate is feasible, given the other constraints facing the firm, the analyst can then use the implied value of sales for the period for constructing the pro forma position statements, income statements, and cash budget. The result is consistent financial constraints and pro forma statements for each period encompassed by the strategic plan.

The disaggregated models can also be used as a tactical planning model to show the decision maker the trade-offs between the various parameters affecting growth. In addition, this application of the disaggregated models demonstrates whether the targeted ratios as developed in the strategic plan are mutually feasible.

As a tactical planning tool, the firm would forecast the size of its assets and current liabilities, the total debt-equity ratio (or long-term debt to equity), any changes in its equity account other than retained earnings, profit margin, dividend payout, and growth. The forecasted variables could be incorporated into equation 5.1 or 5.3 to determine whether they are mutually consistent. For example, suppose Campbell set a target capital structure of 21 percent by the end of 1983 and the other variables of equation 5.1 were accurately forecasted. Given the target capital structure and other variables, the firm would have to grow by 36.75 percent during 1983.

$$g = \frac{(1991526) - (574657) - (1055762 + 216 + 548 - 2017)(1.21)}{(.0501)(1 - .4249)(1.21)(2955646)} - 1$$

$$= .3675 = 36.75\%$$

A target capital structure of 21 percent is feasible, given the other variables, only if the firm can grow at a rate of 36.75 percent. If the firm grows at a lower rate, it must accept a higher capital structure to finance its assets.

We can also use the models to determine a particular parameter that is required, given the forecast of the other variables. For example, if we assume that the firm can accurately forecast its growth, assets, profit margin, changes in its equity other than retained earnings, and dividend payout, we can solve for the required long-term debt-equity or the total debt-equity ratio that is required, given the values of these other variables. We simply insert the forecasted values into equation 5.1 or 5.3 respectively, and solve for the missing ratio.

Exhibits 5.3 through 5.9 present the trade-offs between the various parameters that affect the growth of Campbell Soup Company for 1983. It appears from the data that the firm has a target capital structure that it wants to maintain, since this ratio is stabler than its financial structure ratio. Thus equation 5.1, which assumes a constant capital structure, is the appropriate disaggregated model to use to contrast the key parameters of growth.

Exhibit 5.3 depicts the relation between dividend payout and profit margin for the Campbell Soup Company for 1983, assuming that the other parameters of equation 5.1 have been accurately forecasted. It is apparent that the firm can increase its dividend payout, while maintaining the other variables, by improving its profit margin. The graph depicts the required trade-offs between profit margin and dividend payout necessary to maintain the firm's growth and other variables. If the firm does not lie on the graph—in other words, attempts to pay a higher or lower dividend implied by the corresponding profit margin—one of the other variables of equation 5.1 will be changed.

To support its growth and assets, Campbell can obtain funds through either internal or external sources. Exhibits 5.4 and 5.5 provide information concerning the trade-offs between its capital structure and profit margin, and capital structure and dividend payout, respectively. Both exhibits assume that the change in equity other than retained earnings has been accurately forecasted. Exhibit 5.4 demonstrates that the firm can reduce its reliance on debt by improving its profit margin. Exhibit 5.5 shows that an increase in the dividend payout would require an increase in the targeted capital structure to support the growth and assets. Similar to Exhibit 5.3, the firm must operate on each of the graphs in order to maintain the values of the other variables.

Exhibit 5.6 depicts the relation between growth and total assets. The growth of the firm can be increased with an increase in the size of the assets that can be made operational during the year, assuming that the other parameters of equation 5.1 can be maintained.

Exhibits 5.7 through 5.9 depict the effect of changing growth on profit margin, dividend payout, and capital structure respectively. Exhibit 5.7 shows that there is an inverse relation between the growth in sales and the profit margin, given the values of the other parameters. The higher the firm's profit margin, the lower the required growth that is necessary to finance its assets. From another perspective, for a given asset size the firm can afford to accept a lower profit margin if it can achieve a higher growth in sales.

Exhibit 5.3
Campbell Soup Company, Dividend Payout and Profit Margin, 1983

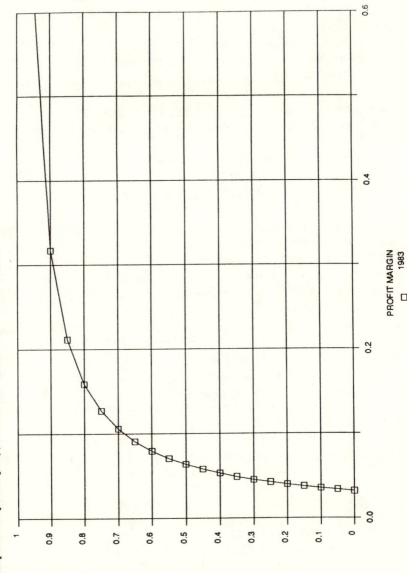

Exhibit 5.4
Campbell Soup Company, Capital Structure and Profit Margin, 1983

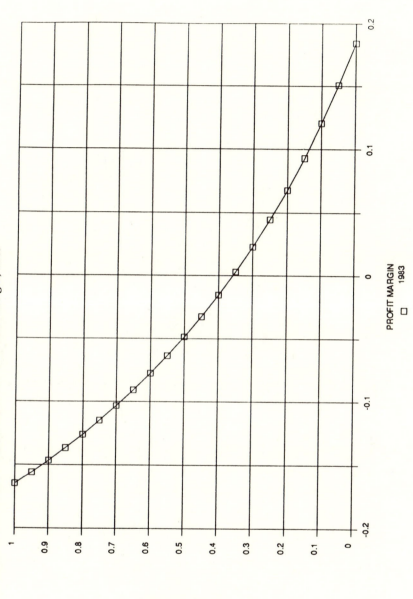

Exhibit 5.5
Campbell Soup Company, Capital Structure and Dividend Payout, 1983

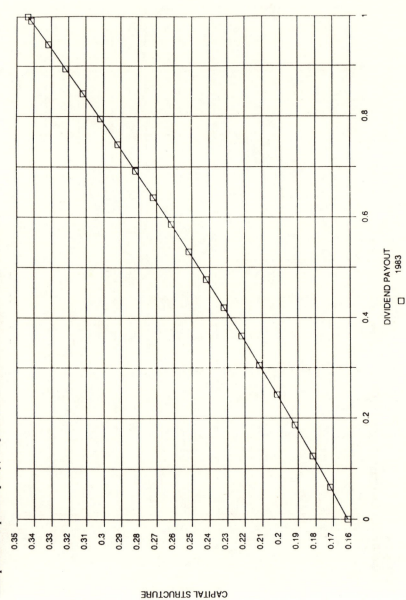

DIVIDEND PAYOUT
□ 1983

CAPITAL STRUCTURE

Exhibit 5.6
Campbell Soup Company, Growth and Total Assets, 1983

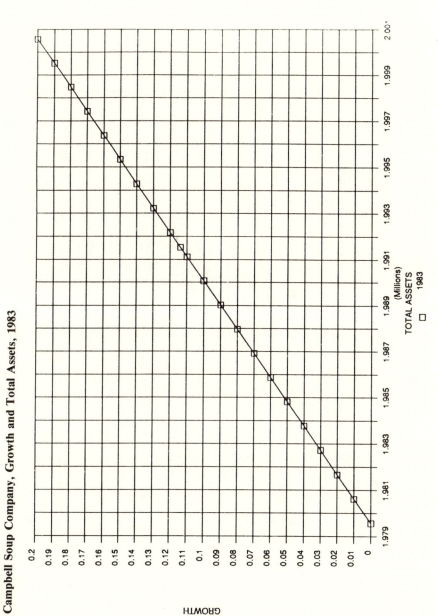

Exhibit 5.7
Campbell Soup Company, Growth and Profit Margin, 1983

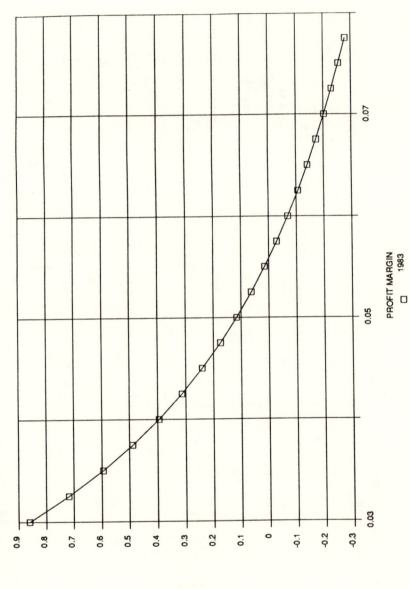

Exhibit 5.8
Campbell Soup Company, Growth and Dividend Payout, 1983

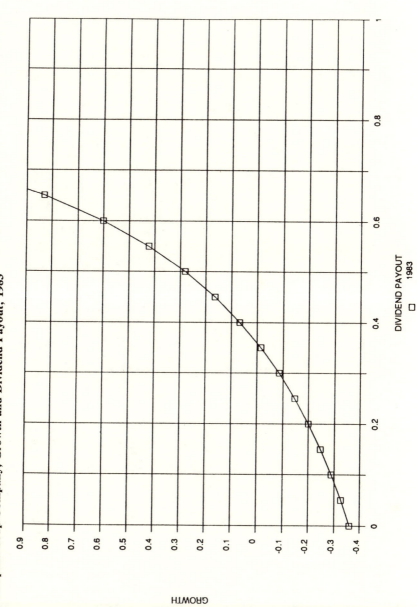

Exhibit 5.9
Campbell Soup Company, Growth and Capital Structure, 1983

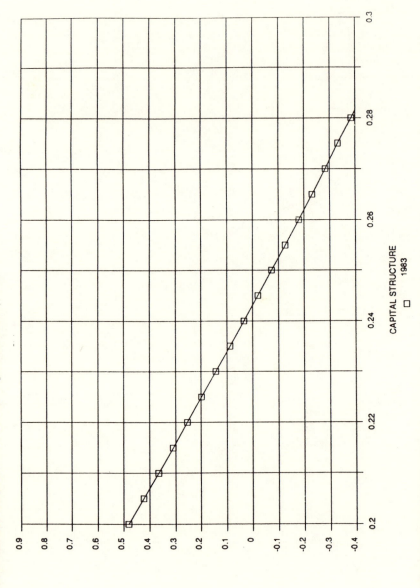

Exhibit 5.8 demonstrates that the firm can afford a higher dividend payout if it can achieve a higher growth in sales. The higher the growth of the firm, the higher the profits, given a constant profit margin. The larger profits can be used by the firm to increase its dividends or to reduce its debt. Exhibit 5.9 depicts the case in which the firm maintains its dividend payout ratio but uses the additional profits to reduce its amount of long-term debt.

It should be noted that Exhibits 5.3 through 5.9 assumed that all the variables of equation 5.1 were held constant except the two that were graphed. It is possible that if one of the graphed variables changes, this might affect some of the other variables that have been assumed constant. In this case the other parameters that vary with a change in one of the graphed variables must be taken into consideration in order to accurately depict the relation between the graphed variables.

REFERENCES

Clark, J., M. Clark, and A. Verzilli. "Strategic Planning and Sustainable Growth," *The Columbia Journal of World Business*, Fall 1985, pp. 47–51.

Eiseman, Peter C. "Another Look at Sustainable Growth," *The Journal of Commercial Bank Lending*, October 1984, pp. 47–51.

Fruhan, William E. "How Fast Should a Company Grow?" *Harvard Business Review*, January/February 1984, pp. 84–93.

Govindarajan, V., and J. K. Shank. "Cash Sufficiency: The Missing Link in Strategic Planning," *Corporate Accounting*, Winter 1984, pp. 23–31.

Higgins, Robert. "Sustainable Growth: New Tool in Bank Lending," *Journal of Commerical Lending*, June 1977, pp. 48–58.

———. "How Much Growth Can a Firm Afford?" *Financial Management*, Fall 1977, pp. 7–15.

———. "Sustainable Growth Under Inflation," *Financial Management*, Fall 1981, pp. 36–40.

Johnson, Dana J. "The Behavior of Financial Structure and Sustainable Growth in an Inflationary Environment," *Financial Management*, Fall 1981, pp. 30–35.

Kefalas, A. G. "Toward a Sustainable Growth Strategy," *Business Horizons*, April 1979, pp. 34–40.

Olson, G. T., J. Clark, and T. Chiang, "Sustainable Growth: A Dynamic Model," *Journal of the Midwest Finance Association*, Vol. 15, 1986, pp. 1–12.

Wittenbent, Fred R. "Bigness v. Profitability," *Harvard Business Review*, January/February 1970, pp. 28–36.

APPENDIX 5.1
DERIVATION OF DISAGGREGATED MODEL

SUSTAINABLE GROWTH WITH TARGET CAPITAL STRUCTURE

A firm's capital structure pertains to amount of funds that are supplied by long-term sources. One measure of the firm's capital structure is the ratio between long-term debt and equity (x, using the notation of the chapter).

To derive a disaggregated model of sustainable growth assuming a target capital structure, we begin with the firm's projected balance sheet for the next period. By definition, the value of the assets as of period 1 must equal the value of the claims as of period 1:

$$(c + r + i + o_c) + (f + o_f) = (a + n + o_L)$$

$$+ L + (e_0 + ms_1(1 - d)). \tag{5.1A}$$

Assuming that the firm wants to achieve or maintain a target capital structure, x, equation 5.1A can be rewritten as

$$(c + r + i + o_c) + (f + o_f) = (a + n + o_L) + (e_0 + ms_1(1 - d))(1 + x).$$

Solving for next period's sales, s_1, yields

$$s_1 = [(c + r + i + o_c + f + o_f) - (a + n + o_L)$$

$$- e_0(1 + x)]/m(1 - d)(1 + x). \tag{5.2A}$$

A firms's growth in sales can be defined as

$$g = (s_1 - s_0)/s_0 = (s_1/s_0) - 1. \tag{5.3A}$$

Substituting equation 5.2A into equation 5.3A yields equation 5.4A, the firm's sustainable growth rate assuming a target capital structure:

$$g^* = \{[c + r + i + o_c + f + o_f - a - n - o_L$$

$$- e_0(1 + x)]/m(1 - d)(1 + x)s_0\} - 1. \tag{5.4A}$$

Equation 5.4 is the firm's disaggregated model, assuming a constant or target capital structure; it is equivalent to equation 5.1 in the chapter.

SUSTAINABLE GROWTH WITH TARGET
FINANCIAL STRUCTURE

A firms financial structure refers to all of its sources of funds, in other words, the right-hand side of a balance sheet. One measure of the firm's financial structure is the ratio of total liabilities to equity—y, using the notation of the chapter. If an objective of the strategic plan were to achieve a target financial structure, y, as opposed to a target capital structure, equation (4) must be modified. By definition,

$$y = (a + n + o_L + L) / (e_0 + ms_1(1 - d)).$$

Rearranging,

$$(a + n + o_L + L) = y(e_0 + ms_1(1 - d)). \tag{5.5A}$$

Substituting equation 5.5A into equation 5.1A and solving for s_1 yields

$$s_1 = [(c + r + i + o_c + f + o_f) - e_0(1 + y)] / m(1 - d)(1 + y). \tag{5.6A}$$

Substituting equation 5.6A into equation 5.3A yields the following equation:

$$g^* = \{[c + r + i + o_c + f + o_f - e_0(1 + y)] /$$

$$(m(1 - d)(1 + y))s_0\} - 1. \tag{5.7A}$$

Equation 5.7A represents the firm's disaggregated growth, assuming a constant or target financial structure; it is equivalent to equation 5.3 in the chapter.

6

FIRM OPTIMAL SUSTAINABLE
GROWTH

In Chapter 3 we stressed that the objective of the firm was not necessarily to maximize growth. Rather, as assumed in financial management literature, management decisions strive to maximize the market value of the common shares. Because common stock constitutes the ownership position in the firm, in theory management thus acts to enhance the wealth position of the common shareholders. This wealth position rests on the risk-return trade-off of the firm's future earnings as evaluated by the securities markets.

Maximum growth need not coincide with the maximum value of the common shares. High growth rates frequently carry a heavier burden or risk. It is quite possible for two stocks—one from a corporation with a zero growth rate and another from a corporation with a positive growth rate—to sell at the same market value. For example, Firm A may have earnings per share of $1 with a zero growth rate but minimum risk, and Firm B may have earnings per share of $3 with an anticipated growth of 7 percent annually but at a higher level or risk, yet both may sell at $10 per share. Risk in relation to return, not growth per se, determines market value.

In the Higgins and Johnson models sustainable growth has been viewed as a derivation of the financial structure or the capital structure, that is, as a function of the degree of financial risk (the ratio of debt to equity) assumed by the firm. For reasons discussed below, management will seek to arrange the financial structure or capital structure to minimize the cost of capital. The point at which the cost of capital is minimized is referred to as the optimal capital structure. Accordingly, the sustainable growth rate calculated from this combination of debt and equity represents the optimal sustainable growth rate. It is that growth rate consistent with maintaining the lowest weighted average cost of capital and maximizing the market value of the common shares.

TRADING ON THE EQUITY

Common stock is the most costly source of capital, for it must compensate investors who accept the risk of a residual claim on the income stream. Within limits, the cost of capital to a firm financed solely by common stock will be higher than if some proportion of debt were inserted into the capital structure. In the case of the all-equity firm, the financial risk—the variability of returns to common shareholders arising from the way the company is financed—would be zero. The risk to common shareholders would originate solely in the variability of the operating income stream, the business risk. As debt, lease commitments, and preferred stock are added to the capital structure, the financial risk to the common mounts. Whether the price of the common declines in concert depends on the earnings generated by the borrowed funds. If these earnings should offset the incremental risk to the common, the yield on the common (K_e) may not increase commensurately, and the average cost of capital (K_{mc}) may actually decline with the substitution of "cheaper" debt for common.

When a firm trades on the equity, it de facto pledges the net worth as security for the protection of creditors. Think of a firm with $100 in assets acquired by $60 of debt and $40 common. The assets would have to decline 40 percent before the position of the creditors is in jeopardy. Net worth acts as a cushion to absorb declines in the market value of assets below book values. The "pledge" of net worth is activated only in the extreme circumstance of liquidation.

More significant to current operations, trading on the equity gives rise to fixed charges (interest or debt service) and so creates a leverage factor, that is, a greater proportionate increase (or decrease) in the rate of profit that follows an increase (or decrease) in sales or earnings before interest and taxes (EBIT) when fixed charges are spread over a larger number of units. Financial risk is measured by the degree of financial leverage (DFL).

Exhibit 6.1 shows four types of capital structures, ranging from no debt (A) to a predominant debt position (D). In each instance, DFL is measured by

$$DFL = \frac{EBIT}{EBT} , \qquad\qquad (6.1)$$

which for capital structure B in period 1 becomes

$$DFL = \frac{10}{7.50}$$

$$= 1.30.$$

Exhibit 6.1
Financial Leverage—Comparison of Four Capital Structures

	A	B	C	D
Bonds[1]	$ 0.00	$ 50.00	$100.00	$150.00
Stocks[2]	200.00	150.00	100.00	50.00
Total	$200.00	$200.00	$200.00	$200.00
	=======	=======	=======	=======
Period 1				
EBIT	$ 10.00	$ 10.00	$ 10.00	$ 10.00
Interest	0.00	2.50	5.00	7.50
EBT	$ 10.00	$ 7.50	$ 5.00	$ 2.50
EPS	0.50	0.50	0.50	0.50
Yield	0.05	0.05	0.05	0.05
Period 2				
EBIT	$ 20.00	$ 20.00	$ 10.00	$ 10.00
Interest	0.00	2.50	5.00	7.50
EBT	$ 20.00	$ 17.50	$ 5.00	$ 2.50
EPS	1.00	1.17	0.50	0.50
Yield	0.10	0.116	0.15	0.25
DFL	1.0	1.3	2.0	4.0

For any level of EBIT, EPS will be larger as the DFL increases.
[1]Interest at 5%.
[2]Issued at $10 par.

Alternatively, DFL could have been calculated by a comparison of percentage changes in EBIT and EBT between periods 1 and 2:

$$DFL = \frac{\text{percentage change in EBT}}{\text{percentage change in EBIT}} \quad (6.2)$$

$$= \frac{133\%}{100\%}$$

$$= 1.30$$

DFL is to be interpreted as a multiplier: for any given percentage of change in EBIT, from the period 1 base year, the result will be a 1.3 time greater percentage change in EBT. With each increment of debt in Exhibit 6.1, the DFL increases, bringing a commensurate increase in the variability of EBT. Note, too, for any given level of EBIT, the earnings per share increases with the infusion of debt—the attractive side of leveraging to the common shareholder, at least on the way up. Between A and D the EPS has increased from $0.50 to $2.50 as the leverage factor rose from 1 to 4. The shareholder in D has more income and risk; what goes up can also come down. Leverage works in both directions. Which capital structure meets your preference?

But leverage effects on EBT are not limited to the financial arrangements of the company. The fixed costs found in the operating stream (depreciation, factory overhead, fixed selling and administrative expenses) magnify the variability of sales revenues. Operating leverage (DOL) relates to the business risk and is measured by

$$DOL = \frac{Q(S - V)}{Q(S - V) - F} , \qquad (6.3)$$

where Q is the number of units; S, the selling price per unit; F, total fixed costs, and V, variable costs per unit. In the manner of equation 6.3, a comparison of percentage changes in the variables gives the same result:

$$DOL = \frac{\text{percentage change in EBIT}}{\text{percentage change in sales}}$$

Similarly, DOL is a multipler: for any given percentage change in sales, the change in EBIT will be so many (DOL) times greater.

Operating and financial leverage combined (DOL × DFL) provide a risk profile of the enterprise: the variability of returns to the common stockholders arising from the business and financial risk. The income statement in Exhibit 6.2 shows the calculations.

The variability of returns induced by leveraging can be quite substantial in particular industries. Take air transport as an example. Typically, debt represents 60 percent of an airline's capital structure, and equity, 40 percent. Operating revenues fluctuate with the number of passengers and the volume of cargo, but operating expenses are inflexible. Flight crews and ground crews are paid the same whether the plane is empty or full; maintenance and depreciation vary little with traffic carried. The overwhelming proportion of costs must be met irrespective of traffic density. It is estimated that once an airline reaches breakeven, 80 to 90 percent of the additional revenues flow down to the pre-tax net. The story of United Airlines in 1963 brings the point home. United's operating expenses advanced 2.8 percent, but net income climbed 121 percent. In 1964 the

Exhibit 6.2
Industrial Company Income Statement This Year

Net Sales		$200,000

Less

Cost of Sales:

Opening Inventory	$ 10,000	
Net Purchases	$ 80,000	
Total	$ 90,000	
Closing Inventory	$ 30,000	$ 60,000
Gross Operating Income		$140,000

Less

Selling Expenses	$ 50,000	
Administrative Expenses	$ 60,000	$110,000
Net Operating Income (EBIT)		$ 30,000
Financial Charges		$ 3,668
Net Income After Taxes (EAT)		$ 24,332

Additional data:	Selling Price (S)	$ 2.00
	Fixed Costs (F)	$100,000
	Variable Costs (V)	$ 0.70 per unit
	Number of Units (Q)	100,000

Operating Leverage (DOL) =

$$\frac{Q \times (S-V)}{Q \times (S-V) - F}$$

$$\frac{100,000 \times (2-.70)}{100,000 \times (2-.70) - 100,000}$$

$$= 4.3$$

Financial Leverage (DFL) =

$$\frac{EBIT}{EBT}$$

$$\frac{30,000}{26,332}$$

$$= 1.14$$

Combined Leverage =

$$(DOL) (DFL)$$

$$= 4.3 \times 1.14 = 4.9$$

respective figures were 7.5 percent, 5 percent, and 86.8 percent. The conclusion is clear. Planning the capital structure or managing financial risk is not undertaken in isolation from the variability of the operating stream (business risk). The anticipated benefits from trading on the equity may be negated if the effect so intensifies the risk characteristics of the firm as to offset the added income.

The combined leverage factor is not a constant. As the company moves up from the breakeven point, the leverage multipler declines. Conversely, at breakeven, the leverage factor is infinity. Moreover, the parameters that enter the calculation—price per unit, variable costs, fixed operating and financial charges—themselves vary from period to period.

The risk of the common shareholders may also be stated, using the standard deviation (σ) of the income stream. In Exhibit 6.3 each company has expected sales (S) of $200,000 subject to a standard deviation of $70,000. For Company A, with only variable costs, the business risk comes from the dispersion around the sales dollar and has a coefficient of variation of .35. Company B has no debt but does have fixed costs embedded in the operating stream. This raises the business risk coefficient to .43. Company C has both fixed operating and financial costs, which produce the highest risk coefficient, .58. The dispersion of returns for each company on the basis of one standard deviation is summarized as follows:

	High	Mean	Low
Company A	$135,000	$100,000	$65,000
Company B	115,000	80,000	45,000
Company C	95,000	60,000	25,000

Sales are normally distributed so that the probability of the low values is approximately 16 percent in each case. For C, however, the advent of the downside variation has ominous implications. If the debt service is not paid, the creditors may declare the entire principal due and payable, precipitating bankruptcy.

The reader will also observe that the effect of price changes (J) on sustainable growth will vary with each company in Exhibit 6.3.

The coefficient of variation relates the dispersion of the income (SD) to the net received by the common shareholders (N). Because the net decreases with the addition of financial charges, the coefficient of variation, and hence relative risk, is larger. Relative risk affects the required rate of return on the common (K_e). K_e comprises a basic interest (I) and a premium for risk (P). One would expect, a priori, that K_e would vary directly with the coefficient of variation:

$$K_e = I + P \tag{6.4}$$

and if so, it follows

Exhibit 6.3
Leverage Effects—Business and Financial Risks

	Company A (all variable costs)	Company B (variable and fixed operating costs	Company C (variable and fixed operating costs; financial fixed costs)
Expected Sales (S)*	$200,000	$200,000	$200,000
Variable Costs**	100,000	100,000	100,000
Net Income (Na)	$100,000		
Operating Fixed Costs (Fo)		$ 20,000	$ 20,000
Net Income (Nb)		$ 80,000	
Financial Fixed Costs (Ff)			$ 20,000
Net Income (Nc)			$ 60,000
Standard Deviation (SD) on Net Income***	$ 35,000	$ 35,000	$ 35,000
Coefficient of Variation (CV): $\frac{SD}{N}$	$\frac{\$ 35,000}{\$100,000}=.35$	$\frac{\$ 35,000}{\$ 80,000}=.43$	$\frac{\$ 35,000}{\$ 60,000}=.58$

* Sales are normally distributed with a standard deviation of $70,000.
** Variable costs are perfectly positively correlated to sales.
*** Since sales and variable costs are perfectly correlated, contributions and net income vary directly with sales. If sales vary by $70,000, contribution varies by 50% of $70,000 or $35,000.

$$K_e = 1 + f\ \frac{SD}{N}\ ,$$
(6.5)

where the risk premium (P) is said to be a function (f) of the coefficient of variation SD/N.

Exhibit 6.3 shows how the coefficient of variation is related to operating and financial leverage for each company. Investors will discount the expected income from equity investment in C at a higher rate because of the greater variability of returns. All things equal, C's cost of common will be higher and the price of its shares lower.

Still the matter is not all that straightforward. There are those who contend that leveraging does not influence the cost of capital, and we have yet to demonstrate how minimizing the cost of capital enhances the market value of the common shares and the enterprise.

LEVERAGING AND THE VALUATION OF THE ENTERPRISE

Assuming that, in the presence of an income tax, leveraging up to some point can be used to lower the cost of capital, there are two basic approaches to the valuation of the enterprise.

Traditional View

Most financial managers subscribe to the view that judicious use of debt lowers the cost of capital and so manage the capital structure with this hypothesis in mind. The scenario runs as follows: As debt is first inserted into the capital structure, the cost of debt will be relatively low. The bonds of the company would merit high ratings from the investment services, since operating earnings (EBIT) cover interest payments with an ample margin to spare. The incremental risk to the common shareholders in consequence is small and investors would probably capitalize common earnings close to the rate (K_{emc}) that was obtained before leveraging. K_{emc}, in this event, primarily reflects the business risk. However, with successive layers of debt, K_{dmc} would tend to rise. Each additional bond issue carries greater risk for earnings coverage declines, and the net worth cushion is likewise diluted. With additional debt the financial risk to the common is joined to the business risk, and K_{emc} eventually increases. So, at some point the average cost of capital (K_{mc}) rises.

Exhibit 6.4 graphs these movements, depicting a U-shaped cost of capital (K_{mc}) curve assumed by the traditional school. As the debt-equity ratio rises to 50 percent, the increased cost of common (K_{emc}), because of additional debt, is more than offset by the savings from the cheaper debt capital. The optimal capital structure is the one that yields the lowest average cost of capital (K_{mc})(i.e., 8 percent). For debt-equity ratios above 50 percent, the lower K_{dmc} no longer compensates for the higher K_{emc}, and average cost (K_{mc}) increases. How do these trends affect the market value of the firm and shareholder wealth?

In Exhibit 6.5 let us posit an EBIT of $20,000 and a total capitalization of $100,000, packaged in bundles of debt and equity according to the indicated ratios in Exhibit 6.4.

As the average cost of capital (K_{mc}) declines, the market value of the common and the firm increases concomitantly. This is so because the net earnings on debt capital after taxes that flow down to the common stock more than compensate initially for the added financial risk assumed by the shareholders. Beyond the optimum capital structure, the phenomenon is reversed and the market value of the shares declines.

Case I <u>No Debt:</u>

EBIT $(\bar{X})$	$20,000
Interest (K_D)	------
EBT	$20,000
Taxes $(T = .50)$	10,000
EAT (Available to Common)	$10,000
Capitalization of Common	
Earnings, $K_{emc} = .10$	
Market Value of Common (S)	$100,000
Market Value of Debt	-------
Market Value of Firm (F)	$100,000
Average Cost of Capital (K_{mc})	10%

Case II <u>Debt, 30%: Equity, 70%</u>

EBIT $(\bar{X})$	$20,000
Interest $(K_D = .08)$	2,400
EBT	$17,600
Taxes $(T = .50)$	8,800
EAT (Available to Common)	$8,800
Capitalization of Common	
Earnings, $K_{emc} = 10.3\%$	
Market Value of Common (S)	$85,437
Market Value of Debt	30,000
Market Value of Firm (F)	$115,437
Average Cost of Capital (K_{mc})	8.4%

Case III Debt, 80%: Equity, 20%

EBIT ($\bar{X}$)	$20,000
Interest (K_D = .15)	12,000
	———
EBT	$8,000
Taxes (T = .50)	4,000
EAT (Available to Common)	$4,000
Capitalization of Common	
Earning, K_{emc} = 16%	
Market Value of Common (S)	$25,000
Market Value of Debt	80,000
Market Value of Firm (F)	$105,000
Average Cost of Capital (K_{mc})	9.2%

Exhibit 6.4
Cost of Capital (K_{mc})

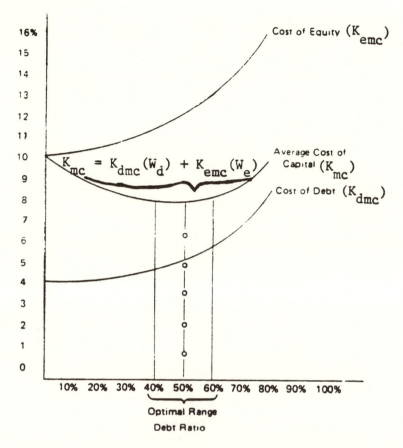

To simplify the illustration, the analysis assumed: constant business risk; constant EBIT over time; all earnings distributed as dividends; and no transaction costs. Modifications to allow for these variables would alter the slope of the average cost curve in Exhibit 6.4 but would not alter the conclusions.

Net Operating Income Approach

This hypothesis states that the market capitalizes the firm as an entity; that is, the market discounts the variability of the operating income (business risk) to secure the market value of the firm. The latter is independent of the D/E ratio. The market discounts financial risk, variability in earnings after interest, solely against the common shares. Hence the average cost of capital (K_{mc}) related to business risk does not vary with the

Exhibit 6.5
Cost of Capital

Percent leverage Debt/Total Invested Capital (1)	Complement of Column(1) (2)	Interst X(1 - t) Where T = 50% (3)	Yield on Stock Equity (4)	Weighted Average Cost [(1) x (3) +(2) x (4)=(5)] (5)
0	100%	--	10.0%	10.0%
10%	90%	4.0%	10.1%	9.5%
20%	80%	4.0%	10.2%	9.0%
30%	70%	4.0%	10.3%	8.4%
40%	60%	4.5%	10.5%	8.1%
50%	50%	5.0%	11.0%	8.0%
60%	40%	6.0%	11.5%	8.2%
70%	30%	7.0%	12.5%	8.7%
80%	20%	7.5%	16.0%	9.2%

Notes: Optimum capital structure comprises 50 percent debt and equity with K_{mc} = 8%. At this point, the pre-tax explicit cost of debt (10%) plus the implicit cost of debt represented by the rise in the cost of equity (1%) for the first time in the series exceeds the basic cost of all equity financing (10%). In a continuous distribution, K_{mc} is a minimum, when the marginal cost of debt (K_{mc}) and the marginal cost of equity (K_{emc}) are equal.

$$K_{mc} = K_{dmc} (W_d) + K_{emc} (W_e)$$

W_d = Proportion of debt in the capital structure (Column 1)
W_e = Proportion of equity in the capital structure (Column 2)
K_{dmc} = After-tax marginal cost of debt (Column 3)
   t = Combined Federal and State Tax Rate (Column 3)
K_{emc} = Marginal return on equity required to maintain market value of common stock (Column 4)
K_{mc} = Weighted average marginal cost of capital (Column 5)

amount of leveraging. With K_{mc} constant, the cost of common (K_{emc}) rises with the risk from leveraging, but this is offset by the presence of cheaper debt capital. The real cost of debt (the explicit interest cost plus the implicit increase in the cost of common owing to the addition of debt to the capital structure) and the real cost of common are equal. Accordingly, there is no single optimal capital structure. Take Case II in the preceding section, where K_{mc} = 8.4 percent.

Case IV

EBIT, after taxes($\bar{X}(1 - T)$), or EBI $10,000

Average Cost of Capital, K_{mc} = 8.4%

Value of the Firm (F), EBI/K $119,048

Market Value of Debt(D)   30,000

Market Value of Stock(S) $89,048

and

EBIT ($\bar{X}$) $20,000

Interest (K_D = .08)   2,400

EBT $17,600

Taxes(T = .50)   8,800

EAT (Available to Common) $8,800

$$K_{emc} = \frac{X - K_D D (1 - T)}{S} = \frac{\$8,800}{89,048} = 9.9\% \qquad (9)$$

Increasing debt to 80 percent of the capital structure:

EBI $10,000

Average Cost of Capital, K_{mc} = 8.4%

Value of the Firm (F), EBI/K $119,048

Market Value of Debt(D)   80,000

Market Value of Stock(S) $39,048

and

EBIT ($\bar{X}$) $20,000

Interest (K_D = .08)   12,000

EBT $8,000

Taxes(T = .50)   4,000

EAT (Available to Common) $4,000

$$K_{emc} = \frac{X - K_D D (1 - T)}{S} = \frac{\$4,000}{39,048} = 10.2\% \qquad (10)$$

The important feature of the NOI approach is the assumption that the average cost of capital (K_{mc}) is a function of the business risk. K_{mc} will change only if the firm accepts capital projects with a greater or lesser variability in the income stream. With K_{mc} remaining constant, there is a trade-off between the cost of debt (K_{dmc}) and the cost of equity (K_{emc}). Although the cost of equity (K_{emc}) rises with the risk from leveraging, the market price per share remains stable, since the number of shares declines proportionate to the increase in debt capital. For example, in the preceding illustration, if the number of shares declined in the ratio of 2.3:1 as debt increased, the market price per share would remain exactly the same.

COST OF CAPITAL[1]

The cost of capital has a prominent role in profit planning, evaluating capital projects, and managing the capital structure. It refers to the returns anticipated by those who contribute to the purchase of the firm's real assets, that is, to the cost of funds used to acquire operating capital. However, while the concept seems quite clear, substantial controversy surrounds the measurement and inclusion of certain component costs. Consequently the calculation in specific cases requires informed judgment.

Generally, the cost of capital represents a composite rate or average cost for the different funds tapped by the firm. With reference to Exhibit 6.6, Munster's assets were financed by current and long-term liabilities, preferred and common stock, and retained earnings. If each source has a "price tag" (implicit or explicit), then Munster's management must strive for a return on the company's assets to match or better its costs of capital.

If Munster should in fact earn a rate of return on its assets at least equal to the cost of capital, the company will maintain the market value of its securities. The point is crucial to understanding the cost of capital concept. When the investor purchases a corporate security, he buys a future stream of income and values the security according to his expectations regarding the size and risk of that income stream. Because the objective of financial management is to maintain or increase the market value of the company's securities, Munster must offer a return on its securities that meets the expectations of investors. The cost of capital, therefore, is not a historical statistic, computed and held constant until the firm attempts to raise new funds. It is a contemporary datum responsive to opinions in the money and capital markets.

But investors do not strive to maximize dollar returns. Investment analysis looks both to expected returns and risk diversification.

Consequently the cost of capital, considered as a rate of return, contains two elements: a basis yield covering the time value of money and a premium for risk. The risk premium varies from industry to industry and from company to company.

Exhibit 6.6
Munster Motors, Inc.—Balance Sheet, December 31, 19__

ASSETS		LIABILITIES	
Current Assets		**Current Liabilities**	
Cash	$514,500	Accounts Payable[1]	$500,000
Receivable	1,400,000	Notes Payable[2]	1,500,000
Inventories	1,000,000		
Prepaid Interest	85,500		
		Long-Term Debt	
		Bonds Payable[3]	2,000,000
Long-Term Assets		**Net Worth**	
Plant and Equipment, at cost			
Less Accumulated		Preferred Stock[4]	2,000,000
Depreciation			
($2,000,000)	12,000,000	Common Stock[5]	2,000,000
Investment in			
Subsidiaries	5,000,000	Capital in Excess of	
		Par Value	5,000,000
		Retained Earnings[6]	7,000,000
Total	$20,000,000		$20,000,000

Notes:

[1] Company policy is to take advantage of all trade discounts.
[2] Represents a continuing, long-established line of credit with Marley National Bank, discount at 6%, for one year.
[3] Issued at par; coupon rate 9%, paid semiannually; 10 year maturity.
[4] Issued at $20 par; 100,000 shares with a stated dividend of $2 per share.
[5] Common stock at par value of $2; 1 million shares outstanding sold at $7 per share.
[6] Munster, Inc., projects an EPS for 19XX at $3.00 and plans to declare a $1.50 dividend. Earnings have been growing at the rate of 7%. The current market price holds at approximately $16.

The applicable tax rate is 50%.

The reason risk weighs so heavily on the cost of capital lies in the competition for investment funds. It matters little to the investor whether he earns a dollar of return from Company X or Y or from a bond rather than from a preferred stock so long as the risk is equal. If the preferred stocks of A and B offer the same yield but B involves greater risk, the rational investor chooses A. Investors have many options, from relatively risk-free U.S. treasury bills to investments in stocks, options, real estate, and so on, with varying degrees of risk. To attract investors, business firms must offer a premium above the risk-free rate to cover the risk of the particular enterprise. The proposition can be stated alternatively: if the yield on the firm's common stock at current market prices does not, in the opinion of investors, adequately compensate for risk, either the market price of the stock will decline to produce a yield commensurate to the risk of the firm, or the firm must improve its earnings to restore the price of the stock.

This reveals another aspect to the cost of capital. It is an opportunity cost for (a) the firm competes against a variety of investor alternatives to obtain funds, and (b) it must select business projects with profit levels that maintain the market value of company securities by providing returns commensurate with investor expectations.

In practice, not every source of funds enters the calculation. Current liabilities are frequently excluded. Some authorities argue that such funds are "free" and that the cost of capital, when used in capital budgeting, relates only to the long-term commitments of invested capital. However, in an economic sense, capital is never "free." Accounts payable and some accruals are only superficially "free" if these debts are discharged within defined penalty periods. Under trade credit terms of 2/10, N/30, the creditor passes on to the debtor the savings in receivable financing that result if the bill is paid within ten days. Otherwise, the debtor, failing to take advantage of the discount, pays 2 percent for the use of the money for twenty days—the equivalent of a 36 percent annual rate. Some firms regularly use trade credit and choose not to accept the discount for prompt payment. Other companies continuously resort to bank credit to acquire current assets. In these instances there are finance charges to be covered out of earnings, just as interest on long-term debt. Also, current liabilities can often be replaced by long-term financing, and the decision to retain short-term debt on a continuing basis presumably rests on the advantages of such financing. In summary, the capital structure consists of diverse capital sources. The amount and cost of one type of capital depends on the proportions raised from other sources. The combinations influence the risk posture of the firm and, in turn, the cost of capital. All in all, judgment dictates the inclusion of current liabilities in the cost of capital.

To hold otherwise creates conceptual problems in the computation of other costs associated with capital structure items. For example, internal financing (which does not carry a unique payout such as interest or dividends) accounts for more than half of the total financing by American corporations. Yet consider the consequence of regarding retained earnings as "free."

In the hypothetical situation of a company expanding solely by retained earnings, management would undertake all capital projects that promise a return above zero if it regarded internal financing as having no cost. Eventually, accepting projects with lower and lower yields, the rate of return on total assets (or invested capital) would decline, although dollars of profit and earnings per share (EPS) would grow at a diminishing rate. If investors evaluated company performance strictly by an EPS criterion, few complaints might descend on the executive suite. Yet, in reality, management is using capital less and less efficiently.

Illustration: A firm has an initial capitalization of 200 shares of common issued at $10 par. Earnings start in the first year at $200 and increase as shown. All earnings are plowed back into the business.

Year	Earnings	Invested Capital	EPS	Percentage Return on Capital	Percentage Growth in EPS
1	$200.00	$2,000.00	$1.00	10.0	—
2	216.00	2,200.00	1.08	9.8	8.0
3	228.96	2,416.00	1.14	9.5	5.5
4	238.12	2,644.96	1.19	9.0	4.3
5	242.88	2,883.08	1.21	8.4	1.6

Earnings per share have increased consistently but the return on invested capital has declined 16 percent.

The missing element is some measure of how earnings should have increased with each increment of capital. That measure is the cost of capital. If the cost of retained earnings is omitted from the calculation, the cost of funds in capital budgeting will be misstated in proportion to the "cost" and relative importance of retained earnings in the company's financial structure. Subsequent investment decisions based on the error may be suboptimal. If the cost of capital is understated and leads to the acceptance of low-yield projects that do not cover the risk premium anticipated by investors, the market value of the common shares will decline. Conversely, if the cost of capital is set too high, opportunities to increase the market value of the common shares are missed.

Although the financial statements record only out-of-pockets expenses, significant opportunity costs—implicit but no less real—accompany all internal financing and affect the market values of outstanding securities. The issue is how to measure these implicit charges in estimating the average cost of capital.

To sumarize, the cost of capital computation relates to invested capital composed of the following:

• Long-term debt
• Preferred stock
• Common Stock
• Retained earnings
• Interest-bearing short-term debt
• Other short-term debt lacking an explicit cost

Although each capital source has an implicit or explicit cost, noninterest-bearing current liabilities are sometimes excluded for convenience; such a practice may overlook a significant component of total capital costs.

WEIGHTED AVERAGE COST OF CAPITAL (K)

Assume that the specific capital costs of Munster include the following:

Source of Funds	After-Tax Cost (%)
Commercial credit (K_c)	3.02
Long-term Debt (K_b)	4.56
Preferred stock (K_{ps})	10.26
Common stock (K_e)	16.30
Retained earnings (K_r)	11.74

These represent the costs of imbedded debt and the contemporary cost of equity. From this, the average cost of capital (K), using book weights, is computed in Exhibit 6.7. Book value weights have the advantages of stability and accessibility, especially for small companies that infrequently seek new financing and lack an active market for their securities. But they express the circumstances of prior periods: the financial and business risk of the firm and conditions in the money and capital markets at the time of original issue. In particular, the market value of common shares in a going concern will vary from the book value. Market values reflect current appraisals by investors of the firm's growth prospects and its financial policies, along with the state of the money and capital markets. In periods of business expansion, market values tend to exceed book values. Book values are static; market values, dynamic.

Munster common currently quotes at $16 per share. Let us further posit that Munster bonds and preferred sell at par. Exhibit 6.8 computes K based on the current market values of the outstanding securities.

Exhibit 6.8 underscores two features of market value weights. When market values exceed book values, equity tends to make up a higher proportion of the capital structure. Because equity shares are also the costlier source of capital, the average cost based on market weights will be higher. Hence, if the firm shapes future financing in the same proportions represented by market weights, the capital structure will evolve toward a higher proportion of equity financing. Yet the "market value" assigned to retained earnings is highly arbitrary: there is no reason to expect that new internal financing will preserve the book value proportions.

Although the case for using market weights is theoretically strong, it must be acknowledged that market values fluctuate more widely than book values. This means that Munster would have to use an average market value for each class for securities. For small companies or those whose

Exhibit 6.7
Munster Motors, Inc.—Average Cost of Capital (Book Weights)

Source of Funds	Amount	Proportion	Cost	Weighted Cost
Notes Payable	$1,414,500*	.073	3.02%	.22
Bonds Payable	2,000,000	.103	4.56	.47
Preferred Stock	2,000,000	.103	10.26	1.06
Common Stock	7,000,000	.360	16.30	5.87
Retained Earnings	7,000,000	.360	11.74	4.23
Total	$19,414,500	1.000		
weighted average cost of Capital ($\underline{K}$)				11.85%

*Net of prepaid interest on discounted note.

Exhibit 6.8
Munster Motors, Inc.—Average Cost of Capital (Market Weights)

Source of Funds	Amount	Proportion	Cost	Weighted Cost
Notes Payable	$1,414,500*	.0660	3.02%	.199
Bonds Payable	2,000,000	.0934	4.56	.425
Preferred Stock	2,000,000	.0934	10.26	.958
Common Stock	8,000,000**	.3740	16.30	6.096
Retained Earnings	8,000,000**	.3740	11.74	4.391
Total	$21,414,500	1.000		
weighted average cost of Capital ($\underline{K}$)				12.070%

*Net of prepaid interest on discounted note.
**Market value of common equity is $16,000,000 divided between paid-in capital and retained earnings as per book proportions, Exhibit 6.6.

securities are sold sporadically at widely separated intervals, the questionable reliability of market averages undermines confidence in the calculated cost of capital. Whether book or market weights, the computation of K in Exhibits 6.7 and 6.8 is of limited usefulness.

K, as calculated above, is basically historical. It may coincide with the firm's true cost of capital (*a*) if the firm raises new funds in the same proportions as the existing capital structure; (*b*) if the earnings potential and risk posture of the enterprise are otherwise unaffected; and (*c*) if fundamental forces that shape the structure of interest rates in the money and capital markets have not altered—not a highly probable confluence of events. The true cost of capital is that return that meets the current expectations of investors and maintains the market price of the firm's securities.

MARGINAL COST OF CAPITAL

The expanding enterprise concentrates on the cost of new debt and new equity, not the prior costs of existing invested capital. Assume now that Munster plans to obtain additional funds of $11,000,000: $4,000,000 in new common, $4,000,000 retained earnings, $1,500,000 new preferred, and $1,500,000 in long-term debt. The new financing represents a three-year plan to expand the invested capital of Munster by one-third. This substantial undertaking, the company has been told, will increase the average cost of capital. The cost of new common and retained earnings are, respectively, 16.7 percent and 11.74 percent. The underwriters judged that a coupon rate of 10 percent would sell the bonds at par and 12 percent yield would dispose of the preferred stock. Exhibit 6.9 calculates the incremental or marginal cost of capital (K_{mc}), the cost of the last composite dollar of capital raised by Munster. Marginal cost is an average cost per dollar of new funds. Munster will pay 13 cents for each dollar of new financing, composed of approximately 68 cents for debt, 1.6 cents for preferred, 6 cents for common, and 4.3 cents for retained earnings. Note that market value weights are used in computing marginal costs, since the market values of new debt and equity approximate the net proceeds received by the company.

The marginal cost of capital for Munster is higher than the average cost, 13 percent compared with 12 percent (based on market value weights). In static analysis, so long as the risk characteristics of the firm do not change—the firm raises new capital projects with the same relative risk—the average (K) and the marginal (K_{mc}) cost of capital will coincide. With the same basic risk-free rate for all firms in the market, the premium above this minimum covers the risk associated with the particular enterprise and determines the firm's cost of capital relative to all other firms. The reasoning holds unless the firm is of such size or the need for funds so substantial in the short term—the case of Munster—as to bid up the price of funds in the marketplace. Otherwise, with risk constant, the firm can

Exhibit 6.9
Munster Motors, Inc.—Marginal Cost of Capital

Source of Funds	Amount	Proportion	Cost	Weighted Cost
Long-term Debt	$1,500,000*	.136	5.00%	.680
Preferred Stock	1,500,000	.136	12.00	1.632
Common Stock	4,000,000	.364	16.70*	6.079
Retained Earnings	4,000,000	.364	11.74	4.273
Total Incremental Investment Capital	$11,000,000	1.000		
Marginal Cost (K_{mc})				12.664 or (13%)

*As in the previous exhibits, the imputed cost of debt is reflected in the cost of equity.

raise funds in the same area of the capital supply curve, and its relative cost of capital would not vary dramatically from period to period.

Dynamically, on the other hand, the actual cost of the next composite dollar of capital may be greater or less than the average cost (K). The risk attributes of net operating income may diminish or intensify over time; debt to equity ratios may change and the firm may seek additional funds in proportions different from the existing capital structure; fiscal and monetary policy may shift the structure of interest rates with perhaps unequal impact or short- and long-term financing arrangements. To these imponderables must be added investor psychology. The expectation of investors, their risk-return trade-off, fixes the risk premium sought by investment in the company. Such perceptions often fluctuate with prevailing moods of optimism or pessimism. In brief, neither K nor K_{mc} is a static figure, computed and enshrined. Alert financial management follows dynamic movements in the money and capital markets to minimize the cost of capital.

The rationale for a composite rate for the cost of capital rather than a single source—for example, K_e—rests on several assumptions. All capital projects are financed by some bundle of debt and equity funds.

• As a corollary, it is not possible to identify a specific source of funds with a specific use. The company raises funds in the financial market that in turn support the whole group of business assets.

• The specific cost of each source of funds interacts with the proportion and cost of all other sources. Up to some point the introduction of debt into the capital structure will lower the average cost of capital, but continued increases in the debt-equity ratio eventually elevates the cost of capital by adding to the financial risk of the business.

The composite rate approach need not assume that the firm has already achieved an optimum capital structure, and strives only to maintain the stated proportions. It will suffice that K_{mc} accurately measures the true cost of future financing. However, if the firm does not have an optimal capital structure, its decisions will also be suboptimal. The optimum capital structure and sustainable growth are discussed below.

OPTIMAL SUSTAINABLE GROWTH

In Chapter 3 we presented Higgins' concept of sustainable growth (equation 3.1) as

$$g^* = \frac{P(1 - D)(1 + L)}{T - [P(1 - D)(1 + L)]} . \tag{3.1}$$

Equation 3.1 primarily deals with sources of funds and not the cost of funds. As such, it is based on accounting numbers, not market values. For example, P represents the profit margin (EAT/Total Sales) and L denotes the book weights for debt and equity. Book weights are the essential ingredients for sustainable growth as thus calculated.

By contrast, equation 6.5 in Exhibit 6.5 describes the weighted average cost of capital:

$$K_{mc} = K_{dmc}(W_d) + K_{emc}(W_e). \tag{6.5}$$

If we assume that debt is selling at par and K_{emc} is the return necessary to maintain the market value of the common stock, then K_{dmc}, K_{emc}, W_d, and W_e coincide as book value and market values. That is the implication of Exhibit 6.10, in which the cost of equity and the cost of debt rise as the financial risk rises with increased leveraging.

Accordingly, there is a manifest link between profit margins (P), return on equity (ROE), leveraging (L), and sustainable growth (g^*). Higgins and Kerin (1983) report:

By far the single most important reason that sample retailers were able to grow faster than their sustainable growth rates was increased use of financial leverage. In every industry studied, the assets-to-equity ratio inexorably rises over the decade. The combined firms' ratio is representative: . . . [Assets to Equity] increased from 2.09 in 1972 to a high of 2.79 in 1980, a 33 percent rise despite the increase in equity from new stock sales.

ROE measures profits per dollar of stockholders' investment or the efficiency with which owners' capital is used. We have also demonstrated above how the introduction of debt into the financial structure will, to some degree, lower the weighted average cost of capital, increase earnings per share and return on equity, and enhance the valuation of the firm.

Exhibit 6.10 relates the calculation of cost of capital to optimal sustainable growth and other key financial variables in a dynamic setting.

Assume a firm with a financial structure of $100,000 initially composed only of common shares. Debt is added in increments of $10,000 at interest indicated in Column 2 of Exhibit 6.10. Net sales are $35,000; operating expenses total $15,000; the ratio of total assets to net sales (T) is $2.86; and a dividend of $3.00 per share is paid on the common stock.

Observe in Exhibit 6.10, under the assumptions of the problem, the behavior of the variables as the degree of financial leverage increases:

1. The after-tax cost of debt ($K_{dmc}[1 - t]$) increases as additional increments of debt are added to the financial structure. The increasing cost of debt reflects the added financial risk with each new issue of debt capital.

2. Similarly, the yield on common stock (K_{emc}) increases with the degree of financial leverage as the added financial risk is discounted against the common stock.

3. The weighted average cost of capital (K_{mc}) takes the form of a U-shaped curve with the bottom of the saucer formed by the lowest weighted average cost of the next dollar of debt and equity (K_{mc}) on line 6.

4. Earnings after taxes (EAT) decreases consistently with the infusion of larger proportions of debt capital (Column 8) but earnings per share (EPS) increases steadily as the *number* of shares decreases (Column 11).

5. The profit margin (P) declines steadily with the growth in interest payments despite the tax savings allowed on interest payments by the IRS Code.

6. Return on equity (ROE) in Column 10, by contrast, rises over the entire range because of the decline in the equity position as the proportion of debt in financial structure increases.

7. The retention ratio ($1 - D$) in Column 14 follows the same behavioral patterns as ROE despite the firm's policy of paying a regular dividend of $3 per share. For each degree of financial leverage there is a corresponding retention ratio.

8. Sustainable Growth (g^*) shows a positive correlation with the degree of financial leverage (Column 15).

9. The value of the firm (Column 16), calculated by the traditional approach (pages 114 to 117), is maximized when K_{mc} is at a minimum.

To summarize, the objective of management is to maximize the market value of the firm, not to maximize the growth rate. This is achieved when $K_{mc} = 8.0\%$ and the value of the firm is $118,182. The growth rate that will sustain the underlying financial structure at this point is the optimal growth rate, 13.6 percent.

SUBSTITUTION OF ROE

The preceding calculations can be simplified by substituting ROE for P in Higgins' equation 3.1

Exhibit 6.10
Weighted Average Cost of Capital and Optimal Sustainable Growth

1	2	3	4	5	6	7
Line	%Debt	%Equity	$K_{dmc}(1-T)$	K_{emc}%	K_{mc}%	L
1	0.00	100.00	0.00	10.00	10.0	0.000
2	10.00	90.00	4.00	10.10	9.5	0.111
3	20.00	80.00	4.00	10.20	9.0	0.250
4	30.00	70.00	4.0	10.30	8.4	0.428
5	40.00	60.00	4.5	10.50	8.1	0.667
6	50.00	50.00	5.0	11.00	8.0	1.000
7	60.00	40.00	6.0	11.50	8.2	1.500
8	70.00	30.00	7.0	12.50	8.7	2.333
9	80.00	20.00	7.5	16.00	9.2	4.000
10	90.00	10.00	8.0	25.00	9.7	9.000

Exhibit 6.10 (continued)

Line	8 EAT $	9 P	10 ROE	11 EPS $	12 D $	13 D(12/11)
1	10,000	0.286	.100	10.00	3	.300
2	9,600	0.274	.107	10.67	3	.281
3	9,200	0.263	.115	11.50	3	.261
4	8,800	0.251	.125	12.57	3	.239
5	8,200	0.234	.137	13.67	3	.220
6	7,500	0.214	.150	15.00	3	.200
7	6,400	0.183	.160	16.00	3	.188
8	5,100	0.146	.170	17.00	3	.176
9	4,000	0.144	.200	20.00	3	.150
10	2,800	0.080	.280	28.00	3	.107

Exhibit 6.10 (continued)

Line	14 1 − D	15 g* %	16 V $
1	.700	7.53	100,000
2	.719	8.29	105,049
3	.739	9.28	110,196
4	.761	10.55	115,437
5	.780	11.92	118,095
6	.800	13.60	118,182
7	.812	14.93	115,652
8	.824	16.30	110,800
9	.850	20.40	105,000
10	.893	33.30	101,200

In a dynamic setting, in which the firm has established a total capitalization for the size of its operations but wants to settle on an optimal proportion of debt to equity and a concomitant sustainable growth rate, the substitution of ROE for P is theoretically justified on the following grounds:

1. The numerator for both variables is the same, EAT. Thus ROE = EAT/equity and P = EAT/sales.

2. The calculation of ROE allows for the prior payments of interest on debt, tax outflows, and the productivity of fixed and current assets;

3. It imparts greater flexibility to the model in two ways: (a) it is no longer necessary to assume that the profit margin on new and existing sales will vary as the debt to equity ratio in the financial structure is changed. Altering the debt to equity ratio affects interest and tax outflows and ipso facto, EAT; and (b) the use of ROE better illustrates the effects of leveraging on sustainable growth. As debt is added to the financial structure and the proportion allocated to equity declines, K_{mc} declines and g^* increases as long as the after-tax cost of debt capital is less than the higher yields required on equity capital.

4. ROE, which considers the proportion of the financial structure devoted to equity and the yield required to maintain the value of equity shares, is explicitly related to dividend policy. Accordingly, dividend payout (D) does not have to be a given as postulated in the Higgins model.

Higgins and Kerin (1983) specifically recognized the close relation between ROE and sustainable growth. They expressed the relation as follows:

$$g^* = \underbrace{\frac{\text{Net profit}}{\text{Sales}}}_{(P)} \times \underbrace{\frac{\text{Sales}}{\text{Assets}}}_{(T)} \times \underbrace{\frac{\text{Assets}}{\text{Equity}}}_{(A)} \times \underbrace{\text{Retention ratio}}_{(R)} \qquad (6.6)$$

$$= \text{ROE} \times \text{Retention ratio}$$

Note that the definition of T has changed. In equation 3.1 T was defined as the "ratio of total assets to net sales," that is, the number of dollars in assets for each dollar of net sales. Because few companies match their assets in a given fiscal period with an equal or greater net sales, T will generally be ≥ 1. In Expression 4.11 above, T is expressed reversely, spelling out the productivity of assets, the number of dollars of sales for each dollar of assets. This will generally be ≤ 1.

Applying Higgins' revised formula to lines 4 and 5 of Exhibit 6.10, we find on line 4

$$g^* = \frac{\$8,800}{\$35,000} \times \frac{\$35,000}{\$100,000} \times \frac{\$100,000}{\$70,000} \times (1 - .239)$$

$$= 0.251485 \times 0.35 \times 1.4285714 \times 0.761$$

$$= 0.0956684 \text{ or } 9.57\% \text{ (rounded)};$$

and on line 5

$$g^* = \frac{\$8,200}{\$35,000} \times \frac{\$35,00}{\$100,000} \times \frac{\$100,000}{\$60,000} \times (1 - .220)$$

$$= 0.2342857 \times 0.35 \times 1.6666 \times 0.780$$

$$= 0.1065955 \text{ or } 10.66\% \text{ (rounded)}.$$

Neither of these results equates to the sustainable growth calculated in Exhibit 6.10. The reason lies in Higgins' misspecification of the revised expression. The correct specification is

$$g^* = \frac{PRAT}{1 - PRAT} \, . \qquad\qquad (6.7)$$

For line 4 in Exhibit 6.10, this becomes

$$g^* = \frac{0.0956684}{1 - .0956684}$$

$$= 0.105789 \text{ or } 10.58\% \text{ (rounded)}$$

and for line 5,

$$g^* = \frac{0.1065955}{1 - 0.1065955}$$

$$= 0.1193138 \text{ or } 11.93\% \text{ (rounded)}.$$

The slight differences between equation 3.1 and the abbreviated version in equation 6.6 is due to the rounding factor.

SUMMARY

This chapter has reviewed the basic theory of managing the capital structure with a view to identifying the optimal sustainable growth rate. The latter identifies that rate of growth in sales that enables the firm to formulate and maintain a financial structure to minimize the weighted average marginal cost of capital.

The weighted average marginal cost of capital reflects the operating and financial risk of the firm. The value of the firm depends on how the market discounts this risk against the trend in future earnings. Thus, while growth per se does not affect the market value of the common stock, the impact of growth on operations and the way growth is financed will affect the stockholder wealth position. A growth rate that intensifies the risk posture of the firm diminishes stockholder wealth unless the increase in earnings is sufficient to compensate for the additional risk.

The issue, then, is one of balance between investment decisions that produce additional revenues and financial decisions that reduce costs. For this purpose we must examine sustainable growth in a capital budgeting context (see Chapter 9).

NOTE

1. The material in this and succeeding sections represents a composite of views expressed in Clark et al., Fama, Myers, and Van Horne.

REFERENCES

Clark, John J., Margaret T. Clark, and Pieter T. Elgers. *Financial Management*. Boston: Holbrook Press, 1976, chs. 10, 11, and 12.

Fama, E. F. "The Effects of a Firm's Investment and Financial Decisions," *American Economics Review*, December 1974, pp. 851–866.

Higgins, Robert C., and Roger A. Kerin. "Managing the Growth-Financial Policy Nexus in Retailing," *Journal of Retailing*, Fall 1983, pp. 19–48.

Myers, Stewart C. "The Search for Optimal Capital Structure," *Financial Management Collection*, Winter 1987.

Van Horne, James C. *Financial Management and Policy*, 5th ed. Englewood Cliffs, N.J.: Prentice-Hall, 1980, chs. 9 and 10.

PART II

APPLICATION OF GROWTH THEORY TO MANAGEMENT DECISION MAKING

7

FORECASTING SUSTAINABLE GROWTH RATES

In an uncertain world the knowledge of future events and outcomes is of particular interest to economic agents in making business decisions. Information about current business conditions and expectations about future events are important inputs for a firm in organizing its productive resources. The main challenge faced by business forecasters is how to effectively use currently available data to derive the necessary business information as an input for the business manager to make managerial decisions consistent with the objective of the company.

In practice, the conduct of business forecasts involves the following procedures: first, the objective or the problem to be solved must be identified; second, data pertinent to the forecasting need must be obtained and selected; third, the forecasting method based on a cost-benefit analysis must be chosen; fourth, appropriate interpretation of the empirical results must be accomplished; fifth, forecasts and suggestions must be made on the basis of the empirial regularities, which then are integrated into the decision process; and finally, diagnostic checking and a post-sample evaluation must be made so as to provide further information for future purposes. A variety of approaches have been suggested in business forecasting. This chapter concentrates on two of them: the accounting-based model and time-series analysis.

ACCOUNTING-BASED MODEL

Because sustainable growth represents the asset growth a firm can support using both internally generated funds and external debt, it is useful to derive the sustainable growth rate by equating the uses of funds to the sources of funds.

Uses of funds = Sources of funds

New assets = Added retained Earnings + New borrowings

Solving this expression for the growth in sale yields

$$\Delta S/S = P(1 - D)(1 + L)T,$$

or

$$g^* = PRAT, \tag{7.1}$$

where g^* = sustainable sales growth; P = profit margin after taxes (profits/sales); $R = (1 - D)$ retention ratio − (profits-dividends)/profits; $A = (1 + L)$ − leverage (assets/equity); and T = asset turnover (sales/assets). By definition, equation (7.1) can be written as

$$g^* = (\text{profits/sales})[(\text{profits-dividends})/\text{profits}]$$
$$(\text{assets/equity})(\text{sales/assets})$$

$$= (\text{profits-dividends})/\text{equity}$$

$$= [(\text{profits-dividends})/\text{profits}][\text{profits/equity}]$$

$$= R(ROE)$$

The sustainable sales growth represented by equation (7.1), which was used by Higgins and Kerin (1983) in their empirical studies, fails to identify the time periods of the sales. It is important to distinguish between the sales at the end of period S_1, which is used to calculate the profit PS_1 and the sales at the beginning of the period, which is the basis to evaluate the growth rate $(S_1 - S_0)/S_0$. With this recognition, the model should be modified as

$$(S_1 - S_0)/T = PS_1(1 - D) + PS_1(1 - D)L$$

$$g^* = PRAT/(1 - PRAT) \tag{7.2}$$

Apparently, the difference between the two versions is the factor $1/(1 - PRAT)$. On the basis of Higgins' expression, sustainable growth is directly related to the accounting components ROE or $P, R, A,$ and T. The predictions by using accounting data are given in detail in Chapter 3.

Because Higgins' formula is derived from an accounting base, it tells us very little about behavioral relations. It can be seen that the relation between g and P, R, A, and T in equations (7.1) and (7.2) are quite different. To estimate the empirical relation, it is convenient to link the actual growth variable, g, to the related variables in a linear (or log-linear) regression form as:

$$g = b_0 + b_1 P + b_2 R + b_3 A + b_4 T + e, \tag{7.3}$$

$$g = a_0 + a_1(ROE) + e, \tag{7.4}$$

where e is an error term, b_0 and a_0 are constant terms, and $b_1, \ldots, b_4$, and a_1 are fixed coefficients, which specify the behavioral relation between the dependent variable and the explanatory (right-hand side) variables. The theory predicts that the coefficients are nonnegative, indicating that an increase in a right-hand side variable will give rise to an increase in the growth rate. If one conducts statistical testing and the result supports the theoretical postulates, the estimated coefficients then can be plugged into equation 7.3 or 7.4 for forecasting purposes. Note that using the regression technique to derive the estimated coefficient shall reflect an average relationship for the estimated model. This can avoid bias arising from the accounting-base approach, where the calculated sustainable growth is conditioned on a particular accounting date.

Because the explanatory variables such as P, T, and ROE depend very much on profits and sales, equation 7.3 or 7.4 is implicitly determined by the factors that govern profits and sales. Standard economic theory suggests that profits are a function of product prices, quantity of the product sold, advertising, fixed and variable costs, and entrepreneurship. It follows that sustainable growth depends not only on the accounting components suggested by Higgins, but also on the fundamental factors that govern the sustainable growth, including the economic variables such as prices, risk, productivity, managerial skills, and marketing strategy. In a well-specified econometric model these elements should be explicitly incorporated into the model.

Although this approach provides more insight concerning the structure of the relation, this may not be the optimal approach to the business because of the consideration of the cost-effectiveness. For this reason the accounting-base approach is capable of serving the purpose, since the accounting figures summarize the net results of the corporation's decisions and strategies.

Decomposition and Regression Fitting

Forecasting future values of growth rate by using time-series analysis is based on extrapolation of historical observations. The classic approach is to separate the time-series factors in a systematic manner. This involves analysis of the components of trend movements, seasonal variations, cyclical fluctuations, and irregular disturbances.

The trend component refers to the growth that characterizes an upward or downward movement (decay). This occurs when a permanent shifts in either the supply-side factors or the demand-side conditions. The former may be attributed to technical innovations, changes in the availability of input factors, improvement in productivity, and industrial expansion; the latter may be due to changes in consumer tastes or preferences, shifts in income and population, and changes in public policies. A linear trend model can be simply represented as

$$g_t = b_0 + b_1(\text{trend}) + e_t. \tag{7.5}$$

The slope of this relation is b_1, while the intercept is b_0. Growth rate (or the level) of sales defined in this model can be described by the trend designated by the straight line combined with random fluctutations, e_t, that cause the actual values to deviate from the trend line.

With the limits of growth or technological constraints, it is sometimes not relevant to fit the model in a linear manner. Alternatively, the quadratic trend model and the logistic growth curve are usually considered. Among the alternative models the criterion for selection should be based on the nature of the product and the empirical regularities.

Next, consider the seasonal factor in the model building. Seasonal fluctuations usually occur within a year and repeat themselves periodically, depending on the length of the season. If sustainable growth is calculated on an annual basis, the seasonal factor may be associated with institutional factors or structural changes, such as tax policy and inventory management. A seasonal model can be expressed as

$$g_t = b_0 + b_1 g_{t-s} + e_t, \tag{7.6}$$

where the subscript s denotes the length of season; s is indexed to be twelve for the monthly data and four for the quarterly data. The maintained hypothesis underlying equation 7.6 states that g_t is correlated to g_{t-s}. Statistical significance of b_1 means that one can use a previous seasonal factor to predict a future value.

Cyclical fluctuations are less periodically, repeating oscillations around the long-term economic trend. Because profits and sales, and in turn the supply of funds, are positively correlated to the business-cycle movements, the growth of sales is expected to display a procyclical phenomenon. Empirically, we can fit the following regression model

$$g_t = b_0 + b_1 (G)_t + e_t, \tag{7.7}$$

where subscript t refers to the time period and G denotes the growth rate of the gross national product (GNP). This model specifies that growth rate of sales at time t is positively correlated to the growth rate of GNP at time t. If the empirical data appear to support the maintained hypothesis, one can conclude that g_t can be predicted by G_t movements. However, in the real world, the impact of G_t on g_t may not be instantaneous; rather, the effect may involve a time lag or last for several periods. If this should be the case, the model may be modified as follows:

$$g_t = b_0 + \sum_{j=0}^{J} b_j(G)_{t-j} + e_t, \qquad j = 0, 1, 2, \ldots, J, \tag{7.8}$$

where subscript j is a finite number. Equation 7.8 states that g_t is correlated to a distributed lag of G, which reflects a dynamic relation between these two variables. The optimal length and the shape of the lags depend on the empirical significance (see Kmenta 1986).

Finally, irregular factors of the time-series component can also affect corporate growth; these factors arise from unexpected disturbances, such as unanticipated institutional changes, public policies, and political incidents affecting corporate financial structure and profits. However, if these disturbances exhibit a particular pattern, the forecasters can use the underlying information to formulate an appropriate policy to deal with these exogenous shocks.

Instead of purely relying on the analysis of long-term trends, seasonal variations, cyclical fluctuations, and irregular disturbances, a conventional approach emphasizes the exploration of historical data in an attempt to discern any underlying pattern. Once the pattern is derived, it then is extrapolated into the future to generate the predicted values. Numerous time-series models have been developed in the literature; here we restrict our discussion to three models: the simple moving average model, the single exponential smoothing model, and the Box–Jenkins model.

Simple Moving Average

The analyst using a moving average model assumes that the pattern embodied in the historical data can best be represented by an arithmetic mean of past observations. The predicted growth rate in a simple moving average model can be expressed by the following equation:

$$g_t = (g_{t-1} + g_{t-2} + \ldots + g_{t-n}) / n, \tag{7.9}$$

where $g_{t-1}, g_{t-2}, \ldots, g_{t-n}$ are past values of g_t. Equation 7.9 states that the growth rate can be predicted by simply using the mean value of g_t. Several features associated with the model merit comment. First, equal weights are imposed on each of the past observations. No consideration is given to the observations before the nth observation. Second, when the new information is available, the process is updated by including the most recent data and discarding the most distant. Third, the forecast value of g_t depends on the number of past observations included in the averaging process; thus the choice of n becomes crucial. The advantages of this model are its simplicity and the ease with which it can be updated. However, in practice, it is often argued that the most recent value should be weighted more heavily than the earlier ones. A variation along this line is the exponential smoothing model.

Exponential Smoothing Model

The exponential smoothing model states that the forecast value for the next period (g^f_{t+1}) is a weighted average of the actual growth rate (g_t) and the previous forecast value (g^f_t). In particular,

$$g^f_{t+1} = ag_t + (1 - a)g^f_t, \tag{7.10}$$

where a is the smoothing constant between 0 and 1 selected by the analyst. Equation 7.10 implies that

$$g^f_{t+1} = ag_t + a(1 - a) g_{t-1} + a(1 - a)^2 g_{t-2} + \ldots +$$

$$a(1 - a)^{n-1} g_{t-(n-1)} + (1 - a)^n g_{t-(n-1)}, \tag{7.11}$$

where the weights, the coefficients of past actual growth rates, decay exponentially over time. Equation 7.11 states that the growth rate can be forecasted by weighting the past actual growth rates. It should be noted that the forecast value is quite sensitive to the chosen value of a, which is usually assumed to be constant. Although the smoothing constant can be derived by a trial-and-error process, a precise algorithm for determining the best parameters is less clear. In contrast, the Box-Jenkins approach provides systematic procedures for modeling and checking the accuracy of the specified model for forecasting.

Box–Jenkins Model

The Box–Jenkins (Box and Jenkins 1976) methodology suggests that the current value of growth is related to its past values and previous shocks. Assuming g_t is a stationary series, a typical Box-Jenkins model can be represented by

$$g_t = a_0 + a_1 g_{t-1} + a_2 g_{t-2} + \ldots + a_p g_{t-p}$$

$$+ e_t - b_1 e_{t-1} - b_2 e_{t-2} - \ldots - b_q e_{t-q}, \tag{7.12}$$

where $a_1, a_2 \ldots, a_p$, and $b_1, b_2, \ldots, b_q$ are coefficients for autoregressive (the history of growth rate) and moving average (the history of shock) terms. This model is usually called an ARIMA (Auto-Regressive Integrated Moving Average) process.

The strategy in the Box–Jenkins methodology is to "identify" the underlying patterns through historical observations of the time series. This usually involves inspection of the autocorrelation function (ACF) and the partial autocorrelation function (PACF). Through the identification of the pattern displayed by ACF and PACF, appropriate orders of autoregressive and/or moving average terms can be selected. Having identified the tentative model, the analyst then can "estimate" the specified model for the unknown parameters. The estimation can be done by using either a least square error method or a maximum likelihood method. To examine the accuracy of the model, "diagnostic checking" by inspecting the randomness of the error terms must be conducted. With these systematic procedures the Box–Jenkins methodology usually leads to an appropriate model that yields a high degree of forecasting accuracy.

The main drawback to the univariate Box–Jenkins model is that the analyst is required to collect and manage a large data base. The data points should cover at least sixty observations. In practice, many financial reports are available only on an annual basis. This can cause difficulty in forecasting certain financial data. In our case, it is difficult to use annual data to forecast sustainable growth rate, since sixty data points involve sixty years. This time horizon may involve a structural change that may not be relevant to the Box–Jenkins methodology.

Estimated Equation and Forecast Values

To illustrate the performance of the models we outlined in the previous section, quarterly data for the period from 1977.Q1 to 1986.Q4 of K-mart and Ford Automobile sales are collected and used to estimate equations 7.4 through 7.12. These equations, excluding 7.7 and 7.11 are labeled as models (a) through (g) in Exhibits 7.1 through 7.6. These models involve the estimations of level of sales, S_t, and growth rate of sales, g_t, for K-mart and Ford, respectively. The results are presented in Exhibits 7.1 through 7.4.

In general, the estimated equations have reasonable explanatory power and the right-hand variables are statistically significant. The exceptions are the trend variable for the growth equations (model [b]) and the ROE variable (model [a]) for Ford Automobile. In these two instances the explanatory variables are statistically insignificant.

The empirical evidence may be summarized as follows: First, the evidence from model (a) suggests tht ROE has a significant explanatory power for K-mart's sales. In particular, 1 percent increase in ROE will support a 1,725-unit increase in sales or 0.37 percent increase in growth rate.

Exhibit 7.1
Estimated Equations for K-mart Sales

Model (a) $S_t = 2795.48 + 1725.56 (ROE_t) + e_t$, $R^2 = 0.43$

　　　　　　(9.97)   (5.12)

Model (b) $S_t = 2137.74 + 100.69T + e_t$, $R^2 = 0.78$

　　　　　　(10.99) (10.98)

Model (c) $S_t = 1386.66 + 0.68 (S_{t-j}) + e_t$ $R^2 = 0.42$

　　　　　　(2.47)   (4.96)

Model (d) $S_t = -487.09 + 7.03 (Y_{t-3}) - 5.51 (Y_{t-4}) + e_t$, $R^2 = 0.77$

　　　　　　(1.03)   (2.78)   (2.16)

Model (e) $S_t = 0.25 (S_{t-1} + S_{t-2} + S_{t-3} + S_{t-4})$

Model (f) $S_t = 0.07 (S_{t-1}) + (1-0.07) [E(S_{t-1})]$

Model (g) $S_t = 380.75 + 0.89 (S_{t-1}) + 0.84 (S_{t-2}) + 0.95 (S_{t-3}) + e_t$

　　　　　　(11.17)   (8.26)   (11.90)

Notes:
[a]The numbers in parentheses are absolute values of *t*-statistic for testing the null hypothesis
to be zero.
[b]R^2 denotes coefficient of determination.

Second, the sales for both K-mart and Ford Automobile are increasing over the secular trend (model [b]) and correlated with the previous season (model [c]). Third, the sales and the growth rate are correlated with the economic activities and the relation involves certain time lags (model [d]). Fourth, the sales (and growth rates) are positively correlated with their own past values. The results from models (e) through (g) indicate that the lag length lasts for no more than four quarters.

Having estimated the above equations, we then use those models to forecast future values. Out-of-sample predictions for four quarters are made. Exhibits 7.5 and 7.6 report the forecast values, actual values, and mean absolute errors (MAE) for the two companies. To compare the performance of the competing models, we define MAE as

$$\text{MAE} = \left(\sum_{j=1}^{4} | A_{t+j} - F_{t+j} | \right) / 4; \quad j = 1, 2, 3, 4,$$

Exhibit 7.2
Estimated Equations for Ford Automobile Sales

Model (a) $S_t = 9772.74 + 375.86(ROE_t) + e_t$, $R^2 = 0.06$

            (14.27) (1.46)

Model (b) $S_t = 8973.55 + 91.70T + e_t$, $R^2 = 0.27$

            (16.26) (3.52)

Model (c) $S_t = 4812.41 + 0.56(S_{t-j}) + e_t$, $R^2 = 0.29$

            (2.92) (3.63)

Model (d) $S_t = 5724.53 + 15.83(Y_{t-1}) - 14.43(Y_{t-2})$, $R^2 = 0.36$

            (4.51)   (2.20)   (1.99)

Model (e) $S_t = 0.25 (S_{t-1} + S_{t-2} + S_{t-3} + S_{t-4})$

Model (f) $S_t = 0.1(S_{t-1}) + (1 - 0.1)[E(S_{t-1})]$

Model (g) $S_t = 80.45 + 0.28(S_{t-1}) + 0.64(S_{t-4}) + e_t$.

            (2.18)   (4.79)

Notes:
[a]The numbers in parentheses are absolute values of *t*-statistic for testing the null hypothsis to be zero.
[b]R^2 denotes coefficient of determination.

where A denotes actual value, F stands for forecast values, and j stands for lead periods. Comparing the figures of MAE, the results show that in most cases the Box–Jenkins model (model [g]) achieves the lowest MAE. The evidence thus concludes that the Box–Jenkins outperforms the competing models.

Conditional Forecasts

One advantage of using the Box–Jenkins model in forecasting is that all the historical data are predetermined. Unlike for the regression model, this will reduce the costs of obtaining the explanatory variables. Moreover, in a

Exhibit 7.3
Estimated Equations for K-mart Growth Rate

Model (a) $g_t = -0.20 + 0.37(ROE_t) + e_t$ $R^2 = 0.57$

$\qquad\qquad$ (4.33) (6.66)

Model (b) $g_t = 0.07 - 0.00032T + e_t$ $R^2 = 0.0002$

$\qquad\qquad$ (0.80)   (0.09)

Model (c) $g_t = 0.10 - 0.77(g_{t-j}) + e_t$ $R^2 = 0.58$

$\qquad\qquad$ (3.71) (6.67)

Model (d) $g_t = 0.1838 - 4.96(G_{t-4}) + e_t$ $R^2 = 0.10$

$\qquad\qquad$ (2.35)   (1.82)

Model (e) $g_t = 0.25 \ (g_{t-1} + g_{t-2} + g_{t-3} + g_{t-4})$

Model (f) $g_t = 0.07(g_{t-1}) + (1 - 0.07)[E(g_{t-1})]$

Model (g) $g_t = 0.13 + 0.6(g_{t-1}) + 0.51(g_{t-2}) + 0.59(g_{t-3}) + e_t$

$\qquad\qquad$ (3.32)   (2.97)   (3.09)

Notes:
[a]The numbers in parentheses are absolute values of *t*-statistic for testing the null hypothesis to be zero.
[b]R^2 denotes coefficient of determination.

Exhibit 7.4

Estimated Equations for Ford Automobile Growth Rate

Model (a) $g_t = -0.008 + 0.015(ROE_t) + e_t$, $R^2 = 0.01$

   (0.14) (0.62)

Model (b) $g_t = 0.01 + 0.00086T + e_t$, $R^2 = 0.003$

   (0.17)   (0.3)

Model (c) $g_t = 0.04 - 0.62(g_{t-j}) + e_t$, $R^2 = 0.38$

   (1.67) (4.41)

Model (d) $g_t = 0.1391 - 4.5(G_{t-2}) + e_t$, $R^2 = 0.14$

   (2.44)   (2.21)

Model (e) $g_t = 0.25 \ (g_{t-1} + g_{t-2} + g_{t-3} + g_{t-4})$

MOdel (f) $g_t = 0.07(g_{t-1}) + (1 - 0.07)[E(g_{t-1})]$

Model (g) $g_t = 0.02 + 0.31(g_{t-1}) + 0.6(g_{t-4}) + e_t$.

   (2.30)   (4.46)

Notes:

[a]The numbers in parentheses are absolute values of *t*-statistic for testing the null hypothesis to be zero.

[b]R^2 denotes coefficient of determination.

Exhibit 7.5
Forecast Values and Errors for K-mart Sales

Model	Actual Sales	Forecast Sales	Actual Growth	Forecast Growth	MAE (Sales)	MAE (Growth)
Model(a)	5212	4003.38	-0.2281	0.0564		
	5979	4313.98	0.1472	0.1228		
	5686	3934.35	-0.049	0.0417		
	7123	6091.31	0.2527	0.5029	1414.25	0.1625
Model(b)	5212	5863.26	-0.2281	0.0536		
	5979	5963.95	0.1472	0.0532		
	5686	6064.64	-0.049	0.0529		
	7123	6165.33	0.2527	0.0527	500.66	0.1694
Model(c)	5212	5982.10	-0.2281	-0.1286		
	5979	4933.97	0.1472	0.2746		
	5686	5455.99	-0.049	- 0.0159		
	7123	5256.68	0.2527	0.1360	977.89	0.0940
Model(d)	5212	5835.72	-0.2281	0.11074		
	5979	5989.15	0.1472	0.1132		
	5686	6030.15	-0.049	0.1019		
	7123	6147.17	0.2527	0.1135	488.46	0.1412
Model(e)	5212	5605.00	-0.2281	0.0174		
	5979	5760.25	0.1472	0.0906		
	5686	5835.06	-0.049	0.0892		
	7123	5988.08	0.2527	0.1225	473.93	0.1426

Model	Actual Sales	Forecast Sales	Actual Growth	Forecast Growth	MAE (Sales)	MAE (Growth)
Model(f)	5212	7077.21	-0.2281	0.0715		
	5979	7224.27	0.1472	0.0731		
	5686	7373.28	-0.049	0.0749		
	7123	7524.23	0.2527	0.0767	1099.13	0.1439
Model(g)	5212	5376.40	-0.2281	-0.2672		
	5979	6000.63	0.1472	0.1964		
	5686	5447.18	-0.049	-0.0860		
	7123	7575.71	0.2527	0.3530	219.29	0.0564

Note: MAE denotes mean absolute errors.

causal model the future values of the right-hand variables (such as ROE in model [a]) are assumed to be given. If these values are not available, one has to assign a probability distribution in order to figure out the predicted values (Granger 1980). For instance, if the empirical relation between g_t and ROE_t for K-mart is

$$g_t = -0.20 + 0.37(ROE_t) + e_t,$$

the one-period-ahead forecast is

$$g_{t+1} = -0.20 + 0.37(ROE_{t+1}).$$

Since ROE_{t+1} is not known at time t, one has to impose some prior set of beliefs about the possible outcomes of ROE at time $t + 1$. In particular, if one assigns:

$ROE_{t+1} = 0.9$ with probability 0.3

$ROE_{t+1} = 0.8$ with probability 0.4

$ROE_{t+1} = 0.7$ with probability 0.2

$ROE_{t+1} = 0.6$ with probability 0.1,

then these beliefs can be transformed into a distribution for forecast sales for K-mart. The forecast values by using model (a) are as follows:

Exhibit 7.6
Forecast Values and Errors for Ford Automobile Sales

Model	Actual Sales	Forecast Sales	Actual Growth	Forecast Growth	MAE (Sales)	MAE (Growth)
Model(a)	14785	10787.6	0.0489	0.0328		
	17303	11283.7	0.1703	0.0533		
	14366	10610.9	-0.1697	0.0255		
	17196	10768.8	0.1970	0.0321	5049.8	0.4932
Model(b)	14785	12366.3	0.0489	0.0428		
	17303	12458.0	0.1703	0.0436		
	14366	12549.7	-0.1697	0.0445		
	17196	12641.4	0.1970	0.0454	3408.6	0.1247
Model(c)	14785	12677.9	0.0489	-0.0945		
	17303	13062.3	0.1703	0.0094		
	14366	14467.3	-0.1697	-0.0666		
	17196	12828.5	0.1970	0.1463	2704.2	0.1145
Model(d)	14785	12269.1	0.0489	0.0647		
	17303	12417.2	0.1703	0.0752		
	14366	11947.7	-0.1697	0.0713		
	17196	12597.2	0.1970	0.1104	3604.7	0.1313
Model(e)	14785	13186.75	0.0489	0.0212		
	17303	13171.93	0.1703	0.0297		
	14366	13014.42	-0.1697	0.0266		
	17196	13367.27	0.1970	0.0731	2727.4	0.1221

Model	Actual Sales	Forecast Sales	Actual Growth	Forecast Growth	MAE (Sales)	MAE (Growth)
Model(f)	14785	17158.7	0.0489	0.0677		
	17303	17509.4	0.1703	0.0698		
	14366	17866.4	-0.1697	0.0721		
	17196	18230.0	0.1970	0.0743	1261.6	0.1210
Model(g)	14785	13829.62	0.0489	-0.0182		
	17303	14501.31	0.1703	0.0622		
	14366	13374.48	-0.1697	-0.0618		
	17196	14762.56	0.1970	0.1129	1795.5	0.0918

Note: MAE denotes mean absolute errors.

$$g_{t+1} = -0.20 + 0.37 (0.90) = 0.13 \text{ with probability } 0.3$$

$$g_{t+1} = -0.20 + 0.37 (0.80) = 0.09 \text{ with probability } 0.4$$

$$g_{t+1} = -0.20 + 0.37 (0.70) = 0.06 \text{ with probability } 0.2$$

$$g_{t+1} = -0.20 + 0.37 (0.60) = 0.02 \text{ with probability } 0.1$$

Alternatively, the future values of ROE can also be derived by fitting ROE_t into its past values using the Box-Jenkins, exponential smoothing, or another econometric method. This is called unconditional forecasting. Further details can be found in the books by Granger (1980) and Abraham and Ledolter (1983).

FORECASTING SUSTAINABLE GROWTH—AN INTEGRATED MODEL

Using the Higgins model in forecasting sustainable growth rate, one has to assume the financial structure to be unchanged throughout the forecast horizon. If the financial structure is subject to the disturbances of a changing economic environment, the Higgins equation may be too rigid to provide a reliable prediction of sustainable growth. To resolve this problem, it is possible to integrate the Higgins model into the time-series analysis. The procedures can be summarized as follows.

First, with the historical information in hand, we choose a particular period as an initial point. Thus we have the values of P_0, R_0, A_0, and T_0. Those figures then can be used to calculate the subsequent period's sustainable growth rate by $g^*_1 = P_0R_0A_0T_0$. Repeating this process for each period, we can generate a vector of sustainable growth rate as $g^*_t = (g^*_1, g^*_2, \ldots g^*_T)$.

Second, fit the g^*_t series into the Box-Jenkins model as

$$g^*_t = a_0 + a_1g^*_{t-1} + \ldots + a_pg^*_{t-p} + e_t - b_1e_{t-1} - \ldots$$

$$- b_qe_{t-q}.$$

If the corporation maintains its financial policy in a systematic manner, the time-series pattern of the model will display this behavior. In this way, we are able to forecast sustainable growth rates with a systematic and stable, rather than a constant, financial policy. This approach thus has a higher degree of flexibility in adjusting corporate financial structures.

SUMMARY

The purpose of this chapter has been to present a survey of some modern computerized forecasting techniques. When sustainable growth is used in a planning approach, projections are required for the pertinent variables on the sales and/or right-hand side of the equation. The reliability of the result, on the other hand, is no better than the quality of the data and the forecasting methodology used to make the projection.

As we have seen, the projections will vary with the methodology selected even when inputs are the same. Similar data will yield different projections, depending on the forecast methodology chosen. Hence the forecasting methodology applied to the data must be appropriate to the degree of accuracy required by the firm's operations. Firms that can rapidly adapt to the changing marketing conditions may find relatively simple techniques adequate to their needs on a cost-effective basis. Firms that require a higher degree of precision will look to more sophisticated models.

In this respect it is well to remember that all forecasts are subject to upside or downside errors. It is a rare (or random) day when a forecast will hit the mark. Hence, in using sustainable growth as a bench mark for planning, management will be thinking g^* plus or minus some factor based on past experience. To this end, the judgmental forecasting should be used as a complementary tool (Armstrong 1985).

REFERENCES

Abraham, Bovas, and Johannes Ledolter. *Statistical Methods for Forecasting.* New York: John Wiley & Sons, 1983.

Armstrong, J. Scott. *Long-Range Forecasting: From Crystal Ball to Computer*, 2nd ed. New York: John Wiley & Sons, 1985.

Box, George E. P., and Gwilym M. Jenkins. *Time Series Analysis: Forecasting and Control*. San Francisco: Holden-Day, 1976.

Granger, Clive W. J. *Forecasting in Business and Economics*. New York: Academic Press, 1980.

Higgins, Robert C. "How Much Growth Can a Firm Afford?" *Financial Management*, Fall 1977, pp. 7–15.

Higgins, Robert C. "Sustainable Growth Under Inflation," *Financial Mangement*, Fall 1981, pp. 36–40.

Higgins, Robert C., and Roger A. Kerin. "Managing the Growth-Financial Policy Nexus in Retailing," *Journal of Retailing*, Fall 1983, pp. 19–48.

Johnson, Dana J. "The Behavior of Financial Structure and Sustainable Growth in an Inflationary Environment," *Financial Management*, Fall 1981, pp. 30–35.

Kmenta, Jan. *Elements of Econometrics*, 2nd ed. New York: Macmillan, 1986.

Makridakis, Spyros, Steven C. Wheelwright, and Victor E. Mcgee. *Forecasting: Methods and Applications*, 2nd ed. New York: John Wiley & Sons, 1983.

8

SUSTAINABLE GROWTH
AND WORKING
CAPITAL MANAGEMENT

Working capital management refers to the determination of the optimal size of the firm's current assets and current liabilities accounts, given the volume of its business. Assuming other aspects of the business are optimal, achieving the optimal current assets and current liabilities will result in the maximum value of the firm.

The optimal size of the current assets and current liabilities will increase as the firm experiences growth. Because these accounts will increase with the growth of the firm, the objective of working capital management requires that the optimal size of each account be determined for each period and that the optimal size be attained. If, however, growth results in a suboptimal current asset and liability size, the expected benefits of growth, increased value of the firm, may not be achieved. In fact, it is possible that the firm may experience financial distress. The purpose of this chapter is to present some possible effects of the firm's growth on each of the current assets and current liabilities. Also discussed will be the effects of a change in each of the current assets and current liabilities on the firm's sustainable growth.

SUSTAINABLE GROWTH AND CASH

Perhaps the most important component of managing the firm's growth is its cash account. Any misplanning may result in a deterioration of the cash position of the firm, which may lead to financial distress. People Express, a discount fare airline, experienced fantastic growth in sales and stock price during the early 1980s. However, only a few years later the firm's stock price plummeted and the firm was taken over by another airline. It appears that the firm attempted to grow at a much faster rate than its sustainable growth. To finance the excessive growth the firm relied heavily on debt financing. Once competition responded to the challenge of the discount fare airline by reducing their prices, sales growth of People Express declined. Unable to support the large debt burden used to finance the past growth, People Express' cash position greatly deteriorated and the firm appeared ready for total collapse, only to be acquired by another airline.

When actual growth exceeds sustainable growth, the firm can finance the excessive growth by issuing additional debt or stock, or reducing its dividends. For many high-growth firms a reduction in dividends may not be feasible, since they do not pay any. Thus growth financing is mainly accomplished by issuing additional debt or stock. Beyond a certain level, however, the firm will not be able to obtain any additional debt financing because of the perception of creditors of the firm's being too risky. The high risk associated with a heavy reliance on debt financing would also reduce the prospects of financing growth by issuing additional stock. The perception of high risk would depress stock prices, making a new issue either unattractive or impossible. Because cash represents the ultimate adjusting account for all aspects of the business, continued attempts to grow at a faster rate than the sustainable growth will eventually result in a deterioration of the cash position.

Several models are available to effectively manage the cash position of the firm. Cash management models developed by Baumol (1952) and Tobin (1956) use the economic ordering quantity (EOQ) methodology used in inventory management. The EOQ model for cash management assumes the following:

1. Cash outflows occur at a constant rate per period.
2. Cash inflows occur at a constant rate per period.
3. Interest rates remain constant during the planning period.
4. Total cash transactions can be accurately forecasted for the planning period.
5. Required funds can be received without delay.

The objective of the model is to determine the optimal average amount of quantity of cash that the firm should maintain. To find the optimal average amount of cash entails minimizing the total cost of managing the firm's cash position. The total cost consists of transaction costs and an opportunity cost. Transaction costs will increase with the number of times the firm converts its marketable securities (or borrows) into cash. Although a large cash balance will reduce the transaction costs, the firm will incur a larger opportunity cost. The opportunity cost consists of interest that could have been earned on marketable securities (or the interest rate that must be paid on the additional debt). By maintaining the average cash balance suggested by the EOQ model, the total cost of managing the cash account will be minimized. The optimal average amount of cash can be determined by the following equation:

$$C^* = (ft/2i)^{.5}, \tag{8.1}$$

where

C^* = optimal average amount of cash;

f = the fixed transaction cost to convert the marketable security into cash or the transaction cost to secure debt financing;

t = total expected funds required for transactions during the period; and

i = the interest rate on marketable securities or debt financing.

To illustrate the use of the model, assume the Lovely Anne's Pie Company estimates that it will need $2,000,000 for transaction purposes for 1987, expects a transaction cost of $100 per order, and can earn 10 percent from its marketable securities. Given this information, the firm should maintain an average cash balance of $31,623.

$$C^* = [(100)(2,000,000)/2(.10)]^{.5}$$

$$C^* = \$31,623.$$

To obtain an average cash balance of $31,623, Lovely Anne's Pie Company must sell $63,246 worth of marketable securities about 32 times during the year.

Required funds to be transferred $= 2(C^*)$

$$\$63,246 = 2(31,623)$$

Number of transactions $= t/2(C^*)$

$$32 \approx 31.62 = 2,000,000/63,246.$$

The usefulness of the EOQ model of cash management rests on the reasonableness of its assumptions. As constructed, the model is completely deterministic; that is, all the variables are known with certainty. If Lovely Anne's Pie Company does not experience constant cash inflows and outflows during the year, it can use a cash model developed by Miller and Orr (1966). The Miller-Orr model allows for uncertainty in the cash inflows and outflows. It assumes the following:

1. Daily cash inflows are completely uncertain.

2. Daily cash outflows are completely uncertain.

3. The interest rate on marketable securities (or new debt) is constant during the planning period.

4. Cash can be received without delay.

The average cash balance using the Miller–Orr model can be specified by the following equation:

$$C* = (1.333)[(3f\sigma^2/4i_d]^{(1/3)}, \qquad\qquad (8.2)$$

where

$C*$ = optimal average amount of cash;

f = the fixed transaction cost to convert the marketable security into cash or the transaction cost to secure debt financing;

σ^2 = the expected variance of daily net cash flows; and

i_d = daily interest rate on marketable securities or the rate on new debt.

To illustrate the use of the model, we can use the data for Lovely Anne's Pie Company described earlier. Assuming a standard deviation of daily net cash flow of $6,000, the optimal average cash balance, using the Miller–Orr model, is $25,866.

$$C* = (1.333)[(3(100)(6,000)^2/4(.10/365)]^{(1/3)}$$

$$= (1.33)(19404.689)$$

$$= \$25,866.$$

One would expect, of course, that the optimal average cash balances based on the EOQ and the Miller–Orr models will be different, since the two models have completely opposite assumptions concerning the firm's cash flows. Whereas the EOQ model assumed a completely deterministic cash flow pattern, the Miller–Orr model assumed a completely random one.

To bridge the gap between the two models, Bagamery (1987) found the standard deviation of daily net cash flows that will yield the same average cash balance for both models. The daily standard deviation required to have the EOQ and Miller–Orr average cash balances be equal is represented by equation 8.3. Thus, for given values of f, i, and t, if the actual standard deviation is equal to equation 8.3, the concern over whether the firm's cash flows correspond more to the assumptions of the EOQ model or the Miller–Orr model is immaterial, since both models will yield the same result.

$$\sigma = [f/(3368454)(i)]^{.25}(t)^{.75} \tag{8.3}$$

To illustrate the use of the Bagamery model, we can refer to the data of Lovely Anne's Pie Company. For the EOQ and Miller–Orr models to provide the same average cash balance requires a standard deviation of cash flows of $6,980.955.

$$\sigma = [100/3368454(.10)]^{.25}(2,000,000)^{.75}$$

$$= (.131263)(53182.959)$$

$$= \$6980.955$$

Equation 8.3 represents the standard deviation that will yield same average cash balance for both the EOQ and Miller–Orr models. Substituting into equation 8.2 the squared value of $6,980.955, we would obtain the same average cash balance as suggested by the EOQ model.

$$C^* = (1.333)[(3)(100)(6980.955)^2/4(.10/365))]^{(1/3)}$$

$$= \$31,623$$

If the standard deviation of daily net cash flows is less than equation 8.3, the average cash balance prescribed by Miller–Orr will be less than the average balance suggested by the EOQ model. In a previous example we assumed a standard deviation of daily net cash flows of $6,000. The result was an average cash balance obtained by the Miller–Orr model ($25,688) that was less than the result using the EOQ model ($31,623). If the standard deviation of daily net cash flows is greater than equation 8.3, the average cash balance prescribed by the Miller–Orr model will be greater than the balance suggested by the EOQ model.

The EOQ model expresses the firm's optimal average cash balance in terms of the total expected volume of transactions per year, t. A contribution of the Bagamery model is that by substituting the squared value of equation 8.3 into equation 8.2, the Miller–Orr model can also be described in terms of the total expected volume of transactions, t.

One would expect that the volume of transactions, t, would increase at the same rate as the growth of the firm. However, by inspecting the EOQ model of cash management it becomes clear that the optimal average cash balance, C^*, will not increase at the same rate as transactions, t. Suppose Lovely Anne's Pie Company grew during 1988 at 15 percent. We would expect that transactions would be \$2,300,000, (\$2,300,000 = 2,000,000 (1.15)) for 1988.

Using the EOQ model described by equation 8.1, we find that the optimal average cash balance is \$33,912.

$$C* = [(100)(2,300,000)/2(.10)]^{.5}$$

$$= \$33,912$$

Although the growth in transactions is equivalent to the growth in sales, the growth in cash is less. The growth in cash is equal to 7.2 percent.

$$\text{Growth in cash} = (C*_{1987} - C*_{1986})/(C*_{1986})$$

$$= (33912 - 31623)/31623$$

$$= .072 = 7.2\%$$

Several of the sustainable growth models assume that the ratio of sales to assets, T, will remain constant during the planning period. This assumption implies that the assets will grow at the same rate as the growth in sales. The cash management models described above, however, imply that cash will grow at a lower rate than sales.

If cash grows at a lower rate than sales, this would suggest that ratio of sales to assets will decrease. A sustainable growth model described in Chapter 5 defined sustainable growth in terms of operating and financial performance ratios. Assuming that the firm wants to maintain a target financial structure, sustainable growth can be described by the following equation:

$$g* = PRAT/(1 - PRAT), \tag{8.4}$$

where

$g*$ = sustainable growth;

P = profit margin;

R = retention ratio = (1 − dividend payout);

A = ratio of assets to equity; and

T = ratio of sales to assets.

With cash growing at a lower rate than sales, the term T in equation 8.4 will decrease. The initial decrease in T will result in a decrease in the firm's sustainable growth. However, because cash requirements will be less than expected, some additional funds from operations can be used to finance additional productive assets. The movement of funds from a nonproductive asset such as cash will allow the firm to increase its growth without the need for additional financing. In other words, with cash growing at a lower rate than sales, more funds than expected become available, thus allowing the firm to grow at a rate in excess of its sustainable growth.

SUSTAINABLE GROWTH AND MARKETABLE SECURITIES

Marketable securities can be used as an income-earning investment for any temporary excess cash. To support the growth, the firm must periodically increase the size of the fixed assets. Before the construction of the fixed assets, the firm may accumulate the required financing and place the funds in a liquid, marketable, low-risk investment. As the marketable securities are liquidated to finance the construction of the fixed assets, there will be no change in sustainable growth as measured by equation 8.4 and the Higgins, Johnson, and Kyd models described in the previous chapters. However, once the fixed assets become operational, the firm's ability to grow will increase owing to the increased productive capacity.

The choice of whether to purchase marketable securities depends on the risk preferences of the managers. A conservative management team may decide to increase marketable securities at the same rate as sales. If, however, the firm decides not to increase marketable securities investment, or not to increase at the same rate, the firm's sustainable growth will increase. This is equivalent to the case in which cash was seen to grow at a rate less than sales. As stated earlier, additional funds will be made available than indicated by the aforementioned sustainable growth models. The additional funds can be used to finance a growth in excess of the sustainable growth without resorting to a higher total debt-equity ratio, a reduced dividend payout, or issuance of additional stock.

The increase in sustainable growth is not without cost, however, since marketable securities represent the firm's first buffer against an unexpected cash shortfall. Thus the choice to stimulate sustainable growth at the expense of marketable securities involves the firm's accepting an additional amount of risk. The risk can be tempered, however, by the firm having access to funds from other sources, such as banks, suppliers, and other lenders.

SUSTAINABLE GROWTH AND ACCOUNTS RECEIVABLE MANAGEMENT

The aforementioned sustainable growth models implicitly assume that accounts receivable will increase at the same rate as sales. At first blush this may be reasonable. However, it is possible that accounts receivable could be expected to grow at a different rate than sales. If this occurs, the firm's sustainable growth will be altered.

In Chapter 1 it was noted that a firm's growth will result in a change in market share if the firm grows at a rate that is greater than the growth of the industry. To achieve a growth greater than the industry certain balance sheet and income statements of the firm may be affected. Accounts receivable is one of them. In order to increase at a faster rate than the industry, the firm may have decided to relax its credit standards and/or credit period.

By relaxing its credit standards to boost sales, the firm's ratio of sales to accounts receivable may change. The ratio will remain constant only if the customers representing the new sales pay for their purchases in the same time as the firm's old customers. In other words, if the average collection period of the firm increases when the firm relaxes its credit standards, the ratio of sales to accounts receivable will decrease. The result will be to reduce the term T in the sustainable growth model depicted by equation 8.4. With a lower T it is readily apparent that the firm's sustainable growth is reduced.

If the firm achieves the growth in sales by relaxing its credit period, the ratio of sales to accounts receivable will decrease. Accounts receivable will increase at a faster rate than sales, thus causing the ratio to decline, owing to the firm's old customers paying later for their purchases and the new customers paying later than the old average collection period. As above, the result will be to lower the ratio of sales to assets, T, and reduce the firm's sustainable growth.

SUSTAINABLE GROWTH AND INVENTORY MANAGEMENT

Depending on the nature of the firm's desired sales growth, its inventory account may increase at a different rate than the sales growth. If the growth is coming from existing product lines, the firm may obtain some economies in its inventory holdings. In other words, the inventory may be growing at a slower rate than the growth in sales.

One model used to manage the size of the firm's inventory is the EOQ. The EOQ model for inventory attempts to minimize the cost of managing the firm's inventory account, just as the EOQ model for cash management attempts to minimize the cost of cash management. The EOQ model for inventory management can be described by the following equation:

$$Q^* = (2fS/c)^{.5}$$ (8.5)

where,

Q^* = the economic ordering quantity;

f = fixed cost of placing an order for inventory;

S = forecasted sales in units for the planning period; and

c = the carrying cost per unit of inventory expressed in dollars.

Maintaining the same assumptions as discussed in the cash managment section, we find the quantity of inventory Lovely Anne's Pie Company should order when in need of inventory. Assuming that the firm expects to sell 500,000 pies in 1987, has a fixed cost per order of $150, and a carrying cost per unit of $.50, the EOQ is 17,321. Each time the firm needs inventory it should order 17,321 pies from its suppliers.

$$Q^* = [2(150)(500000)/.50]^{.5}$$

$$= 17,321$$

Lovely Anne's Pie Company will have an average inventory balance of 8,660 units, (17,321/2). Similar to the cash management EOQ, it is apparent from equation 8.5 that an increase in sales will result in a less than proportionate increase in the quantity of inventory that will be maintained by the firm. Of course, the model as developed here assumed that the firm would experience no order delay and that it chose not to have any safety stock on hand. But these more realistic additions to the basic model do not alter our conclusion that inventory will probably not increase at the same rate as the growth in sales. Given this result, a more than expected amount of funds will be available to finance the firm's growth. As these funds are diverted to some productive use, the ratio of sales to assets will increase, thus increasing the firm's sustainable growth. For the current period the firm will be able to grow at a rate in excess of its sustainable growth as depicted by equation 8.4 and the Higgins, Johnson, and Kyd models.

Another factor to consider is whether the growth in sales is the result of growth into new product areas. In this instance the firm may experience, at least in the short run, a decrease in the ratio of sales to inventory, since it must build up an adequate initial inventory level. Because the additional inventory must be financed, a constraint is placed on the firm's growth in the short run. This is equivalent to the ratio of sales to assets, T, in equation 8.4, declining. The result will be a decrease in the sustainable growth of the firm for the planning period.

SUSTAINABLE GROWTH AND ACCOUNTS PAYABLE

We might expect that accounts payable will grow at the same rate as the growth in sales, since the quantity of purchases should grow at the same rate as the growth in the quantity of sales. However, accounts payable and sales revenue represent quantity multiplied by price. Because the price per unit is greater than the cost per unit, the ratio of accounts payable to sales will decline with the growth in the firm. This suggests that if assets grow at the same rate as the growth in sales, another liability account must increase at a faster rate to maintain the firms sustainable growth, since accounts payable will be growing at a slower rate.

SUSTAINABLE GROWTH AND NOTES PAYABLE

The sustainable growth models developed in Chapters 3 through 5 assumed that the firm wanted to either achieve or maintain a target financial or capital structure. Embodied in this assumption is the firm's expectation of increasing its debt burden each period. The idea of increasing the amount of debt each period may not be what lenders of term loans desire.

The following equation depicts the Higgins model developed in Chapter 3.

$$g^* = P(1 - d)(1 + L)/t - P(1 - d)(1 + L), \qquad (8.6)$$

where

g^* = sustainable growth rate;

P = profit margin;

d = dividend payout ratio;

L = total debt/equity; and

t = total assets/sales.

Data for Joe's Fish Company is presented in Exhibit 8.1. The sustainable growth for the firm using the Higgins model of equation 8.6 is equal to 8.70 percent.

$$g^* = (.05)(1 - .2)(1 + .6)/(.8 - (.05)(1 - .2)(1 + .6)$$

$$= .087 = 8.70\%$$

Given the assumptions of the sustainable growth model, the pro forma balance sheet for Joe's Fish Company for 1988 can be depicted by Exhibit 8.2. It should be noted that the firm's bank loan is expected to increase by $87,000, a situation not especially appealing to the lender.

Exhibit 8.1
Condensed Financial Data: Joe's Fish Company
(December 31, 1987)

Sales	$10,000,000
Net income	500,000
Dividends	100,000

Current Assets	$3,000,000
Net Fixed Assets	5,000,000
Total Assets	$8,000,000

Current Liabilities	$1,000,000
Bank Loans	1,000,000
Long Term Debt	1,000,000
Common Equity	5,000,000
Total Claims	$8,000,000

profit margin = 500,000 / 10,000,000 = .05
dividend payout = 100,000 / 500,000 = .20
assets / sales = 8,000,000 / 10,000,000 = .80
total debt / equity = 3,000,000 / 5,000,000 = .60
nonbank debt /equity = 2,000,000 / 5,000,000 = .40
spontaneous debt / sales = 2,000,000 / 10,000,000 = .20

Exhibit 8.2
Pro Forma Balance Sheet: Joe's Fish Company
(December 31, 1988)

Current Assets	$3,261,000	Current Liabilities	$1,087,000
Net Fixed Assets	5,435,000	Bank Loans	1,087,000
		Long Term Debt	1,087,000
		Common Equity	5,435,000
Total Assets	$8,696,000	Total Claims	$8,696,000

Equation 8.6 assumed that the firm wanted to maintain a constant total debt-equity ratio. Higgins adjusted his basic model to allow for no increase in the funds obtained from the bank. His adjusted model is depicted by the following equation:

$$g^* = P(1 - d)(1 + L')/(t - [P(1 - d][1 + L']), \tag{8.7}$$

where L' = (total debt-bank loans)/equity. Using the data for Joe's Fish Company, the adjusted sustainable growth will be 7.52688 percent. The reduction in sustainable growth is due to the assumption that the firm will not use additional bank financing to support its growth.

$$g^* = (.05)(1 - .2)(1 + .4)/(.8 - (.05)(1 - .2)(1 + .4)$$

$$= .0752688 = 7.52688\%$$

Exhibit 8.3 gives the pro forma balance sheet for Joe's Fish Company, given the adjusted Higgins model. It should be noted that the firm had an 8.6 percent increase in its nonbank debt ([1,086,021 + 1,086,022 − 2,000,000]/2,000,000), although it experienced only a 7.53 percent growth in sales. The excessive growth in nonbank debt, of course, would also not be welcome news to bank lenders.

Eiseman (1984) adjusted the two Higgins models of sustainable growth. The Eiseman model assumes that the firm's nonbank debt increases at the same rate as sales. The Eiseman model of sustainable growth is depicted by the following equation:

$$g^* = P(1 - d)/(t - L'' - P[1 - d]), \tag{8.8}$$

where L'' = spontaneous debt/sales. Given the data for Joe's Fish Company, the sustainable growth using the Eiseman model is equal to 7.14286 percent.

$$g^* = .05(1 - .2)/(.8 - .2 - [.05][1 - .2])$$

$$= .0714286 = 7.14286\%$$

Exhibit 8.3
Pro Forma Balance Sheet: Joe's Fish Company
(December 31, 1988)

Current Assets	$3,225,807	Current Liabilities	$1,086,021
Net Fixed Assets	5,376,344	Bank Loans	1,000,000
		Long Term Debt	1,086,022
		Common Equity	5,430,108
Total Assets	$8,602,151	Total Claims	$8,602,151

Exhibit 8.4
Pro Forma Balance Sheet: Joe's Fish Company
(December 31, 1988)

Current Assets	$3,214,286	Current Liabilities	$1,071,429
Net Fixed Assets	5,357,143	Bank Loans	1,000,000
		Long Term Debt	1,071,429
		Common Equity	5,428,571
Total Assets	$8,571,429	Total Claims	$8,571,429

Exhibit 8.4 gives the pro forma balance sheet for Joe's Fish Company using the Eiseman model of sustainable growth. The constraint of having the growth of nonbank debt be equal to the growth in sales reduces the firm's sustainable growth. However, the reduction in growth may be more than offset by the reduction in the risk of the firm.

REFERENCES

Bagamery, Bruce D. "On the Correspondence Between the Baumol-Tobin and Miller-Orr Optimal Cash Balance Models," *Financial Review*, May 1987, pp. 313–319.

Baumol, W. J. "The Transactions Demand for Cash: An Inventory Theoretic Approach," *Quarterly Journal of Economics*, November 1952, pp. 545–556.

Brigham, E. F., and L. C. Gapenski. *Intermediate Financial Management*. Chicago: Dryden Press, 1985.

Eiseman, Peter. "Another Look at Sustainable Growth." *Journal of Commercial Bank Lending*, October 1984, pp. 47–51.

Miller, M., and D. Orr. "A Model for the Demand for Money by Firms." *Quarterly Journal of Economics*, August 1966, pp. 413–435.

Tobin, J. "The Interest Elasticity of Transactions Demand for Cash." *Review of Economics and Statistics*, August 1956, pp. 241–247.

9

SUSTAINABLE GROWTH AND CAPITAL BUDGETING

As noted in Chapter 4, sustainable growth calculated on a cash flow basis asks the question, what rate of growth in sales can be financed from existing resources that must support the working and capital budgets of the firm? Because the capital budget may represent current outlays that promise no immediate inflow of funds, the issue becomes one of balancing the short- and long-term interests of the firm. For example, in evidencing interest in a takeover of the Boeing Corporation, T. Boone Pickens expressed the view that Boeing should expend greater effort in pushing the sale of its current line of aircraft in competition with the French Airbus. Boeing later announced a slowdown in the development of the airliner of the future.

CAPITAL BUDGETING

Capital budgeting is a form of project analysis (Clark et al. 1976, 1984). However, the latter term is not limited to investment in plant and equip- ment, but includes refunding projects, mergers and acquisitions, long-term advertising programs, and research and development expenditures. On the other side of the coin, the method of analysis is also applied to divestiture proposals and lease-versus-buy options. In general, the technique is applied to long-term projects with a life of five or more years. Thus, the capital budgeting analysis may involve projects with a five-, ten-, fifteen-year—and so on—horizon.

Because capital budgeting techniques are relevant to a wide diversity of projects and are costly in time and money, firms establish a cutoff on the utilization of capital project analysis. A firm may promulgate the rule, for example, that expenditures of $200,000 or less will be expensed and those above $200,000 will be subject to capital analysis.

In brief, the principal characteristics of capital budgeting include the following:

1. It is future oriented. Projections of cash inflows and outflows relating to the project cover five or more periods. Accordingly, the analysis must allow for the time value of money, and this necessitates the discounting of inflows and outflows by an appropriate rate.

2. Because capital budgeting involves future cash flows, the topic cannot be separated from the problem of forecasting. No capital analysis is any better than the quality of the data used. (See Chapter 7, which treats alternative methods of forecasting.) Moreover, the method of forecasting must be appropriate to the data available and the objective of the analysis. It is well to remember, in this regard, that different methods of forecasting applied to the same data may yield different projections.

3. Forecasts always involve a degree of error. The error may run in favor of the project or against it. The probablity of error creates uncertainty, and uncertainty generates risk.

4. The presence of risk requires that the project analyst devise a measurement of risk. Hence, the ultimate object of capital budgeting is to assess the risk and return on each project and from these measurements formulate a capital budget that maximizes the market value of the firm's common stock.

Incremental Cash Flows

Capital budgeting is a *cash inflow analysis*. It is concerned with the incremental cash inflows and outflows that are traceable to a given project and that would disappear if the project were not accepted. Accordingly, project analysis is quantitative, based on monetary estimates of the inflows and outflows. Because it is a cash flow analysis, noncash items—such as depreciation or sunk costs—are not directly included in the analysis. However, the tax savings from depreciation and the after-tax losses on the disposal of previously acquired assets may be included as cash inflows.

The cash impact of depreciation was recorded at the time of purchase. However, the tax savings from the various forms of accelerated depreciation affect the valuation of the project, for they increase the cash flows in the early years of the project and, allowing for the time value of money thereby, enhance the present value of the project.

Irrevocable or sunk costs are irrelevant to economic choice among future alternatives. For this reason the undepreciated portion, or book value, of old equipment being replaced or retired by the acquisition of new equipment does not affect the cash flows of the new project. The importance of unrecovered book values lies in their impact on tax payout of any recorded loss on asset retirement. Although the after-tax loss on the disposal of old equipment is not chargeable against future cash flows, the tax shield from the loss provides a cash inflow for the project under consideration. In the same manner, the scrap or salvage value (net of any taxes) adds to the new project cash flow.

To illustrate, suppose the firm has an obsolete piece of equipment that originally cost $200,000. Accumulated depreciation is $75,000; the salvage value is $25,000; and the firm is in the 40 percent tax range. The plan is to replace the obsolete equipment with a modern version. What are the cash inflows allocable to the new purchase project?

Original cost	$200,000
Less	
Accumulated depreciation	75,000
Book value (sunk cost)	$125,000
Less	
Salvage value	$ 25,000*
Loss on disposal	$100,00
Less	
Tax savings ($100,000 × .40)	$ 40,000*
After-tax loss on disposal of old equipment	$ 60,000

*The salvage value of $25,000 and the tax savings of $40,000 are part of the cash inflows of the new project.

However, the financing charges attributable to the project are not counted as cash outflows. *The general principle in capital budgeting is that the evaluation of proposed capital projects is independent of the financing costs of the projects.* Thus, if a particular project were financed by a special bond issue, the interest cost associated with the bond issue would not constitute a cash outlay. Of course, the financing costs of a project must be accounted for in the analysis and recovered. This is done by discounting the cash flows, using the weighted average marginal cost of capital (K_{mc}), as described in Chapter 6. *The objective of capital project analysis is to calculate a return on the project independent of the cost of financing.* The latter then becomes a cutoff rate for the acceptance or rejection of the project.

Additional taxes attributable to the project include federal, state, and local. The tax charge to the project is the difference between the company's present tax bill and the tax bill that would result if the project were undertaken. This may be a benefit or expense. *It is important to remember that taxable income will not equate with cash flow and may not correspond to accounting income.* (See Chapter 4 for a discussion of accounting data and cash flows.) In any event, as noted earlier, interest is not deducted from the project cash flows and, similarly, is not inserted at this point in ascertaining tax liability. The tax effects of interest are recognized by putting the cost of capital (K_{mc}) on an after-tax basis.

The initiation of a new project may require the services of personnel and facilities already employed by the firm. In these cases such resources may have to be diverted from alternative uses. This creates an opportunity cost chargeable to the proposed project and is measured by the loss of income to the firm as manpower and resources are transferred from current employments to the new project. Opportunity costs are not easy to identify.

An important caveat attends the acceptance of capital projects on the basis of quantitative analysis with a monetary base. Dollars and cents do not always reflect real incomes and real costs and may fail to capture qualitative variables altogether. Several examples will suffice to make the point. Not all companies receive the incomes to which they are entitled because of regulation or violation of law. Historically, this appears to be so in the United States for toll roads, railroads, and public utilities; currently videocassette rental agencies suffer loss of income by renters copying their product. In such cases the real incomes created by the service exceed the money incomes to the provider. Conversely, money costs may not capture the real costs of production. It is fair to say that through the first half of the twentieth century the real costs of labor—unemployment, old-age, illness, and so on—were not covered by the money costs. Similarly today money data may not measure the damage to the environment or other qualitative considerations. Thus a project that appears acceptable by the criteria of quantitative analysis may be rejected because of qualitative elements outside the scope of the analysis.[1]

Operational and Investment Cash Flows

The incremental cash flows associated with a capital project divide into two categories:

Operational Cash Flows. These tend to repeat themselves in each period over the life of the project, albeit not uniformly from period to period. These include the following:

- Cash inflows, which are represented by additional sales or savings in manufacturing, selling, and administrative expenses. Although projects that increase sales are more dramatic, most capital projects are undertaken to reduce costs of operations.
- Cash outflows, which represent additional outlays on manufacturing, selling, and administrative expenses necessitated by the acceptance of the project.

The difference between the cash inflows and outflows in each period in the life of the project equals the net operating cash flows (plus or minus) for the period. In this respect each period in the life of the project is designated by the symbol t; thus a project with ten periods would be displayed by t_1, t_2, t_3, t_4, t_5, and so on.

Investment Cash Flows. These cash flows take place in period t_0, which involves the length of time to acquire the asset and have it in place to produce revenues. This period may be more or less than a year. In capital intensive industries, t_0 may exceed five years. During the investment period the firm must sustain cash outflows without commensurate inflows.

Example: Assume that a firm has decided to acquire a piece of equipment for $500,000. To service the expected increase in revenue the firm will have to invest an additional $60,000 in working capital. The equipment is to replace obsolete equipment with a salvage value of $25,000 and tax savings on disposal of $40,000. The old equipment has a spare-parts inventory that can be liquidated for $10,000. What are the investment cash flows?

Answer:

Cost of new equipment		$500,000
Investment in working capital		60,000
Total		$560,000
Less		
Salvage value: old equipment	$25,000	
Tax savings: disposal of old equipment	40,000	
Liquidation spare-parts inventory	10,000	
Investment tax credit	0	$ 75,000
Net investment cash flow		$485,000

Ranking Capital Projects

Net Present Value. The most common technique in evaluating capital projects, net present value (NPV), is expressed as

$$\text{NPV} = \sum_{t=1}^{N} \frac{A_t}{(1 + K_{mc})t} - I_{t_0}, \tag{9.1}$$

where

N = the number of periods (t) in the life of the project;
t = denotes a given period;
A = net operations cash flow of period (t);
Σ = summarization sign;
($t = 1$) = states that cash flows are payable/receivable at the end of each period; ($t -$ 1) states that the cash flows are payable/receivable at the beginning of each period;

K_{mc} = firm's weighted average cost of capital serving as the discount factor applied to cash flows;

S = salvage value that may be added to operational cash flows of last period or discounted in the next period. Given the greater uncertainty surrounding estimates of salvage values, a higher discount factor is frequently used to determine the present value of salvage;

I = investment cost of project in period (t_0).

Illustration: Alpha, Inc., is considering the acquisition of new equipment that would enable the firm to increase net operating revenues by $500,000 per period for ten periods. The equipment would cost $2,500,000. However, if complementary investments costing $600,000 were made, the operating revenues could be increased 10 percent annually. Alpha's marginal cost of capital (K_{mc}) is 20 percent. At the end of the tenth period the equipment would have an estimated salvage value of $500,000 before applying a 30 percent discount factor. The equipment and complementary investments would be operational at the start of period one. Alpha decides to analyze the project with the complementary investments included. What is the NPV of the project?

Solution:

Growth Factor

Period (t)	Growth Factor @ 10%	
1	$(1 + .10)$	$= 1.100$
2	$(1 + .10)^2$	$= 1.210$
3	$(1 + .10)^3$	$= 1.331$
4	$(1 + .10)^4$	$= 1.461$
5	$(1 + .10)^5$	$= 1.611$
6	$(1 + .10)^6$	$= 1.772$
7	$(1 + .10)^7$	$= 1.949$
8	$(1 + .10)^8$	$= 2.144$
9	$(1 + .10)^9$	$= 2.358$
10	$(1 + .10)^{10}$	$= 2.594$

Projected Operating Cash Flows

1	2	3	4(2×3)
Period (t)	Growth Factor	Cash Flow at Beginning of Period 1	Projected Operating Cash Flow
1	1.100	$500,000	$ 550,000
2	1.210	500,000	605,000
3	1.331	500,000	665,500
4	1.461	500,000	730,500
5	1.611	500,000	805,500
6	1.772	500,000	886,000
7	1.949	500,000	974,500
8	2.144	500,000	1,072,000
9	2.358	500,000	1,179,000
10	2.594	500,000	1,297,000

Present Value of Net Operating Cash Flows

1 ($t = 1$) Period	2 Projected Operating Cash Flow	3 Discount Factor (K_{mc}) = .20	4(2×3) Present Value*
1	$ 550,000	$1/(1 + 20)$ = .833	$ 458,150
2	605,000	$1/(1 + 20)^2$ = .694	419,870
3	665,500	$1/(1 + 20)^3$ = .579	385,324
4	730,500	$1/(1 + 20)^4$ = .482	352,101
5	805,500	$1/(1 + 20)^5$ = .402	323,811
6	886,000	$1/(1 + 20)^6$ = .335	296,810
7	974,500	$1/(1 + 20)^7$ = .279	271,886
8	1,072,000	$1/(1 + 20)^8$ = .233	249,776
9	1,179,000	$1/(1 + 20)^9$ = .194	228,726
10	1,297,000	$1/(1 + 20)^{10}$ = .162	210,114

Present value of operating cash flows $3,196,658

Add

Present value of salvage at end of $t = 11$;
(30%) for 11 periods yields discount factor
of 0.056. $500,000 × 0.056 =   28,000

Present value of total cash inflow $3,224,658

Less

Investment cash flows (t_0)		
Equipment cost	$2,500,000	
Complementary equipment	600,000	

Total   3,100,000

Net present value $ 124,658

NPV indicates that Alpha has recaptured its investment outlay, earned a return of 20 percent on its investment, and has an excess of $124,658. In theory, Alpha should continue to accept capital projects until NPV = 0. In practice, this dictum may be subject to management and/or financial constraints.

NPV is an absolute, rather than a relative, measure of project value and, in some circumstances, can obscure problems in the selection process. For example, in the presence of a capital constraint, two projects of quite different investment magnitudes may have the same NPV, but they might not have the same return per dollar of invested capital. A *profitability index* (PI) could assist the analyst here.

$$PI = \frac{\text{Present value of net cash inflows}}{\text{Present value of cash outflows}} \qquad (9.2)$$

And in the case of Alpha, Inc.,

$$PI = \frac{\$3,224,658}{3,100,000}$$

= 1.0402122 or 1.04 (rounded).

Internal Rate of Return. The internal rate of return (IRR) is that discount rate which will equate the present value of the forecasted cash outflows with the present value of the expected inflows. The method discounts the stream of future cash inflows to equal investment outflows. Using present value tables, the internal rate evolves by a process of trial and error.

Illustration: Assume the same fact situation of Alpha, Inc. What discount rate will equate the net cash inflows ($3,224,658) to equal the investment outflows ($3,100,000)? Experimenting with three discount rates yields the following:

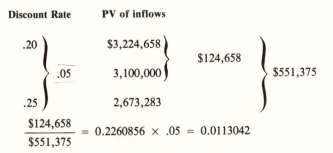

Discount Rate   PV of inflows

.20 $3,224,658

.05   3,100,000 $124,658

.25   2,673,283 $551,375

$$\frac{\$124,658}{\$551,375} = 0.2260856 \times .05 = 0.0113042$$

Then,

$$0.0113042 + .20 = 0.2113042 \text{ or } 21.13\% \text{ (rounded)}.$$

If the IRR $\geq K_{mc}$, the project would be considered for possible acceptance by the firm. Subject to some assumptions, when NPV = 0, IRR = K_{mc}.

Payback. Payback asks the question, how many periods will it take to recapture the investment in the project? Simply accumulate the cash inflows to equal the investment outlay. In the case of Alpha, the project investment is recaptured in the fifth period.

Cash flows are on an after-tax, before-depreciation basis. The firm sets the cutoff payback period. Alpha, for example, may rule that projects with a payback of five years or less would be considered for acceptance; projects with a payback of more than five years would be rejected.

The payback method of ranking capital projects has the advantage of simplicity but suffers significant drawbacks. Unlike NPV or IRR, payback does not measure profitability or allow for the time value of money. Neither does it attempt to measure the risk inherent in the project unless we assume that risk varies directly with the life of the project—many times a false assumption. Moreover, the analysis has a built-in bias that favors projects with heavy cash flows in the early years and does not consider the cash flows in the periods after the cutoff period. If the firm ranks projects from low to high paybacks, therefore, the rankings may differ from those produced by NPV and IRR.

Despite such manifest drawbacks, payback continues as a commonly used method of ranking, either alone or as a supplement to more sophisticated approaches. Simple to compute and for operating people to understand, payback also provides a rough measure of project liquidity, that is, the early recovery of invested funds.

Average Rate of Return. This method is referred to as the accounting method, since it evaluates capital projects by accounting numbers rather than by cash flows. It describes the impact of the project on the conventional financial statements. The average rate of return (AR) represents the ratio of

$$AR = \frac{\text{Average annual income after taxes and depreciation}}{\text{Original investment or average investment}} \qquad (9.3)$$

Often the average annual income represents the difference between the current income statement and the pro forma statement that would result if the project were accepted. This figure is then projected over the life span of the project.

Illustration: Assume three projects each requiring a $60,000 investment depreciated over five years. No salvage value is anticipated from the investments. The projects have the following book profits (after taxes and depreciation) and cash flows (after taxes):

	Project A		Project B		Project C	
Period (t)	Book Profit	Net Cash Flow	Book Profit	Net Cash Flow	Book Profit	Net Cash Flow
1	$8,000	$16,000	$4,200	$8,400	$1,000	$ 1,000
2	6,000	12,000	4,200	8,400	2,000	4,000
3	4,000	8,000	4,200	8,400	4,000	8,000
4	2,000	4,000	4,200	8,400	6,000	12,000
5	1,000	2,000	4,200	8,400	8,000	16,000

The AR on Project A is either

$$\frac{\$21,000/5}{\$60,000/2} = \frac{\$ 4,200}{\$30,000} = 14\%$$

or

$$\frac{\$21,000/5}{\$60,000} = \frac{\$ 4,200}{\$60,000} = 7\%.$$

The same AR could be calculated for Projects B and C despite the marked differences in cash flows. Thus, like payback, AR makes no allowance for the time value of money and does not afford a viable measure of risk. Also, book profit is subject to vagaries of available accounting options, which may adversely affect the comparability of projects.

All things considered, the only theoretically correct procedures are NPV or IRR. However, the other methods—payback and AR—do have a story to tell, albeit a limited one. The liquidity of the project is a valuable datum to consider, and management will always want to assess the impact of capital projects on the conventional accounting statements. Accordingly, a good practice to follow in capital budgeting is to rank projects by each method and investigate the conflicts in rankings. The disparity in rankings may indicate the need for better data and/or further investigation of the projects.

Capital projects are grouped together to form capital budgets. Under NPV or IRR, the preferred budget—assuming no managerial or financial constraints—is the one that gives the highest NPV or the highest IRR. This is accomplished when projects are accepted to the point where, for the last project, NPV = 0 or IRR = K_{mc}. Under payback, the preferred budget is the combination of projects with payback periods within the stipulated cutoff. Under AR, the choice budget is the one that offers the highest AR. Different combinations of projects may result, depending on the method of ranking.

The preceding material constitutes no more than a cursory introduction to capital budgeting. Much more could have been said about risk management, the affects of managerial and financial constraints, the issue of project comparability, the sources of conflicts in rankings, the utility of programming in capital budgeting, capital budgeting in an international context, and so forth. Our comments are primarily intended as a threshold for the discussion of the relation between sustainable growth and the capital budget.

SUSTAINABLE GROWTH AND CAPITAL BUDGETING

In dealing with sustainable growth and capital budgeting, we shall use the Govindarajan and Shank cash flow approach to sustainable growth described in Chapter 4. We shall also posit a hypothetical firm, the LCB company, with financial statements contained in Exhibits 9.1, 9.2, and 9.3. These statements further assume that LCB has made no expenditure on plant and equipment in 1987. Appendixes 9.1, 9.2, and 9.3 calculate sustainable growth using the Higgins and Johnson models (Chapter 3) and depict the results from the Govindarajan and Shank cash flow model (Chapter 4).

The calculations in the exhibits show that the Higgins and Johnson models in the hypothetical case yield 8.9 percent sustainable growth. By contrast, the cash flow model gives a sustainable growth of 10.1 percent. The difference is traceable to the addback of depreciation that, correctly so, is recognized as a source of funds. Thus, in the generic case, the cash flow model will yield a higher sustainable growth whenever the addback of depreciation, deferred income taxes, and accrued expenses that do not use

Exhibit 9.1
LCB Company Income Statement, 1987 (000 omitted)

Net Sales	$640,310
Cost of Sales	(533,909)
Gross Profit	$106,401
Selling, General, and Administrative Expenses	(15,741)
Depreciation Expense	(26,786)
Maintenance	(10,000)
Earnings Before Interest and Taxes (EBIT)	$53,874
Interest Expense	(9,424)
Earnings Before Taxes (EBT)	$44,450
Income Tax Expense	(19,800)
Net Income (EAT)	$24,650
Dividends	7,184
Addition to Retained Earnings	$17,466

Additional Data Taken From Financial Statements:

1 - Previous period(s) Net Sales (1986) were $599,534. Sales increased by $40,776 or 6.8%

2 - Change in Receivables   : $(7,156)

3 - Change in Inventory   : $(10,853)

4 - Change in Accounts Payable   : $ 3,642

5 - Change in Prepaid Expenses   : $(984)

6 - Change in Accruals   : $ 4,605

7 - Current Portion of Long-Term Debt : $ 6,211

current funds exceed accrued incomes and prepaid expenses not currently providing funds.

Now assume that LCB had spent $20,000,000 on new plant construction and equipment during 1987. However, the new construction is not expected to provide additional earnings until 1989 ($t_0 = 2$ years). These two items would be financed out of cash reserves. The accounting entry to record the transaction

Exhibit 9.2
LCB Company Balance Sheet, 1987 (000 omitted)

Assets

Current Assets:

Cash	$ 21,368
Accounts Receivable	77,924
Inventory	118,184
Prepaid Expenses	10,711
Total Current Assets	$228,187

Fixed Assets	$358,984	
Less		
Accumulated Depreciation	(145,857)	
Net-Fixed Assets		$213,127
Total Assets		$441,314

Liabilities

Current Liabilities:

Current Portion of Long Term Debt	$ 6,211
Accounts Payable	39,658
Accrued Expenses	50,141
Accrued Taxes	13,695
Total Current Liabilities	$109,705
Long Term Debt	117,863
Total Liabilities	$227,568

Shareholders Equity

Common Stock	$ 509
Paid-in Capital	29,910
Retained Earnings	183,327
Total Shareholders Equity	$ 213,746
Total Liabilities & Shareholders Equity	$441,314

Exhibit 9.3
LCB Company Statement of Changes in Financial Condition, 1987
(000 omitted)

Cash Provided By:

Operations:

Net Earnings (EAT)		$24,650
Add		
Depreciation	$26,786	
Increase (Decrease) in		
Working Capital[1]	(10,746)	16,040
Cash Provided by Operations (FPO)		$40,690

External Financing

Current Portion of Long Term Debt	$(6,211)	
Issuance of Long Term Debt	18,467	
Issuance of Common Stock	20,000	$32,256

Cash Used For:

Dividends	$ 8,204	
Fixed Asset under Construction	20,000	$28,204
Increased (Decrease) in Cash		$44,742

Increase (Decrease) in Working Capital

Receivables (net)	$(7,156)	
Change in Accounts Payable	3,642	
Change in Prepaids	(984)	
Change in Accruals	4,605	
Changes in Inventory	(10,853)	$(10,746)

———

[1]Exclusive of increase (decrease) in cash.

	Debit	**Credit**
Fixed assets in progress	$20,000,000	
Cash		$20,000,000

would not affect the 1987 income statement. However, the balance sheet would reflect the transfer of asset values from cash to fixed assets and the statement of changes in financial condition would highlight the addition to funds required for investment. Appendixes 9.1 and 9.3 reflect the changes on the financial statements. Appendix 9.1 calculates the revised sustainable growth figures.

Note also, however, that we are making essentially an "unproductive" investment, that is, an investment that will not contribute cash inflows for two periods. In a wider sense, goodwill and other intangible assets may also be termed nonproductive. Firms also accumulate assets for political ends: to fend off takeovers, to strengthen the position of management, to provide against the occurrence of specified contingencies, and so on. But the models discussed in the preceding chapters are not sufficiently sensitive to pick up the distinction between operational and nonoperational investments. They implicitly assume that all assets are productive. In the extant case, they will not reflect the implications of the transfer of assets from cash to fixed assets in progress. On the other hand, the Govindarajan and Shank model can easily be modified to incorporate nonoperational asset investments. The revised Govindarajan–Shank model becomes

$$g_c^* = \frac{\text{FPO} + (\text{FPO} \times R) - M}{(F + U_a + W + M - \text{FPO}) - (\text{FPO} \times R)}, \tag{9.4}$$

where U_a = investment in nonoperational assets/EAT and all other parameters remain the same as previously described.

Without adjustment, the Higgins and Johnson models give the same results as before the investment in nonoperational plant and equipment (i.e., a sustainable growth of 8.9 percent). The modified Govindarajan–Shank model, by contrast, picks up the impact of the investment on sustainable growth. The firm's ability to finance current sales is reduced to 3.74 percent by the capital investment of $20,000,000. Appendix 9.1 presents the full array of calculations.[2]

If LBC chose to finance the nonoperational investment by new debt, the Govindarajan–Shank approach would *raise* sustainable growth to 5.96 percent. The Higgins and Johnson models would register a slight decline to 8.5. Earnings after taxes (EAT) are reduced by higher interest payments and spread out over a higher dollar investment in total assets. Appendix 9.2 shows the impact of bond financing for nonoperational assets on sustainable growth.

Conversely, if LCB resorted to stock financing, sustainable growth would rise from the base value of 3.74 percent (under internal financing) to 4.93 percent using the Govindarajan–Shank model. The Higgins and Johnson models would register further declines to 7.6 percent, reflecting the lower degree of financial leveraging. But neither model—Higgins or Johnson—underscores the true issue, the investment in nonoperational assets and the relation of sustainable growth to capital budgeting. Appendix 9.3 details the calculations.

The hypothetical case of LCB does illustrate the relation between sustainable growth and the size and method of financing the capital budget. If the firm cannot raise additional funds by debt or stock financing—if it must rely on retained earnings for required funds—then it may have to trade-off the present value of current earnings against the expected gains accruing from the capital budget. Stated differently, the capital budget is not the product of a simplistic process of accepting projects until NPV = 0 or IRR = K_{mc}. In the presence of fixed resources, this could unduly penalize current operations. Under these conditions the firm must investigate the opportunity costs of shifting resources from current to future operations or vice versa.

In keeping with the conceptual framework of financial management, we may think of the firm achieving an equilibrium between current sales (financed by net working capital and operational fixed assets) and future benefits (represented by the capital budget) when the present value of current sales equals the present value of the capital budget. Given the opportunity costs and benefits in deploying assets between current and future operations, K_{mc} would appear to be the appropriate discount rate in arriving at the respective present values. However, the selection of a discount rate is always a matter of some argument in financial management, and the reader should not take our use of K_{mc} as the final word on the subject. The advantage to this conception, on the other hand, is that it forces management to view the firm as a whole with an eye on the present and future; the capital budget is no longer an exercise in future expectations without regard to its impact on current operations.

Nor can we assume that difficult choices can be avoided by hypothesizing that every dollar of internally generated funds will be supplemented by externally recruited resources. New debt may not be quickly or easily obtainable, especially if the firm's debt to equity ratio already approximates the average for its size and industry. Equally, new stock issues involve a preparatory time period and are a costly form of financing.

Sustainable growth calculated on a cash basis highlights the connections to the working and capital budgets. It further suggests the importance of ascertaining the firm's strategic plan as a primary input to interpreting the financial statements.

NOTES

1. The distinction between capital budgeting and strategic management has blurred in recent years. Strategic management models, while incorporating quantitative analysis, also attempt to incorporate qualitative factors.

2. The reader should not infer that retained earnings represent "free capital." Actually, it is discounted at the same rate as common stock, a costly form of financing. Moreover, the rate of growth is limited by the rate of accumulation in retained earnings.

REFERENCES

All references to capital budgeting are adapted from the following volumes:

Clark, John J., Margaret T. Clark, and Pieter Elgers, *Financial Management*. Boston: Holbrook Press, 1976.

Clark, John J., Thomas J. Hindelang, and Robert Pritchard, *Capital Budgeting*. Englewood Cliffs, N.J.: Prentice-Hall, 1984.

Govindarajan, V. and John K. Shank, "Cash Sufficiency: The Missing Link in Strategic Planning," *Corporate Accounting*, Winter 1984, pp. 23–30.

APPENDIX 9.1
FINANCING CAPITAL EXPENDITURES
BY RETAINED EARNINGS

LCB Company

Income Statement
1987

(000 omitted)

Net Sales	$640,310
Cost of Sales	(533,909)
Gross Profit	$106,401
Selling, General, and Administrative Expenses	(15,741)
Depreciation Expense	(26,786)
Maintenance	(10,000)
Earnings Before Interest and Taxes (EBIT)	$53,874
Interest Expense	(9,424)
Earnings Before Taxes (EBT)	$44,450
Income Tax Expense	(19,800)
Net Income (EAT)	$24,650
Dividends	(7,184)
Addition to Retained Earnings	$17,466

LCB Company

Balance Sheet
1987

(000 omitted)

<u>Assets</u>

Current Assets:

Cash		$ 1,368
Accounts Receivable		77,924
Inventory		118,184
Prepaid Expenses		<u>10,711</u>
Total Current Assets		$208,187
Fixed Assets	$358,984	
Less: Accumulated Depreciation	<u>145,857</u>	
Net Fixed Assets	$213,127	
Fixed Assets in Progress[1]	<u>20,000</u>	<u>233,127</u>
Total Assets		$441,314

LCB Company Balance Sheet (Continued)

Liabilities

    Current Liabilities:

Current Portion of Long Term Debt	$6,211
Accounts Payable	39,658
Accrued Expenses	50,141
Accrued Taxes	13,695
Total Current Liabilities	$109,705
Long Term Debt	$117,863
Total Liabilities	$227,568

Shareholders Equity:

Common Stock	$509
Paid-in Capital	29,910
Retained Earnings	183,327
Total Shareholders Equity	$213,746
Total Liabilities and Shareholders Equity	$441,314

---

[1]Fixed Assets in Progress are non-operational; that is, they do not contribute to cash inflows.

LCB Company

Statement of Changes in Financial Condition
1987

(000 omitted)

Cash Provided by:

Operations:

Net Earnings (EAT)		$24,650
Add:		
Depreciation	$26,786	
Increase (Decrease) in		
Working Capital	(10,746)	16,040
Cash Provided by Operations		$40,690

External Financing

Current Portion of Long Term Debt	$(6,211)	
Issuance of Long Term Debt	18,467	12,256
Cash Available for Investment (FAI)		$52,946

Cash Used For:

Dividends	$ 7,184	
Fixed Asset Construction	20,000	
Cash Required for Investment		$27,184
Increase (Decrease) in Cash		$25,762

LCB Company Statement of Changes (Continued)

Increase (Decrease) in Working Capital

Receivables (Net)	$(7,156)	
Change in Accounts Payable	3,642	
Change in Prepaids	(984)	
Change in Accruals	4,605	
Change in Inventory	(10,853)	$(10,746)

Revised Sustainable Growth: Higgins and Johnson Models

LCB Company
End of 1987

Model Parameters

P = EAT/Net Sales = $24,650/$640,310 = 0.0384969

D = Dividend Payout Ratio = Dividends Paid/EAT =
$7,184/$24,650 = 0.2914401

L = Total Debt/Equity = $227,568/$213,746 = 1.0646655

T = Total Assets/Net Sales = $441,314/$640,310 = 0.6892192

W = Net Working Capital/Net Sales = $98,482/$640,310 = 0.1538036

L_L = Long Term Debt/Equity = $117,863/$213,746 = 0.5514161

F = Net Fixed Assets/Net Sales = $213,127/$640,310 = 0.3328437
(Does not include Non-Operational Assets)

J = Price Change = Assume 0

Higgins Model

$$g^* = \frac{P(1-D)(1+L)}{T-[P(1-D)(1+L)]} \qquad (3.1)$$

$$= \frac{0.0384969\,(1-0.2914401)(1+1.0646655)}{0.6892192-[0.0384969\,(1-0.2914401)(1+1.0646655)]}$$

= 0.0889847 or 8.9% (rounded)

Sustainable Growth: Higgins and Johnson Models (Continued)

Johnson Model

$$g_R{}^* = \frac{Y(1 + J) - WJ}{F - [(1 + J)Y] + [W(1 + J)]}$$

where

$$Y = P(1 - D)(1 + L_L)$$

Then,

$$Y = (0.0384969)(1 - 0.2914401)(1 + 0.5514161)$$

and

$$g_R{}^* = \frac{0.0423184(1 + 0) - 0.1538036(0)}{0.3640845 - [(1 + 0)0.0423184] + [0.1538036(1 + 0)]}$$

$$= \frac{0.0423184}{0.4755697}$$

$$= 0.0889846 \text{ or } 8.9\% \text{ (rounded)}$$

Govindarajan and Shank Model

Excess Cash Scenario
LCB Company
End of 1987

(000 omitted)

Model Parameters

F = Fixed Asset Investment Rate = Net Fixed Assets Purchased/Change

in Net Sales = 0 (Excludes Non-Operational Assets)

W = Change in Working Capital/Change in Net Sales = \$15,016/\$40,776 =

0.3682558

Note: Change in Working Capital per Statement of Changes in

Financial Condition = \$(10,746) + \$ 25,762 = \$15,016

M = Maintenance Expense/Net Sales = \$10,000/\$640,310 = 0.0156174

P = EBIT/Net Sales = \$53,874/\$640,310 = 0.0841373

i = Interest Expense/Net Sales = \$9,424/\$640,310 = 0.0147178

D_p = Depreciation Expense/Net Sales = \$26,786/\$640,310 = 0.0418328

D = Dividend Payout Rate = Dividends Paid/EAT =\$7,184/\$24,650 =

0.2914401

U_A = Investment in Non-Operational Assets/EAT = \$20,000/\$24,650 =

0.811359

T = Income Tax Rate = Income Tax Expense/EBT = \$19,800/\$44,450 =

0.4454443

Govindarajan and Shank Model (Continued)

R = Debt Supplement to Internally Generated Funds = Change in Long and

Intermediate Debt/Cash Retained by Company,

where Cash Retained by Company =

Cash Provided by Operations (FPO)	$51,436
Plus: Change in Working Capital	(10,746)
Less: Dividends Paid	(7,184)
	$33,506

$$R = \frac{\$12,256}{\$33,506} = 0.3657852$$

Solution

I - Funds Provided by Operations (FPO)

$= (P - i) \times (1 - T) \times (1 - D) + D_p$

$= (0.0841373 - 0.0147178) \times (1 - 0.445443) \times$

$(1 - 0.2914401) + 0.0418328$

$= 0.0691101$

II - Funds Available for Investment (FAI)

$FPO \times (1 \times g_c^*) \times (1 \times R)$

$= 0.0691101 \times (1 + g_c^*) \times (1 + 0.3657852)$

Govindarajan and Shank Model (Continued)

III – Funds Required for Investment (FRI)

$$(g_C^* \times F) + (g_C^* \times W) + ([1 + g_C^*] \times M) \text{ modified to:}$$

$$= (g_C^* \times F) + (g_C^* \times U_A) + (g_C^* \times W) + ([1 + g_C^*] \times M)$$

$$= (g_C^* \times 0) + (g_C^* \times 0.811359) + (g_C^* \times 0.3682558) +$$

$$([1 + g_C^*] \times 0.0156174)$$

IV – $g_C^* = \dfrac{FPO + (FPO \times R) - M}{(F + UA + W + M - FPO) - (FPO \times R)}$.

$$= \dfrac{0.0691101 + (0.0691101 \times 0.3657852) - 0.0156174}{(0 + 0.811359 + 0.3682558 + 0.0156174 - 0.0691101) - (0.0691101 \times 0.3657852)}$$

$$= \dfrac{0.4117124}{(1.1261221) - (0.0252794)}$$

$$= \dfrac{0.4117124}{1.1008427} = 0.0373997 \text{ or } 3.74\% \text{ (rounded)}$$

APPENDIX 9.2
FINANCING CAPITAL EXPENDITURES
BY DEBT ISSUES

LCB Company
Income Statement
1987

(000 omitted)

Net Sales	$640,310
Cost of Sales	(533,909)
Gross Profit	$106,401
Selling, General, and Administrative Expenses	(15,741)
Depreciation Expense	(26,786)
Maintenance	(10,000)
Earnings Before Interest and Taxes (EBIT)	$53,874
Interest Expense	(10,824)
Earnings Before Taxes (EBT)	$43,050
Income Tax Expense	(19,176)
Earnings After Taxes (EAT)	$23,874
Dividends	(7,184)
Additions to Retained Earnings	$16,690

LCB Company

Balance Sheet
1987

(000 omitted)

Assets

Current Assets:

Cash	$ 21,368
Accounts Receivable	77,924
Inventory	118,184
Prepaid Expenses	10,711
Total Current Assets	$228,187

Fixed Assets	$358,984	
Less: Accumulated Depreciation	(145,857)	
Net Fixed Assets	$213,127	
Fixed Assets in Progress[1]	20,000	233,127
Total Assets		$461,314

Liabilities

Current Liabilities:

Current Portion of Long Term Debt	$ 6,211
Accounts Payable	39,658
Accrued Expenses	50,141

LCB Company Balance Sheet (Continued)

Accrued Taxes	13,695
Total Current Liabilities	$109,705
Long Term Debt[2]	137,863
Total Liabilities	$247,568

Shareholders Equity

Common Stock	$509
Paid-in Capital	29,910
Retained Earnings	183,327
Total Shareholders Equity	$213,746
Total Liabilities and Shareholders Equity	$461,314

(1) Fixed Assets in Progress are non-operational; that is, they do not contribute to cash inflows.

(2) $20,000,000 in long term debt sold at par to yield 7 percent.

LCB Company

Statement of Changes in Financial Condition
End of 1987

(000 omitted)

Cash Provided by:

Operations

Net Earnings (EAT) $23,874

Add:

Depreciation $26,786

Increase (Decrease)

Working Capital   (10,746)   16,040

Cash Provided by Operations $39,914

External Financing

Current Portion of Long Term Debt $(6,211)

Insurance of Long Term Debt   38,467   32,256

Cash Available for Investment (FAI) $72,170

Cash Used For:

Dividends $7,184

Fixed Asset Construction   20,000

Statement of Changes (Continued)

Cash Required for Investment		<u>27,184</u>
Increase (Decrease) in Cash		<u>$44,986</u>
Increase (decrease) in Working Capital		
Receivable (Net)	$(7,156)	
Changes in Account Receivable	3,642	
Changes in Prepaids	(984)	
Changes in Accruals	4,605	
Changes in Inventory	<u>(10,853)</u>	<u>($10,746)</u>

Sustainable Growth: Higgins & Johnson Models

LCB Company
1987

P = EAT/Net Sales = $23,874/$640,310 = 0.037285

D = Dividend Payout Ratio = Dividends Paid/EAT =
$7,184/$23,874 = 0.3009131

L = Total Debt/Equity = $247,568/$213,746 = 1.1582345

T = Total Assets/Net Sales = $461,314/$640,310 = 0.7204541

W = Net Working Capital/Net Sales = $118,482/$640,310 = 0.1850384

L_L = Long Term Debt/Equity = $137,863/$213,746 = 0.6449851

F = Net Fixed Assets/Net Sales = $233,127/$640,310 = 0.3640845

Higgins Model:

$$g_c^* = \frac{P(1-D)(1+L)}{T-[P(1-D)(1+L)]}$$

$$= \frac{0.037285\,(1-0.3009131)(1+1.1582345)}{0.7204541-[0.0372185\,(1-0.3009131)(1+1.1582345)}$$

$$= \frac{0.0562551}{0.6641989}$$

$$= 0.0846964 \text{ or } 8.5\% \text{ (rounded)}$$

Sustainable Growth: Higgins & Johnson Models (Continued)

Johnson Model:

$$gR^* = \frac{Y(1+J) - WJ}{F - [(1+J)Y] + [W(1+J)]}$$

where,

$$Y = (P(1-D)(1+L_L))$$

Then,

$$Y = (0.037285(1-.3009131)(1+0.6449851) = .0428771$$

and,

$$gR^* = \frac{0.0428771(1+0) - (0.1850384 \times 0)}{0.3640845 - [(1+0)0.0428771] + [0.1850384(1+0)]}$$

$$= \frac{0.0428771}{0.5062458}$$

$$= 0.0846962 \text{ or } 8.5\% \text{ (rounded)}$$

Govindarajan and Shank Model

Bond Financing
LCB Company
End of 1987

Model Parameters

F = No change = 0

W = Change in Working Capital/Change in Net Sales =

$34,240/$40,776 = 0.8397096

Note: Change in Working Capital per Statement of Changes in

Financial Condition = $(10,746) + $44,986 = $34,240

M = No change   0.0156174

P = No change   0.0841373

i = Interest Expense/Net Sales = $10,824/$640,310 = 0.0169043

Includes interest of $1,400 on new $20,000 bond issue.

D_p = No change   0.0418328

D = No change   0.2914401

U_A = Investment in Non-Operational Assets/EAT

= $20,000/$23,874   0.8377314

T = No change   0.4454443

Govindarajan and Shank Model (Continued)

R = Debt Supplement to Internally Generated Funds =

Change in Long and Intermediate Debt/Cash

Retained by Company,

where Cash Retained by Company =

Cash Provided by Operations (FPO)	$50,660
Plus: Change in Working Capital	(10,746)
Less: Dividends Paid	(7,184)
	$32,730

R = $20,000
    $32,730

= 0.6110602

Solution

I - Funds Provided by Operations (FPO)

= (P - I) x (I - T) x (I - D) + D_p

= (0.0841373 - 0.0169043) x (I - 0.4454443)
  (I - 0.2914401) + 0.0418328

= 0.068251

II - <u>Funds Available for Investment (FAI)</u>

$$FPO \times (1 + g_c^*) \times (1 + R)$$

$$= 0.068251 \times (1 + g_c^*) \times (1 + 0.6110602)$$

III - <u>Funds Required for Investment (FRI)</u>

$$= (g_c^* \times F) + (g_c^* \times U_A) + (g_c^* \times W) + ([1 + g_c^*] \times M)$$

$$= (g_c^* \times 0) + (g_c^* \times 0.8377314) + (g_c^* \times 0.8397096) +$$
$$([1 + g_c^*] \times 0.0156174)$$

IV - $g_c^* = \dfrac{FPO + (FPO \times R) - M}{(F + U_a + W + M - FPO) - (FPO \times R)}$

$$= \frac{0.068251 + (0.068251 \times 0.6110602) - 0.0156174}{(0 + 0.8377314 + 0.8397096 + 0.0156174 - 0.068251) - (0.068251 \times 0.6110602)}$$

$$= \frac{0.09433907}{(1.62480740) - (0.04170547)}$$

$$= \frac{0.09433907}{1.58310193}$$

$$= 0.05959128 \text{ or } 5.96\% \text{ (rounded)}$$

APPENDIX 9.3
FINANCING CAPITAL EXPENDITURES
BY STOCK FINANCING

LCB Company

Income Statement
1987

(000 omitted)

Net Sales	$640,310
Cost of Sales	(533,909)
Gross Profit	$106,401
Selling, General, and Administrative Expenses	(15,741)
Depreciation Expense	(26,786)
Maintenance	(10,000)
Earnings Before Interest and Taxes (EBIT)	$53,874
Interest Expense	(9,424)
Earnings Before Taxes (EBT)	$44,450
Income Tax Expense	(19,800)
Net Income (EAT)	$24,650
Dividends	(8,204)
Addition to Retained Earnings	$16,466

LCB Company

Balance Sheet
1987

(000 omitted)

Assets

Current Assets	$ 21,368
Accounts Receivable	77,924
Inventory	118,184
Prepaid Expenses	10,711
Total Current Assets	$228,187

Fixed Assets	$358,984	
Less: Accumulated Depreciation	145,857	
Net Fixed Assets	$213,127	
Fixed Assets in Progress	20,000	233,127
Total Assets		$461,314

Liabilities

Current Liabilities	
Current Portion of Long Term Debt	$ 6,211
Accounts Payable	39,658
Accrued Expenses	50,141
Accrued Taxes	13,695
Total Current Liabilities	$109,705
Long Term Debt	117,863
Total Liabilities	$227,568

Shareholders Equity

Common Stock ($25 Par)	$ 10,509[1]
Paid-in Capital	39,910
Retained Earnings	183,327
Total Shareholders Equity	$233,746
Total Liabilities and Stockholder Equity	$461,314

---

[1] LCB sold 400,000 shares, par value $25, for $50 per share. Total shares outstanding 410,180. LCB paid $20 per share dividend over the fiscal year.

LCB Company

Statement of Changes in Financial Condition

(000 omitted)

Cash Provided By:
  Operations:
    Net Earnings (EAT) $24,650
    Add
    Depreciation $26,786
    Increase (Decrease) in
    Working Capital[1]   (10,746)   16,040
    Cash Provided by Operations (FPO) $40,690

  External Financing:
    Current Portion of Long Term Debt $(6,211)
    Issuance of Long Term Debt   18,467
    Issuance of Common Stock   20,000 $32,256

Cash Used For:
  Dividends $ 8,204
  Fixed Asset under Construction   20,000   ($28,204)
Increase (Decrease) In Cash $44,742

Increase (Decrease) in Working Capital
  Receivables (net) $(7,156)
  Change in Accounts Payable   3,642
  Change in Prepaids   (984)
  Change in Accruals   4,605
  Changes in Inventory   (10,853) $(10,746)

---

[1]Exclusive of Increase (Decrease) in Cash.

Sustainable Growth: Higgins & Johnson Models

LCB Company
End of 1987

Model Parameters

P = EAT/Net Sales = $24,650/$640,310 = 0.0384969

D = Dividend Payout Ratio = Dividends Paid/EAT =
$8,204/$24,650 = 0.3328194

L = Total Debt/Equity = $227,568/$233,746 = 0.9735696

T = Total Assets/Net Sales = $461,314/$640,310 = 0.7204541

W = Net Working Capital/Net Sales = $118,482/$640,310 = 0.1850384

L_L = Long Term Debt/Equity = $117,863/$233,746 = 0.5042353

F = Net Fixed Assets/Net Sales = $233,127/$640,310 = 0.3640845

J = Price change = Assume 0.

Higgins Model

$$g_c^* = \frac{P(1-D)(1+L)}{T - [P(1-D)(1+L)]} \qquad (3.1)$$

$$= \frac{.0384969\,(1 - .3328194)\,(1 + 0.9735696)}{0.7204541 - [0.0384969\,(1 - .3328194)\,(1 + 0.9735696)_c}$$

$$= \frac{0.0506897}{0.6697644}$$

$$= 0.0756828 \text{ or } 7.6\% \text{ (rounded)}$$

Higgins & Johnson Models (Continued)

Johnson Model

$$g_R^* = \frac{Y(1+J) - WJ}{F - [(1+J)Y] + [W(1+J)]} \qquad (3.3)$$

where,

$$Y = P(1-D)(1+L_L)$$

$$Y = 0.0384969(1 - .3328194)(1 + .5042353)$$

$$= 0.0386352$$

and

$$g_R^* = \frac{0.0386352(1+0) - (0.1850384 \times 0)}{0.3640845 - [(1+0)0.0384969] + [0.1850384 - (1+0)]}$$

$$= \frac{0.0386352}{0.510626}$$

$$= 0.0756624 \text{ or } 7.6\% \text{ (rounded)}$$

Govindarajan and Shank Model

LCB Company
Stock Financing
End of 1987

F = No change   0

W = Change in Working Capital/Change in Net Sales =
$33,996/$40,776 = 0.8337257
Note: Change in Working Capital per Statement of Changes in
Financial Condition = $(10,746) + $44,742 = $33,996.

M = No Change   0.0156174

P = No change   0.0841373

I = Interest Expense/Net Sales = $9,424/$640,310 = 0.0147178

D_p = No change   0.0418328

D = Dividend Payout Ratio = Dividends Paid/EAT = $8,204/$24,650 =
0.3328194

U_a = Investment in Non-Operational Assets/EAT =$20,000/$24,650 =
0.811359

T = No change   0.4454443

R = Debt Supplement to Internally Generated Funds =
Change in Long and Intermediate Debt/Cash Retained
by Company
where. Cash Retained by Company =
Cash Provided by Operations (FPO) $51,436
Plus: Change in Working Capital   (10,746)
Less: Dividends Paid   (8,204)
                                          $32,486

$R = \dfrac{$12,256}{$32,486} = 0.3772702$

Govindarajan and Shank Model (Continued)

Solution

I - Funds Provided by Operations (FPO)

$$= (P - I) \times (I - T) \times (I - D) + D_p$$

$$= (0.0841373 - 0.0147178) \times (1 - 0.4454443) \times (1 - 0.3328194) + 0.0418328$$

$$= 0.0675172$$

II - Funds Available for Investment (FAI)

$$FPO \times (I + g_C^*) \times (I + R)$$

$$= 0.0675172 \times (I + g_C^*) \times (I + 0.3772702)$$

III - Funds Required for Investment (FRI)

$$= (g_C^* \times F) + (g_C^* \times U_A) + (g_C^* \times W) + ([I + g_C^*] \times M)$$

$$= (g_C^* \times 0) + (g_C^* \times 0.811359) + (g_C^* \times 0.8337257) + [(I + g_C^*) \times 0.0156174)]$$

IV - $g_C^* = \dfrac{FPO + (FPO \times R) - M}{(F + Ua + W + M - FPO) - (FPO \times R)}$

$$= \frac{0.0675172 + (0.0675172 \times 0.3772702) - 0.0156174}{(0 + 0.811359 + 0.8337257 + 0.0156174 - 0.0675172) - (0.0675172 \times 0.33772702)}$$

$$= \frac{0.077372}{1.5931849 - 0.0228023}$$

$$= \frac{0.077372}{1.570382}$$

$$= 0.0492695 \text{ or } 4.93\% \text{ (rounded)}$$

10

MERGERS: TERMS OF COMBINATION AND SUSTAINABLE GROWTH

The variables incorporated in the sustainable growth models are pertinent to the design of the financial and capital structures of business combinations. The financial or capital structure reflects the type and kinds of consideration paid to the shareholders of the acquired company and in turn determines the accounting method (purchase or pooling) used to record the transaction.* For example, if the Burroughs Corporation (Chapter 3) were financed entirely with common stock, the sustainable rate of growth after taxes in 1981 would fall to 1.01 percent; if the financial structure were 50 percent debt and 50 percent common, the sustainable growth rate would approximate 1.68 percent. These compare with a sustainable growth rate of 1.88 percent based on a 1981 debt-equity ratio of 1.036.

Mergers and acquisitions, to judge from the evidence, have a spotty record of success, at least by the expectations of their promotors (Clark 1985). The phenomenon makes them an interesting subject for the calculation of sustainable growth (g^*), since promotors count success in terms of synergistic effects, and the quality of earnings is an important component of the risk-return trade-off of market valuation. Exhibit 10.1 presents pertinent data on two hypothethical firms negotiating a merger. Exhibit 10.2 shows the financial statements and sustainable growth rate if the combination were affected as a

---

*The accounting rules have changed since 1970. Combinations put together in the 1960s were subject to Accounting Research Bulletin (ARB 48). Under ARB 48, the liberal interpretation of the pooling provisions allowed almost any combination to be recorded as a pooling. Accounting Principles Board Opinion 16, 17, and 18, adopted in 1970 and 1971, set tighter criteria for distinguishing between purchase and pooling as well as the treatment of goodwill (Accounting Principles Board 1967; Accounting Research Bulletin 1957).

Exhibit 10.1
Balance Sheet of Alpha, Inc., and Delta, Inc., December 31, 1984

	Acquiring Firm (A)	Acquired Firm (B)
	Alpha, Inc.	Delta, Inc.
Assets		
Current Assets	$ 80,000	$ 28,000
Fixed Assets	450,000	200,000
Total Assets	$530,000	$228,000
Liabilities and Equity		
Current Liabilities	$ 10,000 (5%)	$ 5,000 (5%)
Fixed Liabilities	40,000(10%)	$ 5,000(10%)
Capital Stock ($10par)	300,000	100,000
Excess over par	50,000	
Retained Earnings	150,000	100,000
Treasury Stock	(20,000)	
Total	$530,000	$228,000

Income Statement of Alpha, Inc., and Delta, Inc.

Sales	$342,000	$130,242
Less		
Cost of Sales	100,000	50,000
Gross Profit	$242,000	$ 80,242
Less		
Selling and Administrative Expenses	50,000	20,000
EBIT	$192,000	$ 60,000
Less		
Interest	4,500	2,550
EBT	$187,500	$ 57,692
Less		
Taxes (52%)	97,500	27,692
EAT	$ 90,000	$ 30,000

Exhibit 10.1 (continued)

	Acquiring Firm (A)	Acquired Firm (B)
	Alpha, Inc.	Delta, Inc.
Profit Margin (P) = EAT/Sales	.263	.23
Earnings Per Share (EPS)	3.00	3.00
Dividend Payout Ratio (D)	.33	.33
Retention Ratio After Taxes (1-D)	.67	.67
Total Assets/Sales Ratio (T)	1.55	1.75
Financial Structure Objective (L=D/E)	.104	.14
Price Trend (J)	stable	stable
Current Assets/Current Sales (C)	.234	.215
Fixed Assets/Sales (F)	1.316	1.536

Sustainable Growth: Stable Prices

$$g^* = \frac{P(1-D)(1+L)}{T-[P(1-D)(1+L)]}$$

$$\text{Firm A} = \frac{.263(1-.33)(1+.104)}{1.55-[.263(1-.33)(1+.104)]} = \frac{.1945358}{1.3554641}$$

$$= .1435196 \text{ or } 14.4\% \text{ rounded}$$

$$\text{Firm B} = \frac{.23(1-.33)(1+.14)}{1.75-[.23(1-.33)(1+.14)]} = \frac{.175674}{1.574326}$$

$$= .1115867 \text{ or } 11.2\% \text{ rounded}$$

purchase, and Exhibit 10.3 illustrates the financial statements and sustainable growth rate if the combination were affected as a pooling.

The objective of Exhibits 10.1 through 10.3 is to demonstrate the impact on the sustainable growth of the merged companies as determined by the purchase price paid for the acquired company, the type of consideration (cash and/or securities), the size of the premium over market value, and the choice of accounting options (purchase or pooling) required by the structure of the deal.

To understand the relation between the consideration package for a business combination and the available accounting options, it is necessary to understand the issue of purchase or pooling.

A purchase is a business combination in which a significant proportion of the existing management (the common shareholders) of the acquired company is displaced (Accounting Principles Board 1967). Philosophically, the definition implies the occurrence of a real economic event (an investment)

Exhibit 10.2
Combination of Alpha-Delta, Affected by Purchase Method

Accounting to Record Combination on Alpha's Books:

A - Terms of Combination: On December 31, 1984, Alpha agrees to purchase a 90 percent interest in Delta for $432,000 in bonds (paying 8 percent annually) in exchange for 9000 shares of Delta common stock selling at $48 per share. Two-thirds of the excess of the market value paid over the value of the assets received will be allocated to depreciable assets and the remaining one-third is to be recorded as Goodwill. The latter will be immediately written off against retained earnings rather than amortized. The incremental value in fixed assets will be depreciated over 20 years. Alpha is in the 52 percent tax bracket (Federal and State).

B - Accounting Entry: (December 31, 1984)

Current Assets	$ 28,000	
Fixed Assets	368,000	
Goodwill	84,000	
Current Liabilities		$ 5,000
Fixed Liabilities		23,000
Minority Interest		20,000
Bonds Payable		432,000
Retained Earnings	$ 84,000	
Goodwill		$ 84,000

Exhibit 10.2 (continued)

C - <u>Financial Statements</u> (One Year Later)

Consolidated Balance Sheet

December 31, 1985

<u>Assets</u>		<u>Liabilities and Equity</u>	
Current	$108,000	Current Liabilities (5%)	$ 15,000
Fixed Assets	818,000	Fixed Liabilities (10%)	63,000
		Bonds Payable (8%)	432,000
		Capital Stock ($10 par)	300,000
		Excess Over Par	50,000
		Retained Earnings	66,000
		Treasury Stock	(20,000)
		Minority Interest	20,000
	$926,000		$926,000

Consolidated Income Statement

December 31, 1985

Sales	$472,242
<u>Less</u>	
Cost of Sales	150,000
Gross Profit	$322,242
<u>Less</u>	
Selling & Adminstrative Expenses	70,000
EBIT	$252,242
<u>Less</u>	
Interest	41,610
EBT	$210,632
<u>Less</u>	
Taxes (52%)	109,529
EAT	101,103

Exhibit 10.2 (continued)

Profit Margin (P) = EAT/Sales	.214
Earnings Per Share (EPS)	$3.37
Dividend Payout Ratio (D)	.33
Retention Ratio After taxes (1-D)	.67
Total Assets / Sales Ratio (T)	1.961
Financial Structure Objective (L=D/E)	1.226
Price Trend (J) :	Stable
Current Assets / Current Sales (C)	.229
Fixed Assets / Sales (F)	1.73

Sustainable Growth : Stable Prices

$$g^* = \frac{P(1-D)(1+L)}{T-[P(1-D)(1+L)]}$$

$$= \frac{.214(1-.33)(1+1.226)}{1.961-[.214(1-.33)(1+1.226)]} = \frac{.319638}{1.6408}$$

$$= .1945171 \text{ or } 19.45\% \text{ rounded}$$

and a discontinuity in voting participation, financial structure, and accountability. The characteristics of a purchase transaction follow from the definition.

1. The acquiring corporation views the transaction as an investment; if the value of the consideration (cash and/or securitires) exceeds the appraised value of the assets acquired, the excess may be recorded as goodwill. Accounting Principles Board (APB) Opinon No. 17 requires that the portion of the excess recorded as goodwill be amortized against earnings over some reasonable period, not to exceed forty years. The charge against earnings, on the other hand, while lowering account net income, does not qualify as a tax deduction (Accounting Principles Board 1967). Other things equal, taxable income exceeds accounting income.

2. The surviving firm records the acquired assets at their cost (i.e., current value), not at the book value, to the selling corporation. A new basis of accountability is established, possibly resulting in higher depreciation charges against income with sequential effects on the bottom line.

3. Consideration may take the form of debt securities, stock, and/or cash. Securities issued by the acquiring corporation are deemed to have been issued at current market values. Debt securities and cash are frequently used to reduce the participation of the acquired firm's shareholders in the management of the surviving corporation. If the surviving corporation had acquired its own voting stock (treasury stock) in contemplation of the combination, the transaction must be recorded as a purchase.

Exhibit 10.3
Combination of Alpha-Delta, Affected by Pooling Method

Accounting to Record Combination on Alpha's Books:

A - Terms of Combination: On December 31, 1984, Alpha agrees to issue 10,800 shares of common stock (market value: $40 per share) in exchange for 9,000 shares of Delta, Inc. representing a 90 percent interest. The 2,000 shares of Treasury Stock were acquired for an employee pension fund. Hence all shares offered to Delta are new shares. Alpha is in the 52 percent tax bracket (Federal and State).

B - Accounting Entry: (December 31, 1984)

Current Assets	$ 28,000	
Fixed Assets	200,000	
Goodwill	18,000	
Current Liabilities		$ 5,000
Fixed Liabilities		23,000
Capital Stock - Alpha		108,000
Retained Earnings - Delta		90,000
Minority Interest		20,000

C - Financial Statements (One Year Later)

Consolidated Balance Sheet

December 31,1985

Assets		Liabilities and Equity	
Current	$108,000	Current Liabilities (5%)	$ 15,000
Fixed Assets	650,000	Fixed Liabilities (10%)	63,000
		Capital Stock ($10 par)	408,000
		Excess Over Par	32,000
		Retained Earnings	240,000
		Treasury Stock	(20,000)
		Minority Interest	20,000
	$758,000		$758,000

Exhibit 10.3 (continued)

Consolidated Income Statement

December 31,1985

Sales	$472,242
Less	
Cost of Sales	150,000
Gross Profit	$322,242
Less	
Selling & Adminstrative Expenses	70,000
EBIT	$252,242
Less	
Interest	7,050
EBT	$245,192
Less	
Taxes (52%)	127,500
EAT	117,692

Profit Margin (P) = EAT/Sales	.250
Earnings Per Share (EPS)	$2.88
Dividend Payout Ratio (D)	.33
Retention Ratio After Taxes (1-D)	.67
Total Assets / Sales Ratio (T)	1.610
Financial Structure Objective (L=D/E)	.115
Price Trend (J) :	Stable
Current Assets / Current Sales (C)	.229
Fixed Assets / Sales (F)	1.38

Sustainable Growth : Stable Prices

$$g^* = \frac{P(1-D)(1+L)}{T-[P(1-D)(1+L)]}$$

$$= \frac{.25(1-.33)(1+.115)}{1.61-[.25(1-.33)(1+.115)]} \quad \frac{=.1867625}{1.4232375}$$

$$= .1311973 \text{ or } 13.12\% \text{ rounded}$$

4. Liabilities of the seller corporation become the obligations of the surviving firm. However, the retained earnings of the seller are not added to those of the surviving firm. Purchase accounting in effect capitalizes the retained earnings of the seller. The basic notion is that one company cannot increase its retained earnings by buying another company.

The strictures of the purchase option may not appeal to promoters who are seeking to quickly demonstrate the wisdom of the combination. The following are some drawbacks.

1. Given the presence of goodwill and/or a higher basis of accountability on depreciable assets, net income will be lower than if the transaction were completed as a pooling.

2. There are negotiation problems. If the consideration includes cash, the seller may incur substantial taxable gains and demand a higher price to offset the tax bite. Or, the acquiring firm may want the purchase price allocated to assets, which can be amortized to reduce taxable income, while the seller may seek to allocate purchase price against assets that reduce his taxable gains. The sets may not match.

3. The investor corporation requires earnings projections on the seller under a variety of purchase terms. This implies an understanding of the accounting methods adopted by the seller in calculating net income and an estimate of the current value of the seller's assets.

An important limitation of the purchase option should be mentioned at this point. Under purchase, the acquiring corporation includes all assets and liabilities of the seller in its consolidated statement, no matter when during the fiscal period the transaction was consummated. However, on the consolidated income statement, it picks up only the income of the seller applicable to the period between the transaction date and the end of the fiscal period.

The choice between purchase and pooling depends on the state of the economy, earning capacity of the combining firms, their financial structures, and the objectives of the ownership interests. In general, focusing only on the accounting numbers, purchase is the choice if the book value of the acquired assets exceeds their fair market value and the effective yield on the financing used is less than the return on assets for the acquired company. These conditions frequently prevail in prolonged periods of decline in the financial markets and business activity. Conversely, in a period of expansion, market values tend to exceed book values, and pooling may seem to be the attractive option.

Apropos of pooling, APB Opinion No. 16 describes pooling as a business combination in which the holders of substantially all of the ownership interest in the constituent corporations become the owners of a single corporation that owns the assets and businesses of the constituent corporations (Accounting Principles Board 1967). Continuity of voting participation and operations is the core of a pooling arrangement. From this flows the specific features of the accounting treatment.

1. The acquisition is not viewed as an investment; rather, the two predecessor corporations combine into a single entity.

2. The original accounts—assets and liabilities—are carried over to the combined entity at book values. The transaction does not create a new basis of accountability or generate goodwill.

3. A pooling must be accomplished by an exchange of voting stock between previously independent companies. Bond and preferred stocks that alter the structure of ownership may not form part of the consideration. For the same reason, cash is ruled out, along with treasury stock acquired in comtemplation of the merger.

4. Because assets and liabilities carry over at book values, the retained earnings of the seller corporation carry over to the combination.

The par or stated capital of the pooled companies may be greater or less than the total capita of the individual units. If the former is true, the excess is deducted first from the total of any other contributed capital and then from the consolidated retained earnings. If the latter is true, the difference is reported on the consolidated balance sheet as excess over par.

Distinct advantages can accrue to management through executing a pooling of interests.

1. The transaction may qualify as a tax-free exchange if it also meets Internal Revenue criteria.

2. The transaction does not drain liquid assets or increase the debt-equity ratio of the combination.

3. All things equal, pooling results in a higher net income because of the absence of goodwill and no change in the basis of accountability.

4. Regardless of market values, the post-combination entity bears responsibility only for the dollar amounts that existed before the combination. Hence, if synergism results, pooling can create "instant growth" in earnings. As a general rule, pooling is desirable if the assets of the acquired company at book are undervalued in relation to actual or potential earning power.

5. Retention of retained earnings may permit the combination to write off any deficit on the books of the acquiring firm.

6. In contrast to the purchase transaction, the combination may pick up not only the assets and liabilities of the constituents, but also their full income irrespective of the transaction date—even after the close of the fiscal year or before the auditors arrive.

The advantages to pooling are easily demonstrated in a situation in which all variables are basically similar except for the choice of accounting method. The real world, on the other hand, shows few instances that afford such simple laboratory comparisons. Instead, the relative advantage to pooling will depend on the specific terms of the combination: the asset value, type and amounts of consideration, presence of goodwill, and so on. Earnings per share could be higher under purchase accounting, depending on the consideration mix and asset values. This complicates the researchers' problem of assessing whether security markets ignore accounting numbers in pricing the common shares of a business combination. The accounting effects may be clouded by the presence of other variables. More on this topic later.

Exhibits 10.1 and 10.2 demonstrate that the sustainable growth (g^*) after combination can be significantly affected by the terms of combination and the option chosen to record the merger. From the exhibits, these effects are summarized:

Sustainable Growth

Pre-Combination
Alpha, Inc.	14.4%
Delta, Inc.	11.2%

Post-Combination
Purchase accounting	19.45%
Pooling accounting	13.12%

The reader, however, should not quickly generalize that purchase accounting tends to result in higher sustainable growth rates, all things being equal. The primary affect of the decision whether to purchase or pool will be on the debt-equity ratio. The consideration in pooling is, for the most part, restricted to an exchange of stock; purchase accounting, on the other hand, allows for the use of cash, debt, and preferred stock as well as common stock in the consideration package. But combinations are complex transactions and have to be examined in the light of the special circumstances of prior decisions. They are primarily important in terms of the information they convey to investors. It is a consequence, not a cause.

ESTABLISHING FINANCIAL POLICY IN RELATION TO A TARGET GROWTH RATE

As we noted in Chapter 3, the growth equations can be used to solve for any unknown value. For example, suppose that Alpha, Inc., planning to merge with a compatible firm, established a target growth rate of 11.2 percent for the combination. What debt to equity ratio is compatible with the stated objective, if Alpha projects a profit margin (P) of .25, a payout percentage (D) of .33, and a total assets to sales ratio (T) of 2.83?

Solution: Using the original Higgins model expressed in Equation 3.1 (Chapter 3), we have

$$g^* = \frac{P(1 - D)(1 + L)}{T - [P(1 - D)(1 + L)]} \tag{3.1}$$

$$11.2 = \frac{.25(1 - .33)(1 + L)}{2.83 - [.25(1 - .33)(1 + L)]}$$

$$11.2 = \frac{.1675(1 + L)}{2.83 - .1675(1 + L)}.$$

Let $(1 + L) = X$. Then

$$.112 = \frac{.1675(X)}{2.83 - .1675(X)} \, ,$$

and let $Y = .1675(X)$.

Hence

$$.112(2.83 - Y) = Y$$

$$.112 \times 2.83 = Y + .112Y$$

$$.112 \times 2.83 = 1.112Y$$

$$Y = \frac{.112 \times 2.83}{1.112}$$

$$= .285$$

Then,

$$X = \frac{Y}{.1675}$$

$$X = \frac{.285}{.1675}$$

$$X = 1.7,$$

since $X = (1 + L)$, $L = X - 1$ or $1.7 - 1 = .70$. The debt to equity ratio consistent with the targeted growth rate is .70.

In like manner, Alpha may test for other parameters critical to the calculation of sustainable growth in business combinations, such as dividend payout, total assets-sales ratio, and profit margins. The testing procedure can also encompass projected price trends by using the Johnson model (Equation 3.3, Chapter 3). For example, assume the following projections for a proposed combination:

$$P = .25$$

$$D = .33$$

$$J = .10$$

$$W = .67$$

$$F = 2.67$$

What is the capital structure (L_L) consistent with a growth rate of 7.3 percent, where W represents the net working capital-sales ratio, F equals fixed assets/sales, and J, an anticipated rise in the price level? Recall that

$$g_R{}^* = \frac{Y(1 + J) - WJ}{F - (1 + J)Y + W(1 + J)} , \tag{3.3}$$

where $Y = P(1 - D)(1 + L_L)$.

Inserting the disaggregated value of Y into the primary equation, $g_R{}^*$ becomes

$$g_R{}^* = \frac{[P(1 - D)(1 + L_L)](1 + J) - WJ}{F - [(1 + J)P(1 - D)(1 + L_L)] + W(1 + J)} .$$

Then

$$.073 = \frac{[.25(1 - .33)(1 + L_L)](1 + .10) - (.67)(.10)}{2.67 - [(1 + .10).25(1 - .33)(1 + L_L)] + .67(1 + .10)}$$

$$.073 = \frac{[.1675(1 + L_L)](1.10) - .067}{2.67 - [(1 + .10).1675(1 + L_L)] + .737}$$

Let $X = (1 + L_L)$.

Then

$$.073 = \frac{[.1675(X)](1.10) - .067}{2.67 - [(1.10).1675(X)] + .737}$$

If $Z = .1675(X)$,

then

$$.073 = \frac{Z(1.10) - .067}{2.67 - Z(1.10) + .737}$$

$$.073(2.67 - 1.1Z + .737 = 1.1Z - .067$$

$$.19491 - .0803Z + .053801 = 1.1Z - .067$$

$$.19491 + .053801 + .067 = 1.1Z + .0803Z$$

$$.315711 = 1.1803Z$$

$$.2674836 = Z$$

Accordingly, since

$Z = .2674836$ or $.1675(X)$, then

$X = 1.596917$ or 1.6 (rounded),

and if $X = (1 + L_L)$, then $1.6 = (1 + .60)$ and $L_L = .60$. A long-term debt-equity ratio of .60 is compatible with a growth rate of 7.3 percent.

EMPIRICAL DATA

Appendix 10.1 contains a sample, designated as the Clark, Clark, Olson (CCO) sample, of thirty-five business combinations selected from the 1965–1970 merger wave and the current, continuing merger wave from 1977. Twenty-one cases fell into the first period and fourteen cases into the second period. For each combination in the sample, sustainable growth was calculated six to eight months before the combination; at the time of the combination, sustainable growth was calculated on the basis of the pro forma consolidated financial statements. The cases selected were those with only one major combination in the year under study although a minor combination (less than 10 percent of the acquiring firm's size) was tolerated.

Of the thirty-five combinations in the sample, sixteen showed a higher sustainable growth rate (calculated by the Higgins model) compared with the pre-acquisition rates of the independent entities. In nineteen combinations the sustainable growth rate dropped below pre-acquisition levels. Of the nineteen combinations with lower sustainable growth rates, the calculated sustainable growth rate in fifteen cases located in the range set by the minimum and maximum rates of the companies in their pre-acquisition status.

There were twenty poolings; eight were associated with higher post-acquisition sustainable growth rates and twelve with lower post-acquisition growth rates. Fifteen purchase transactions were recorded; nine were with higher sustainable growth rates and six with lower sustainable growth rates. The literature tends to assert that when market values exceed book values, pooling is the preferred option, and when book values exceed market values, the purchase option is the preferred strategy (Anderson and Lounderback 1973; Copeland and Wojdak 1969). Exhibits 10.4 and 10.5 present the overall results of the CCO survey and the tests for statistical significance.

A second sample, designated as the Anderson, Jaksina, Kutch, Maurizio (AJKM) sample, and displayed in Appendix 10.2, reviewed thirty-five combinations in the period from 1980 to 1985. The study concentrated on cash tender acquisitions, and the combinations, on the average, comprised smaller companies. However, the investigation developed a more extensive analysis of intercompany relations.

Exhibit 10.4
CCO Sample Summary

Sample Size: 35

	Average Sustainable Growth	Standard Deviation
Acquiring Firms	9.60%	4.55%
Target Firms	7.89%	6.98%
Post-Combination Firms	10.28%	8.06%

Comparison	t-statistic	
Acquiring - Target	1.072	not significant
Acquiring - Post-Combination	.5845	not significant

In the second sample twenty-four of the cash tender acquisitions generated higher sustainable growth rates, while eleven had lower sustainable growth rates; that is 69 percent of the combinations generated higher growth rates and 31 percent, lower growth rates. By contrast, the CCO sample showed that 49 percent of the acquiring firms had higher sustainable growth after the combination, while 51 percent had lower sustainable growth rates. Thus, when the two samples are compared, no trend is evident.

However, when the firms in the CCO survey are classified as purchase or pooling combinations (Exhibit 10.5), a pattern emerges. Sixty percent of the companies in the CCO study recorded as purchases had higher sustainable growth rates, and 40 percent, lower rates. In the case of pooling, the CCO study shows that only 40 percent of the acquiring companies had higher sustainable growth rates after combination, as compared with 60 percent that were lower. These results were consistent with the findings of the AJKM survey (Exhibit 10.6). The apparent advantage to the purchase approach may possibly be attributed to the leverage effects discussed in Chapter 6. For example, cash tender acquisitions that draw down liquidity of the acquiring company may coincide with the issuance of debt to restore the liquidity position.

The AJKM survey adduced other points of interest to the evaluation of sustainable growth in business combinations.

1. The *average* sustainable growth rate of the acquiring companies as a group increased after the combination from an average value of 12.31 percent before combination to 14.29 percent after combination.

2. The *average* premium paid by the acquiring companies was 35.48 percent, yet most acquiring firms achieved a positive percentage in sustainable growth post-combination (Exhibit 10.7). There was some indication of an

Exhibit 10.5
CCO Sample: Comparison of Purchase/Pooling Combinations

	Average Sustainable Growth	Standard Deviation
Purchase:		
Acquiring Firms	8.12%	4.74%
Target Firms	9.27%	6.91%
Post-Combination Firms	9.98%	9.06%
Pooling:		
Acquiring Firms	10.71%	6.48%
Target Firms	7.11%	7.06%
Post-Combination Firms	10.86%	7.57%

Comparison	t-statistic	
Purchase:		
Acquiring - Target	.5834	not significant
Acquiring - Post-Combination	.9240	not significant
Pooling:		
Acquiring - Target	1.621	not significant
Acquiring - Post-Combination	.1373	not significant
Purchase-Pooling:		
Acquiring - Target	1.304	not significant
Acquiring - Post-Combination	.9053	not significant
Post-Combination	.3164	not significant
Acquiring - Target	.5834	not significant
Acquiring - Post-Combination	.9240	not significant

adverse relation between the premium paid and post-combination sustainable growth; that is, the higher the premium paid, the lower the sustainable growth rate for the acquiring company. However, the data are not conclusive.

SUMMARY

Applied to mergers and acquisitions, the sustainable growth rate constitutes a valuable tool in the construction of a business combination.

Exhibit 10.6
Number of Companies with Higher Sustainable Growth after Merger

	Total	Percent
Sample #2 - All Cash Tender (Purchases)		
Sample Size = 35		
Higher Growth	24	69%
Lower Growth	11	31
	35	100%
Sample Size = 32		
Higher Growth	22	69%
Lower Growth	10	31
	32	100%
Sample #1 - Purchases and Poolings		
Sample Size = 35		
Higher Growth	17	49%
Lower Growth	18	51
	35	100%
Sample Size = 15		
Higher Growth	9	60%
Lower Growth	6	40
	15	100%
Sample Size = 20		
Higher Growth	8	40%
Lower Growth	12	60
	20	100%

1. It can assist in the evaluation of a target company. If the target company has a low sustainable growth rate, the acquiring firm may have to insert new resources to raise the rate or reallocate excess rescources if a higher growth rate in sales is not otherwise attainable. In the latter case the sustainable growth rate of the combination may decline (Fruhan 1984).

2. The nature and the amount of the consideration to consummate the transaction affects the component variables of sustainable growth. Payment of excessive premiums for the target company (as in the Dupont-Conoco and Texas-Getty cases) can reduce sustainable growth and trigger a

Exhibit 10.7
Summary Sample No. 1 (CCO) and Sample No. 2 (AJKM)

	Average			Standard Deviation		
Sustainable Growth	#1	#2	#2	#1	#2	#2
(# of points)	(35)	(32)	(35)	(35)	(32)	(35)
Acquiring Firms	9.60	12.31	11.40	4.55	21.62	20.88
Target Firms	7.89	6.87	7.08	6.98	27.12	25.95
Post-Combination Firms	10.28	14.29	13.38	8.06	12.93	12.77

	Average		Standard Deviation	
(# of points)	(32)	(35)	(32)	(35)
Average Premium in Percent Paid	35.84	40.68	31.71	40.73
Average % Change in Growth	73.80	205	169.2	1141

Comparison of Premium in % Paid vs. % Change in Growth from

Sample #2

	(32)	(35)
(# of points)		
R^2	.20%	.10%
t	.24%	.14%

Comparison - Purchases	t-statistics		R^2	
Sample Size	(32)	(35)	(32)	(35)
Acquiring - Target	.76	.73	1.7%	1.6%
Acquiring - Post-Combination	1.06	1.27	3.6%	4.7%

sell-off of assets to reorganize the financial and/or capital structure. On the other hand, the consideration package may leverage up sustainable growth.

3. Awareness of the sustainable growth concept in the planning stage should affect the type and kind of consideration paid as well as the choice of available tax options.

4. Estimation of a feasible sustainable growth rate may deter combinations with marginal probabilities for success. In addition, if the planners posit a desired growth rate, they can reverse the formulae to design an appropriate financial and/or capital structure (Clark et al. 1985).

REFERENCES

Accounting Principles Board (APB). *Omnibus Opinion*, 1966. American Institute of Certified Public Accountants (AICPA), 1967.

———. Opinion No. 16, *Business Combinations*, 1970. AICPA, 1970.

———. Opinion No. 17, *Intangible Assets*, 1970. AICPA, 1970.

———. Opinion No. 18, *The Equity Method of Accounting for Investments in Common Stock*, 1971. AICPA, 1971.

———. Opinion No. 23, *Accounting for Income Taxes—Special Areas*, 1972. AICPA, 1972.

———. Opinion No. 24, *Accounting for Income Taxes—Investments in Common Stock Accounted for by the Equity Method*, 1972. AICPA, 1972.

———. Opinion No. 28, *Interim Financial Reporting*, 1973. AICPA, 1973.

———. Opinion No. 29, *Accounting for Non-Monetary Transactions*, 1973. AICPA, 1973.

———. Opinion No. 30, *Reporting the Results of Operations*, 1973. AICPA 1973.

AICPA. Accounting Research Bulletin, No. 48. *Business Combinations*, January 1957.

Anderson, John C., and Joseph G. Lounderback III. "Income Manipulation and Purchase-Pooling: Some Additional Results," *Journal of Accounting Research*, Autumn 1973, pp. 338–343.

Clark, John J. *Business Merger and Acquisitions Strategies*. Englewood Cliffs, N.J.: Prentice-Hall, 1985.

Clark, John J., Margaret T. Clark, and Andrew Verzilli. "Strategic Planning and Sustainable Growth," *The Columbia Journal of World Business*, Fall 1985, pp. 47–51.

Copeland, Ronald M., and Joseph W. Wojdak. "Income Manipulation and the Purchase-Pooling Choice," *Journal of Accounting Research*, Autumn 1969, pp. 188–195.

Financial Accounting Standards Board. *Accounting for Business Combinations and Purchased Intangibles*, August 19, 1976.

Fruhan, William E. "How Fast Should a Company Grow?" *Harvard Business Review*, January/February 1984, pp. 84–93.

Govindarajan, V., and John K. Shank. "Cash Sufficiency: The Missing Link in Strategic Planning," *Corporate Accounting*, Winter 1984, pp. 23–31.

Higgins, Robert. "Sustainable Growth: New Tool in Bank Lending," *The Journal of Commercial Lending*, June 1977, pp. 48–58.

Higgins, Robert. "How much Growth Can a Firm Afford," *Financial Management*, Fall 1977, pp. 7–15.

Higgins, Robert. "Sustainable Growth Under Inflation," *Financial Management*, Fall 1981, pp. 36–40.

Johnson, Dana J. "The Behavior of Financial Structure and Sustainable Growth in an Inflationary Environment," *Financial Management*, Fall 1981, pp. 30–35.

Mueller, Dennis C. "The Effects of Conglomerate Mergers: A Survey of the Empirical Evidence," *Journal of Banking and Finance*, Vol. 1, 1977, p. 339.

APPENDIX 10.1
SUSTAINABLE GROWTH: SELECTED BUSINESS COMBINATIONS, 1965–1970 AND 1977–1986 (HIGGINS MODEL)

John J. Clark, Margaret T. Clark, and Gerard T. Olson

Company A: American Hospital Supply, Inc.   Company B: Haemonetics Corp.

Date of Combination: 1983   Method of Accounting: Pooling

Pre-Acquisition Sustainable Growth:

	Rate
Company A: American Hospital Supply, Inc.	14.96%
Company B: Haemonetics Corp.	13.50%
Post-Combination Sustainable Growth:	12.89%

Company A: Anaconda   Company B: ARCO

Date of Combination: 1977   Method of Accounting: Purchase

Pre-Acquisition Sustainable Growth:

	Rate
Company A: Anaconda	7.29%
Company B: ARCO	10.41%
Post-Combination Sustainable Growth:	6.58%

Company A: Armour & Co.   Company B: Baldwin-Lima-Hamilton

Date of Combination: 1965   Method of Accounting: Pooling

Pre-Acquisition Sustainable Growth:

	Rate
Company A: Armour & Co.	6.95%
Company B: Baldwin-Lima-Hamilton	14.95%
Post-Combination Sustainable Growth:	1.98%

Company A: Avon Products, Inc.   Company B: Tiffany & Co.

Date of Combination: 1979   Method of Accounting: Pooling

Pre-Acquisition Sustainable Growth:

	Rate
Company A: Avon Products, Inc.	12.12%
Company B: Tiffany & Co.	8.94%
Post-Combination Sustainable Growth:	11.04%

Company A: Bausch & Lomb, Inc.   Company B: Charles River Breed-
                                                          ing Laboratories, Inc.

Date of Combination: 1983   Method of Accounting:Pooling

Pre-Acquisition Sustainable Growth:

	Rate
Company A: Bausch & Lomb, Inc.	4.56%
Company B: Charles River Breeding Laboratories, Inc.	9.47%
Post-Combination Sustainable Growth:	9.41%

Company A: Beatrice Foods Co.   Company B: E.R. Moore Co.

Date of Combination: 1969   Method of Accounting: Pooling

Pre-Acquisition Sustainable Growth:

	Rate
Company A: Beatrice Foods	9.76%
Company B: E. R. Moore	7.76%
Post-Acquisition Sustainable Growth:	9.06%

Company A: Brown Co.   Company B: KVP Sutherland
                                                    Paper Co.

Date of Combination: 1966   Method of Accounting: Pooling

Pre-Acquisition Sustainable Growth:
                                                            Rate

    Company A: Brown Co.   1.57%

    Company B: KVP Sutherland Paper Co.   2.73%

Post-Combination Sustainable: 2.66%

Company A: Caterpillar Tractor   Company B: Townmotor Corp.

Date of Combination: 1965   Method of Accounting: Pooling

Pre-Acquisition Sustainable Growth:
                                                            Rate

    Company A: Caterpillar Tractor Co.   18.87%

    Company B: Townmotor Corp.   14.40%

Post-Combination Sustainable Growth: 18.67%

Company A: Certain-Teed Corp.   Company B: Gustin-Bacon
                                                    Manufacturing Co.

Date of Combination: 1966   Method of Accounting: Pooling

Pre-Acquisition Sustainable Growth:
                                                            Rate

    Company A: Certain-Teed Corp.   4.76%

    Company B: Gustin-Bacon Manufacturing Co.   4.31%

Post-Combination Sustainable Growth: 1.73%

Company A: Cross Co.   Company B: Kearney & Trecker

Date of Combination: 1979   Method of Accounting: Pooling

Pre-Acquisition Sustainable Growth:
                                                            Rate

    Company A: Cross Co.   16.35%

    Company B: Kearney & Trecker   12.93%

Post-Combination Sustainable Growth: 14.67%

Company A: Diebold, Inc.   Company B: Lamson Corp.

Date of Combination: 1965   Method of Accounting: Purchase

Pre-Acquisition Sustainable Growth:

	Rate
Company A: Diebold, Inc.	9.85%
Company B: Lamson Corp.	5.21%
Post-Combination Sustainable Growth:	11.19%

Company A: Dun & Bradstreet Corp.   Company B: A. C. Nielsen Co.

Date of Combination: 1984   Method of Accounting: Pooling

Pre-Acquisition Sustainable Growth:

	Rate
Company A: Dun & Bradstreet Corp.	15.89%
Company B: A. C. Nielsen Co.	16.07%
Post-Acquisition Sustainable Growth	10.54%

Company A: DuPont   Company B: Conoco

Date of Acquisition 1982   Method of Accounting: Purchase

Pre-Acquisition Sustainable Growth:

	Rate
Company A: DuPont	5.12%
Company B: Conoco	16.40%
Post-Combination Sustainable Growth:	2.76%

Company A: Federal -Mogul Corp.   Company B: Sterling Aluminum
                                               Products, Inc.

Date of Combination: 1965   Method of Accounting: Pooling

Pre-Acquisition Sustainable Growth:

	Rate
Company A: Federal-Mogul Corp.	8.94%
Company B: Sterling Aluminum Products, Inc.	0.64%
Post-Combination Sustainable Growth:	5.51%

Company A: H. J. Heinz Co.   Company B: Ore-Ida Foods, Inc.

Date of Combination: 1965   Method of Accounting: Pooling

Pre-Acquisition Sustainable Growth:

                                                           Rate

    Company A: H. J. Heinz Co.   5.34%

    Company B: Ore-Ida Foods, Inc.   7.72%

Post-Combination Sustainable Growth: 6.25%

Company A: Hershey Chocolate Corp.   Company B: Cory Corp.

Date of Combination: 1967   Method of Accounting: Purchase

Pre-Acquisition Sustainable Growth:

                                                           Rate

    Company A: Hershey Chocolate Corp.   9.85%

    Company B: Cory Corp.   7.55%

Post-Combination Sustainable Growth: 16.80%

Company A: Holiday Inns   Company B: Harrah's Corporation

Date of Combination: 1980   Method of Accounting: Purchase

Pre-Acquisition Sustainable Growth:

                                                           Rate

    Company A: Holiday Inns   5.90%

    Company B: Harrah's Corporation   8.00%

Post-Combination Sustainable Growth: 8.40%

Company A: Kellogg Co.   Company B: Fearn International,
                                             Inc.

Date of Combination: 1970   Method of Accounting: Pooling

Pre-Acquisition Sustainable Growth:
                                                           Rate

    Company A: Kellogg Co.   7.67%

    Company B: Fearn International, Inc.   2.03%

Post-Combination Sustainable Growth: 8.16%

Company A: Monsanto Co.   Company B: Fisher Governor Co.

Date of Combination: 1969   Method of Accounting: Purchase

Pre-Acquisition Sustainable Growth:

		Rate
Company A: Monsanto Co.		5.10%
Company B: Fisher Governor Co.		6.80%
Post-Combination Sustainable Growth:		4.96%

Company A: Mosinee Paper Corp.   Company B: Sorg Paper Corp.

Date of Combination: 1983   Method of Accounting: Purchase

Pre-Acquisition Sustainable Growth:

		Rate
Company A: Mosinee Paper Corp.		5.46%
Company B: Sorg Paper Corp.		0.83%
Post-Combination Sustainable Growth:		7.47%

Company A: Philips Van Heuesen Corp.   Company B: Joseph Feiss,
                                                 Inc.

Date of Combination: 1966   Method of Accounting: Pooling

Pre-Acquisition Sustainable Growth:

		Rate
Company A: Philips Van Heuesen Corp.		13.48%
Company B: Joseph Feiss, Inc.		8.26%
Post-Combination Sustainable Growth:		9.03%

Company A: Levi Strauss & Co.   Company B: Koracorp Indus-
                                                 tries, Inc.

Date of Combination: 1979   Method of Accounting: Purchase

Pre-Acquisition Sustainable Growth:

		Rate
Company A: Levi Strauss & Co.		18.02%
Company B: Koracorp Industries, Inc.		28.17%
Post-Combination Sustainable Growth:		32.93%

Company A: Litton Industries, Inc.   Company B: Itek Corp.

Date of Combination: 1983   Method of Accounting: Purchase

Pre-Acquisition Sustainable Growth:

	Rate
Company A: Litton Industries, Inc.	17.2%
Company B: Itek Corp.	3.4%
Post-Combination Sustainable Growth:	13.2%

Company A: Midland-Ross Corp.   Company B: National Castings Co.

Date of Combination: 1965   Method of Accounting: Pooling

Pre-Acquisition Sustainable Growth:

	Rate
Company A: Midland-Ross Corp.	5.30%
Company B: National Castings Co.	3.29%
Post-Combination Sustainable Growth:	7.65%

Company A: Pitney Bowes Inc.   Company B: Dictaphone Corp.

Date of Combination: 1979   Method of Accounting: Purchase

Pre-Acquisition Sustainable Growth:

	Rate
Company A: Pitney Bowes Inc.	7.54%
Company B: Dictaphone Corp.	3.40%
Post-Combination Sustainable Growth:	7.71%

Company A: Quaker Oats Co.   Company B: Stokley-Van Camp, Inc.

Date of Combination: 1983   Method of Accounting: Purchase

Pre-Acquisition Sustainable Growth:

	Rate
Company A: Quaker Oats Co.	8.68%
Company B: Stokley-Van Camp, Inc.	8.06%
Post-Combination Sustainable Growth:	14.22%

Company A: Revlon, Inc.   Company B: U. S. Vitamin &
                                                      Pharmaceutical Corp.

Date of Combination: 1966   Method of Accounting: Pooling

Pre-Acquisition Sustainable Growth:

                                                           Rate

        Company A: Revlon, Inc.   10.97%

        Company B: U. S. Vitamin   3.34%

Post-Combination Sustainable Growth: 8.25%

Company A: Smithkline Corporation   Company B: Beckman Instruments,
                                                         Inc.

Date of Combination: 1981   Method of Accounting: Pooling

Pre-Acquisition Sustainable Growth:

                                                           Rate

        Company A: Smithkline Corporation   22.90%

        Company B: Beckman Instruments, Inc.   10.60%

Post-Combination Sustainable Growth: 16.80%

Company A: Susquehanna Corp.   Company B: Atlantic Research

Date of Combination: 1967   Method of Accounting: Purchase

Pre-Acquisition Sustainable Growth:

                                                           Rate

        Company A: Susquehanna Corp.   1.50%

        Company B: Atlantic Research   13.15%

Post-Combination Sustainable Growth: 19.36%

Company A: U.S. Steel Corp.   Company B: Alside, Inc.

Date of Combination: 1968   Method of Accounting: Purchase

Pre-Acquisition Sustainable Growth:

                                                           Rate

        Company A: U.S. Steel Corp.   1.26%

        Company B: Alside, Inc.   12.14%

Post-Combination Sustainable Growth: 3.81%

```
Company A: U.S. Steel Corp.              Company B: Marathon Oil

Date of Combination: 1982        Method of Accounting: Purchase

Pre-Acquisition Sustainable Growth:
                                                    Rate

     Company A: U.S. Steel Corp.                    7.36%

     Company B: Marathon Oil                       15.00%

Post-Combination Sustainable Growth:               (7.81%)
```

```
Company A: Union Oil of California    Company B: The Pure Oil Co.

Date of Combination:  1965        Method of Accounting: Pooling

Pre-Acquisition Sustainable Growth:
                                                    Rate

     Company A: Union Oil of California             7.28%

     Company B: The Pure Oil Co.                    5.46%

Post-Combination Sustainable Growth                 9.25%
```

```
Company A: Ward Foods              Company B: Honolulu Iron Works

Date of Combination: 1966        Method Of Accounting: Pooling

Pre-Acquisition Sustainable Growth:
                                                    Rate

     Company A: Ward Foods                          2.66%

     Company B: Honolulu Iron Works                11.32%

Post-Combination Sustainable Growth:               18.66%
```

```
Company A: White Consolidated Industries, Inc.

Company B: Scott & Williams, Inc.

Date of Combination: 1966        Method of Accounting: Pooling

Pre-Acquisition Sustainable Growth:
                                                    Rate

     Company A: White Consolidated Industries, Inc.   24.10%

     Company B: Scott & Williams, Inc.               (15.50%)

Post-Combination Sustainable Growth:               35.29%
```

APPENDIX 10.2
SUSTAINABLE GROWTH: CASH TENDER
COMBINATIONS (HIGGINS MODEL)

Sallie Anderson, Jan Jaksina, Don Kutch, and Amelia Maurizio

EXECUTIVE SUMMARY OF STATISTICS REGARDING MERGER

Using Higgins' Model With Corporate Tax & Stable Prices
(INSERT INFORMATION IN 'AS' COLUMN)

ACQUIRING COMPANY	DOVER CORPORATION	:
ACQUIRED COMPANY	MEASUREMENT SYSTEMS, INC.	:
ANNOUNCEMENT DATE	OCT. 6, 1982	:
COMPLETION DATE	NOV. 24, 1982	:
PRICE PAID (IN MILLIONS)	15.5000	:
PREMIUM PAID (IN PERCENT)	0.0000	:
BETA VALUE OF ACQUIRING COMPANY BEFORE MERGER	0.8500	:
BETA VALUE OF ACQUIRED COMPANY BEFORE MERGER		:
BETA VALUE OF ACQUIRING COMPANY AFTER MERGER	1.0500	:

TABLE OF $g*$ VALUES (in percent)

USING HIGGINS' MODEL WITH CORPORATE TAX
& STABLE PRICES

$g*$ OF ACQUIRING COMPANY BEFORE MERGER	23.725308	:
$g*$ OF ACQUIRED COMPANY BEFORE MERGER	23.348307	:
$g*$ OF ACQUIRING COMPANY AFTER MERGER	11.509897	:

EXECUTIVE SUMMARY OF STATISTICS REGARDING MERGER

Using Higgins' Model With Corporate Tax & Stable Prices
(INSERT INFORMATION IN 'AS' COLUMN)

ACQUIRING COMPANY	GOLDEN WEST FINANCIAL CORP.	:
ACQUIRED COMPANY	FIRST S & L SHARES, INC.	:
ANNOUNCEMENT DATE	FEB. 2, 1982	:
COMPLETION DATE	JUNE 2, 1982	:
PRICE PAID (IN MILLIONS)	18.8000	:
PREMIUM PAID (IN PERCENT)	87.5000	:
BETA VALUE OF ACQUIRING COMPANY BEFORE MERGER	1.2500	:
BETA VALUE OF ACQUIRED COMPANY BEFORE MERGER		:
BETA VALUE OF ACQUIRING COMPANY AFTER MERGER	1.4500	:

TABLE OF g* VALUES (in percent)

USING HIGGINS' MODEL WITH CORPORATE TAX
& STABLE PRICES

g* OF ACQUIRING COMPANY BEFORE MERGER	-12.46991	:
g* OF ACQUIRED COMPANY BEFORE MERGER	2.948302	:
g* OF ACQUIRING COMPANY AFTER MERGER	48.019633	:

EXECUTIVE SUMMARY OF STATISTICS REGARDING MERGER

Using Higgins' Model With Corporate Tax & Stable Prices
(INSERT INFORMATION IN 'AS' COLUMN)

ACQUIRING COMPANY	SUN COMPANY	:
ACQUIRED COMPANY	EXETER OIL CO.	:
ANNOUNCEMENT DATE	NOV. 18, 1983	:
COMPLETION DATE	JAN. 11, 1984	:
PRICE PAID (IN MILLIONS)	75.6000	:
PREMIUM PAID (IN PERCENT)	196.9000	:
BETA VALUE OF ACQUIRING COMPANY BEFORE MERGER	1.1500	: :
BETA VALUE OF ACQUIRED COMPANY BEFORE MERGER		: :
BETA VALUE OF ACQUIRING COMPANY AFTER MERGER	1.2000	: :

TABLE OF g* VALUES (in percent)

USING HIGGINS' MODEL WITH CORPORATE TAX
& STABLE PRICES

g* OF ACQUIRING COMPANY BEFORE MERGER	5.42086 :
g* OF ACQUIRED COMPANY BEFORE MERGER	13.156702 :
g* OF ACQUIRING COMPANY AFTER MERGER	5.461592 :

EXECUTIVE SUMMARY OF STATISTICS REGARDING MERGER

Using Higgins' Model With Corporate Tax & Stable Prices
(INSERT INFORMATION IN 'AS' COLUMN)

ACQUIRING COMPANY	WARNACO, INC.	:
ACQUIRED COMPANY	OLGA COMPANY	:
ANNOUNCEMENT DATE	APRIL 5, 1984	:
COMPLETION DATE	JUNE 5, 1984	:
PRICE PAID (IN MILLIONS)	27.7000	:
PREMIUM PAID (IN PERCENT)	2.9000	:
BETA VALUE OF ACQUIRING COMPANY BEFORE MERGER	1.1500	: :
BETA VALUE OF ACQUIRED COMPANY BEFORE MERGER		: :
BETA VALUE OF ACQUIRING COMPANY AFTER MERGER	1.1000	: :

TABLE OF g* VALUES (in percent)

USING HIGGINS' MODEL WITH CORPORATE TAX
& STABLE PRICES

g* OF ACQUIRING COMPANY BEFORE MERGER	14.185133 :
g* OF ACQUIRED COMPANY BEFORE MERGER	29.012478 :
g* OF ACQUIRING COMPANY AFTER MERGER	6.244413 :

EXECUTIVE SUMMARY OF STATISTICS REGARDING MERGER

Using Higgins' Model With Corporate Tax & Stable Prices
(INSERT INFORMATION IN 'AS' COLUMN)

ACQUIRING COMPANY	DAMSON OIL CORP.	:
ACQUIRED COMPANY	DORCHESTER GAS CORP.	:
ANNOUNCEMENT DATE	JAN. 26, 1984	:
COMPLETION DATE	MAY 11, 1984	:
PRICE PAID (IN MILLIONS)	391.0000	:
PREMIUM PAID (IN PERCENT)	30.4000	:
BETA VALUE OF ACQUIRING COMPANY BEFORE MERGER		: :
BETA VALUE OF ACQUIRED COMPANY BEFORE MERGER		: :
BETA VALUE OF ACQUIRING COMPANY AFTER MERGER		: :

TABLE OF g* VALUES (in percent)

USING HIGGINS' MODEL WITH CORPORATE TAX
& STABLE PRICES

g* OF ACQUIRING COMPANY BEFORE MERGER	6.99997	:
g* OF ACQUIRED COMPANY BEFORE MERGER	1.443610	:
g* OF ACQUIRING COMPANY AFTER MERGER	12.969819	:

EXECUTIVE SUMMARY OF STATISTICS REGARDING MERGER

Using Higgins' Model With Corporate Tax & Stable Prices
(INSERT INFORMATION IN 'AS' COLUMN)

ACQUIRING COMPANY	TEXAS EASTERN CORP.	:
ACQUIRED COMPANY	PETROLANE CORP.	:
ANNOUNCEMENT DATE	JUNE 22, 1984	:
COMPLETION DATE	SEPT. 28, 1984	:
PRICE PAID (IN MILLIONS)	1044.5000	:
PREMIUM PAID (IN PERCENT)	66.7000	:
BETA VALUE OF ACQUIRING COMPANY BEFORE MERGER	1.0500	: :
BETA VALUE OF ACQUIRED COMPANY BEFORE MERGER	1.2000	: :
BETA VALUE OF ACQUIRING COMPANY AFTER MERGER	1.0000	: :

TABLE OF g* VALUES (in percent)

USING HIGGINS' MODEL WITH CORPORATE TAX
& STABLE PRICES

g* OF ACQUIRING COMPANY BEFORE MERGER	3.49896	:
g* OF ACQUIRED COMPANY BEFORE MERGER	1.929928	:
g* OF ACQUIRING COMPANY AFTER MERGER	-4.993291	:

EXECUTIVE SUMMARY OF STATISTICS REGARDING MERGER

Using Higgins' Model With Corporate Tax & Stable Prices
(INSERT INFORMATION IN 'AS' COLUMN)

ACQUIRING COMPANY	HOLLYWOOD PARK REALTY ENTER. INC.	:
ACQUIRED COMPANY	LOS ALAMITOS RACE COURSE CORP.	:
ANNOUNCEMENT DATE	JULY 30, 1984	:
COMPLETION DATE	AUG. 10, 1984	:
PRICE PAID (IN MILLIONS)	27.7000	:
PREMIUM PAID (IN PERCENT)	21.3000	:
BETA VALUE OF ACQUIRING COMPANY BEFORE MERGER		: :
BETA VALUE OF ACQUIRED COMPANY BEFORE MERGER		: :
BETA VALUE OF ACQUIRING COMPANY AFTER MERGER		: :

TABLE OF g* VALUES (in percent)

USING HIGGINS' MODEL WITH CORPORATE TAX
& STABLE PRICES

g* OF ACQUIRING COMPANY BEFORE MERGER	4.86614	:
g* OF ACQUIRED COMPANY BEFORE MERGER	-2.011038	:
g* OF ACQUIRING COMPANY AFTER MERGER	7.707324	:

```
          EXECUTIVE SUMMARY OF STATISTICS REGARDING MERGER
          -------------------------------------------------------
          Using Higgins' Model With Corporate Tax & Stable Prices
                    (INSERT INFORMATION IN 'AS' COLUMN)
```

```
--------------------------------------------------------------------
ACQUIRING COMPANY                  MINSTAR, INC.                    :
--------------------------------------------------------------------
ACQUIRED COMPANY                   AEGIS CORP.                      :
--------------------------------------------------------------------
ANNOUNCEMENT DATE                  APRIL 6, 1984                    :
--------------------------------------------------------------------
COMPLETION DATE                    NOV. 13, 1984                    :
--------------------------------------------------------------------
PRICE PAID (IN MILLIONS)           59.0000                          :
--------------------------------------------------------------------
PREMIUM PAID (IN PERCENT)          50.0000                          :
--------------------------------------------------------------------
BETA VALUE OF ACQUIRING                                             :
COMPANY BEFORE MERGER                                               :
--------------------------------------------------------------------
BETA VALUE OF ACQUIRED                                              :
COMPANY BEFORE MERGER                                               :
--------------------------------------------------------------------
BETA VALUE OF ACQUIRING                                             :
COMPANY AFTER MERGER                                                :
--------------------------------------------------------------------
```

```
                         TABLE OF g* VALUES (in percent)
                         ------------------------------
                   USING HIGGINS' MODEL WITH CORPORATE TAX
                              & STABLE PRICES
          ------------------------------------------------------
          g* OF ACQUIRING COMPANY BEFORE MERGER    110.05416 :
          ------------------------------------------------------
          g* OF ACQUIRED COMPANY BEFORE MERGER       8.436410 :
          ------------------------------------------------------
          g* OF ACQUIRING COMPANY AFTER MERGER      15.173393 :
          ------------------------------------------------------
```

EXECUTIVE SUMMARY OF STATISTICS REGARDING MERGER

Using Higgins' Model With Corporate Tax & Stable Prices
(INSERT INFORMATION IN 'AS' COLUMN)

ACQUIRING COMPANY	LIMITED STORES, INC.	:
ACQUIRED COMPANY	LANE BRYANT, INC.	:
ANNOUNCEMENT DATE	APRIL, 29, 1982	:
COMPLETION DATE	JUNE 1, 1982	:
PRICE PAID (IN MILLIONS)	105.7000	:
PREMIUM PAID (IN PERCENT)	52.6000	:
BETA VALUE OF ACQUIRING COMPANY BEFORE MERGER	1.4000	:
BETA VALUE OF ACQUIRED COMPANY BEFORE MERGER	0.9000	:
BETA VALUE OF ACQUIRING COMPANY AFTER MERGER	1.4500	:

TABLE OF $g*$ VALUES (in percent)

USING HIGGINS' MODEL WITH CORPORATE TAX
& STABLE PRICES

$g*$ OF ACQUIRING COMPANY BEFORE MERGER	32.25202	:
$g*$ OF ACQUIRED COMPANY BEFORE MERGER	6.686062	:
$g*$ OF ACQUIRING COMPANY AFTER MERGER	49.465930	:

EXECUTIVE SUMMARY OF STATISTICS REGARDING MERGER

Using Higgins' Model With Corporate Tax & Stable Prices
(INSERT INFORMATION IN 'AS' COLUMN)

ACQUIRING COMPANY	HOVANIAN ENTERPRISES, INC.	:
ACQUIRED COMPANY	CALTON, INC.	:
ANNOUNCEMENT DATE	SEPT. 12, 1984	:
COMPLETION DATE	OCT. 19, 1984	:
PRICE PAID (IN MILLIONS)	9.4000	:
PREMIUM PAID (IN PERCENT)	0.0000	:
BETA VALUE OF ACQUIRING COMPANY BEFORE MERGER		:
BETA VALUE OF ACQUIRED COMPANY BEFORE MERGER		:
BETA VALUE OF ACQUIRING COMPANY AFTER MERGER		:

TABLE OF g* VALUES (in percent)

USING HIGGINS' MODEL WITH CORPORATE TAX
& STABLE PRICES

g* OF ACQUIRING COMPANY BEFORE MERGER	26.60836	:
g* OF ACQUIRED COMPANY BEFORE MERGER	34.607885	:
g* OF ACQUIRING COMPANY AFTER MERGER	40.187145	:

EXECUTIVE SUMMARY OF STATISTICS REGARDING MERGER

Using Higgins' Model With Corporate Tax & Stable Prices
(INSERT INFORMATION IN 'AS' COLUMN)

ACQUIRING COMPANY	GENERAL HOST CORP.	:
ACQUIRED COMPANY	FRANK'S NURSERY & CRAFTS INC.	:
ANNOUNCEMENT DATE	JAN. 31, 1983	:
COMPLETION DATE	AUG. 23, 1983	:
PRICE PAID (IN MILLIONS)	44.0000	:
PREMIUM PAID (IN PERCENT)	1.3000	:
BETA VALUE OF ACQUIRING COMPANY BEFORE MERGER		:
BETA VALUE OF ACQUIRED COMPANY BEFORE MERGER		:
BETA VALUE OF ACQUIRING COMPANY AFTER MERGER		:

TABLE OF g* VALUES (in percent)

USING HIGGINS' MODEL WITH CORPORATE TAX
& STABLE PRICES

g* OF ACQUIRING COMPANY BEFORE MERGER	5.12702 :
g* OF ACQUIRED COMPANY BEFORE MERGER	12.6341 :
g* OF ACQUIRING COMPANY AFTER MERGER	13.4588 :

EXECUTIVE SUMMARY OF STATISTICS REGARDING MERGER

Using Higgins' Model With Corporate Tax & Stable Prices
(INSERT INFORMATION IN 'AS' COLUMN)

ACQUIRING COMPANY	DART & KRAFT, INC.	:
ACQUIRED COMPANY	HOBART CORP.	:
ANNOUNCEMENT DATE	FEB 18, 1981	:
COMPLETION DATE	APRIL 30, 1981	:
PRICE PAID (IN MILLIONS)	456.9000	:
PREMIUM PAID (IN PERCENT)	97.5000	:
BETA VALUE OF ACQUIRING COMPANY BEFORE MERGER	0.6500	: :
BETA VALUE OF ACQUIRED COMPANY BEFORE MERGER	0.8500	: :
BETA VALUE OF ACQUIRING COMPANY AFTER MERGER	0.6500	: :

TABLE OF $g*$ VALUES (in percent)

USING HIGGINS' MODEL WITH CORPORATE TAX
& STABLE PRICES

$g*$ OF ACQUIRING COMPANY BEFORE MERGER	9.604612 :
$g*$ OF ACQUIRED COMPANY BEFORE MERGER	9.234047 :
$g*$ OF ACQUIRING COMPANY AFTER MERGER	6.340763 :

EXECUTIVE SUMMARY OF STATISTICS REGARDING MERGER

Using Higgins' Model With Corporate Tax & Stable Prices
(INSERT INFORMATION IN 'AS' COLUMN)

ACQUIRING COMPANY	FABRI-CENTERS OF AMERICA, INC.:
ACQUIRED COMPANY	DISCOUNT FABRICS, INC. :
ANNOUNCEMENT DATE	JUNE 1, 1981 :
COMPLETION DATE	JUNE 30, 1981 :
PRICE PAID (IN MILLIONS)	3.6000 :
PREMIUM PAID (IN PERCENT)	107.1000 :
BETA VALUE OF ACQUIRING COMPANY BEFORE MERGER	1.1500 : :
BETA VALUE OF ACQUIRED COMPANY BEFORE MERGER	: :
BETA VALUE OF ACQUIRING COMPANY AFTER MERGER	: :

TABLE OF g* VALUES (in percent)

USING HIGGINS' MODEL WITH CORPORATE TAX
& STABLE PRICES

g* OF ACQUIRING COMPANY BEFORE MERGER	9.321961 :
g* OF ACQUIRED COMPANY BEFORE MERGER	8.276020 :
g* OF ACQUIRING COMPANY AFTER MERGER	14.583038 :

EXECUTIVE SUMMARY OF STATISTICS REGARDING MERGER

Using Higgins' Model With Corporate Tax & Stable Prices
(INSERT INFORMATION IN 'AS' COLUMN)

ACQUIRING COMPANY	SOUTHEASTERN PUBLIC SERVICE CO:	
ACQUIRED COMPANY	GRANITEVILLE CO.	:
ANNOUNCEMENT DATE	MAY 2, 1983	:
COMPLETION DATE	JULY 28, 1983	:
PRICE PAID (IN MILLIONS)	66.5000	:
PREMIUM PAID (IN PERCENT)	41.4000	:
BETA VALUE OF ACQUIRING COMPANY BEFORE MERGER		:
BETA VALUE OF ACQUIRED COMPANY BEFORE MERGER		:
BETA VALUE OF ACQUIRING COMPANY AFTER MERGER		:

TABLE OF g* VALUES (in percent)

USING HIGGINS' MODEL WITH CORPORATE TAX
& STABLE PRICES

g* OF ACQUIRING COMPANY BEFORE MERGER	0.106675	:
g* OF ACQUIRED COMPANY BEFORE MERGER	19.327257	:
g* OF ACQUIRING COMPANY AFTER MERGER	-0.038084	:

EXECUTIVE SUMMARY OF STATISTICS REGARDING MERGER

Using Higgins' Model With Corporate Tax & Stable Prices
(INSERT INFORMATION IN 'AS' COLUMN)

ACQUIRING COMPANY	MacANDREWS & FORBES GROUP, INC:
ACQUIRED COMPANY	TECHNICOLOR, INC. :
ANNOUNCEMENT DATE	NOV. 1, 1982 :
COMPLETION DATE	JAN. 25, 1983 :
PRICE PAID (IN MILLIONS)	99.9000 :
PREMIUM PAID (IN PERCENT)	38.3000 :
BETA VALUE OF ACQUIRING COMPANY BEFORE MERGER	:
BETA VALUE OF ACQUIRED COMPANY BEFORE MERGER	:
BETA VALUE OF ACQUIRING COMPANY AFTER MERGER	1.4000 :

TABLE OF g* VALUES (in percent)

USING HIGGINS' MODEL WITH CORPORATE TAX
& STABLE PRICES

g* OF ACQUIRING COMPANY BEFORE MERGER	35.557039 :
g* OF ACQUIRED COMPANY BEFORE MERGER	3.439735 :
g* OF ACQUIRING COMPANY AFTER MERGER	35.472228 :

EXECUTIVE SUMMARY OF STATISTICS REGARDING MERGER

Using Higgins' Model With Corporate Tax & Stable Prices
(INSERT INFORMATION IN 'AS' COLUMN)

ACQUIRING COMPANY	BORG-WARNER CORP.	:
ACQUIRED COMPANY	BURNS INTERNATIONAL SECURITY	:
ANNOUNCEMENT DATE	FEB. 28, 1982	:
COMPLETION DATE	JUNE 3, 1982	:
PRICE PAID (IN MILLIONS)	80.9000	:
PREMIUM PAID (IN PERCENT)	8.7000	:
BETA VALUE OF ACQUIRING COMPANY BEFORE MERGER	1.0500	:
BETA VALUE OF ACQUIRED COMPANY BEFORE MERGER	1.0500	:
BETA VALUE OF ACQUIRING COMPANY AFTER MERGER	1.0500	:

TABLE OF g* VALUES (in percent)

USING HIGGINS' MODEL WITH CORPORATE TAX
& STABLE PRICES

g* OF ACQUIRING COMPANY BEFORE MERGER	7.107543	:
g* OF ACQUIRED COMPANY BEFORE MERGER	7.949727	:
g* OF ACQUIRING COMPANY AFTER MERGER	8.604319	:

EXECUTIVE SUMMARY OF STATISTICS REGARDING MERGER

Using Higgins' Model With Corporate Tax & Stable Prices
(INSERT INFORMATION IN 'AS' COLUMN)

ACQUIRING COMPANY	NATIONAL SEMI-CONDUCTOR	:
ACQUIRED COMPANY	DATA TERMINAL SYSTEMS	:
ANNOUNCEMENT DATE	JAN 18, 1983	:
COMPLETION DATE	JUNE 2, 1983	:
PRICE PAID (IN MILLIONS)	45.7000	:
PREMIUM PAID (IN PERCENT)	-9.0000	:
BETA VALUE OF ACQUIRING COMPANY BEFORE MERGER	1.4500	:
BETA VALUE OF ACQUIRED COMPANY BEFORE MERGER	1.2500	:
BETA VALUE OF ACQUIRING COMPANY AFTER MERGER	1.4500	:

TABLE OF g* VALUES (in percent)

USING HIGGINS' MODEL WITH CORPORATE TAX
& STABLE PRICES

g* OF ACQUIRING COMPANY BEFORE MERGER	3.286327	:
g* OF ACQUIRED COMPANY BEFORE MERGER	34.226568	:
g* OF ACQUIRING COMPANY AFTER MERGER	11.507636	:

EXECUTIVE SUMMARY OF STATISTICS REGARDING MERGER

Using Higgins' Model With Corporate Tax & Stable Prices
(INSERT INFORMATION IN 'AS' COLUMN)

ACQUIRING COMPANY	NATIONAL DISTILLERS & CHEMICAL CO.	:
ACQUIRED COMPANY	SUBURBAN PROPANE GAS COMPANY	:
ANNOUNCEMENT DATE	JAN. 3, 1983	:
COMPLETION DATE	FEB. 22, 1983	:
PRICE PAID (IN MILLIONS)	269.3000	:
PREMIUM PAID (IN PERCENT)	34.2000	:
BETA VALUE OF ACQUIRING COMPANY BEFORE MERGER	0.9500	: :
BETA VALUE OF ACQUIRED COMPANY BEFORE MERGER	1.0000	: :
BETA VALUE OF ACQUIRING COMPANY AFTER MERGER	0.9500	: :

TABLE OF g* VALUES (in percent)

USING HIGGINS' MODEL WITH CORPORATE TAX
& STABLE PRICES

g* OF ACQUIRING COMPANY BEFORE MERGER	-0.148838	:
g* OF ACQUIRED COMPANY BEFORE MERGER	12.250609	:
g* OF ACQUIRING COMPANY AFTER MERGER	-2.615118	:

EXECUTIVE SUMMARY OF STATISTICS REGARDING MERGER

Using Higgins' Model With Corporate Tax & Stable Prices
(INSERT INFORMATION IN 'AS' COLUMN)

ACQUIRING COMPANY	CSX CORPORATION	:
ACQUIRED COMPANY	TEXAS GAS RESOURCES CORP.	:
ANNOUNCEMENT DATE	JUNE 8, 1983	:
COMPLETION DATE	SEPT. 20, 1983	:
PRICE PAID (IN MILLIONS)	1053.5000	:
PREMIUM PAID (IN PERCENT)	43.4000	:
BETA VALUE OF ACQUIRING COMPANY BEFORE MERGER	0.9500	:
BETA VALUE OF ACQUIRED COMPANY BEFORE MERGER		:
BETA VALUE OF ACQUIRING COMPANY AFTER MERGER	1.1000	:

TABLE OF g* VALUES (in percent)

USING HIGGINS' MODEL WITH CORPORATE TAX
& STABLE PRICES

g* OF ACQUIRING COMPANY BEFORE MERGER	8.061869	:
g* OF ACQUIRED COMPANY BEFORE MERGER	17.185014	:
g* OF ACQUIRING COMPANY AFTER MERGER	6.762450	:

EXECUTIVE SUMMARY OF STATISTICS REGARDING MERGER

Using Higgins' Model With Corporate Tax & Stable Prices
(INSERT INFORMATION IN 'AS' COLUMN)

ACQUIRING COMPANY	WILLIAMS COMPANIES	:
ACQUIRED COMPANY	NORTHWEST ENERGY CO.	:
ANNOUNCEMENT DATE	SEPT. 12, 1983	:
COMPLETION DATE	DEC. 12, 1983	:
PRICE PAID (IN MILLIONS)	711.2000	:
PREMIUM PAID (IN PERCENT)	45.8000	:
BETA VALUE OF ACQUIRING COMPANY BEFORE MERGER	1.2500	: :
BETA VALUE OF ACQUIRED COMPANY BEFORE MERGER	1.2500	: :
BETA VALUE OF ACQUIRING COMPANY AFTER MERGER	1.1500	: :

TABLE OF g* VALUES (in percent)

USING HIGGINS' MODEL WITH CORPORATE TAX
& STABLE PRICES

g* OF ACQUIRING COMPANY BEFORE MERGER	−0.133230 :
g* OF ACQUIRED COMPANY BEFORE MERGER	2.583715 :
g* OF ACQUIRING COMPANY AFTER MERGER	8.495867 :

EXECUTIVE SUMMARY OF STATISTICS REGARDING MERGER

Using Higgins' Model With Corporate Tax & Stable Prices
(INSERT INFORMATION IN 'AS' COLUMN)

ACQUIRING COMPANY	QUAKER OATS CO.	:
ACQUIRED COMPANY	STOKLEY-VAN CAMP	:
ANNOUNCEMENT DATE	JULY 18,1983	:
COMPLETION DATE	NOV.7, 1983	:
PRICE PAID (IN MILLIONS)	211.4000	:
PREMIUM PAID (IN PERCENT)	91.3000	:
BETA VALUE OF ACQUIRING COMPANY BEFORE MERGER	0.8500	: :
BETA VALUE OF ACQUIRED COMPANY BEFORE MERGER	0.7500	: :
BETA VALUE OF ACQUIRING COMPANY AFTER MERGER	0.7500	: :

TABLE OF g* VALUES (in percent)

USING HIGGINS' MODEL WITH CORPORATE TAX
& STABLE PRICES

g* OF ACQUIRING COMPANY BEFORE MERGER	9.990175	:
g* OF ACQUIRED COMPANY BEFORE MERGER	7.426092	:
g* OF ACQUIRING COMPANY AFTER MERGER	14.366247	:

```
        EXECUTIVE SUMMARY OF STATISTICS REGARDING MERGER
        -------------------------------------------------
        Using Higgins' Model With Corporate Tax & Stable Prices
                 (INSERT INFORMATION IN 'AS' COLUMN)


    --------------------------------------------------------------
    ACQUIRING COMPANY           R.J. REYNOLDS IND. INC.        :
    --------------------------------------------------------------
    ACQUIRED COMPANY            BEAR CREEK                     :
    --------------------------------------------------------------
    ANNOUNCEMENT DATE           OCT. 11, 1983                  :
    --------------------------------------------------------------
    COMPLETION DATE             JAN. 4, 1984                   :
    --------------------------------------------------------------
    PRICE PAID (IN MILLIONS)    74.1000                        :
    --------------------------------------------------------------
    PREMIUM PAID (IN PERCENT)   9.9000                         :
    --------------------------------------------------------------
    BETA VALUE OF ACQUIRING     0.9000                         :
    COMPANY BEFORE MERGER                                      :
    --------------------------------------------------------------
    BETA VALUE OF ACQUIRED                                     :
    COMPANY BEFORE MERGER                                      :
    --------------------------------------------------------------
    BETA VALUE OF ACQUIRING     0.9500                         :
    COMPANY AFTER MERGER                                       :
    --------------------------------------------------------------



                    TABLE OF g* VALUES (in percent)
                    -------------------------------
                USING HIGGINS' MODEL WITH CORPORATE TAX
                        & STABLE PRICES
        --------------------------------------------------------
        g* OF ACQUIRING COMPANY BEFORE MERGER   12.507013 :
        --------------------------------------------------------
        ġ* OF ACQUIRED COMPANY BEFORE MERGER     6.694703 :
        --------------------------------------------------------
        g* OF ACQUIRING COMPANY AFTER MERGER    21.561945 :
        --------------------------------------------------------
```

EXECUTIVE SUMMARY OF STATISTICS REGARDING MERGER

Using Higgins' Model With Corporate Tax & Stable Prices
(INSERT INFORMATION IN 'AS' COLUMN)

ACQUIRING COMPANY	BROWN-FORMAN DISTILLERS CORP.	:
ACQUIRED COMPANY	LENOX, INC.	:
ANNOUNCEMENT DATE	JUNE 9, 1983	:
COMPLETION DATE	AUG. 2, 1983	:
PRICE PAID (IN MILLIONS)	814.3000	:
PREMIUM PAID (IN PERCENT)	59.3000	:
BETA VALUE OF ACQUIRING COMPANY BEFORE MERGER	1.0000	:
BETA VALUE OF ACQUIRED COMPANY BEFORE MERGER		:
BETA VALUE OF ACQUIRING COMPANY AFTER MERGER	1.0000	:

TABLE OF g* VALUES (in percent)

USING HIGGINS' MODEL WITH CORPORATE TAX
& STABLE PRICES

g* OF ACQUIRING COMPANY BEFORE MERGER	20.360227	:
g* OF ACQUIRED COMPANY BEFORE MERGER	8.394794	:
g* OF ACQUIRING COMPANY AFTER MERGER	10.903360	:

EXECUTIVE SUMMARY OF STATISTICS REGARDING MERGER

Using Higgins' Model With Corporate Tax & Stable Prices
(INSERT INFORMATION IN 'AS' COLUMN)

ACQUIRING COMPANY	IBM CORPORATION	:
ACQUIRED COMPANY	ROLM CORPORATION	:
ANNOUNCEMENT DATE	JUNE 13, 1983	:
COMPLETION DATE	AUG. 1, 1983	:
PRICE PAID (IN MILLIONS)	227.8000	:
PREMIUM PAID (IN PERCENT)	-0.8000	:
BETA VALUE OF ACQUIRING COMPANY BEFORE MERGER	0.9500	: :
BETA VALUE OF ACQUIRED COMPANY BEFORE MERGER	1.3500	: :
BETA VALUE OF ACQUIRING COMPANY AFTER MERGER	1.0500	: :

TABLE OF g* VALUES (in percent)

USING HIGGINS' MODEL WITH CORPORATE TAX
& STABLE PRICES

g* OF ACQUIRING COMPANY BEFORE MERGER	13.384233	:
g* OF ACQUIRED COMPANY BEFORE MERGER	22.950980	:
g* OF ACQUIRING COMPANY AFTER MERGER	18.139674	:

EXECUTIVE SUMMARY OF STATISTICS REGARDING MERGER

Using Higgins' Model With Corporate Tax & Stable Prices
(INSERT INFORMATION IN 'AS' COLUMN)

ACQUIRING COMPANY	NORTEK, INC.	:
ACQUIRED COMPANY	JENSEN INDUSTRIES, INC.	:
ANNOUNCEMENT DATE	DEC. 19, 1984	:
COMPLETION DATE	MAR. 9, 1985	:
PRICE PAID (IN MILLIONS)	16.2000	:
PREMIUM PAID (IN PERCENT)	36.5000	:
BETA VALUE OF ACQUIRING COMPANY BEFORE MERGER	0.9500	: :
BETA VALUE OF ACQUIRED COMPANY BEFORE MERGER		: :
BETA VALUE OF ACQUIRING COMPANY AFTER MERGER	1.0500	: :

TABLE OF g* VALUES (in percent)

USING HIGGINS' MODEL WITH CORPORATE TAX
& STABLE PRICES

g* OF ACQUIRING COMPANY BEFORE MERGER	6.450852	:
g* OF ACQUIRED COMPANY BEFORE MERGER	19.310590	:
g* OF ACQUIRING COMPANY AFTER MERGER	10.479426	:

EXECUTIVE SUMMARY OF STATISTICS REGARDING MERGER

Using Higgins' Model With Corporate Tax & Stable Prices
(INSERT INFORMATION IN 'AS' COLUMN)

ACQUIRING COMPANY	TEXTRON, INC.	:
ACQUIRED COMPANY	AVCO CORP.	:
ANNOUNCEMENT DATE	DEC. 3, 1984	:
COMPLETION DATE	MAR. 1, 1985	:
PRICE PAID (IN MILLIONS)	1169.6000	:
PREMIUM PAID (IN PERCENT)	68.1000	:
BETA VALUE OF ACQUIRING COMPANY BEFORE MERGER	1.0000	:
BETA VALUE OF ACQUIRED COMPANY BEFORE MERGER	1.4500	:
BETA VALUE OF ACQUIRING COMPANY AFTER MERGER	1.0500	:

TABLE OF g* VALUES (in percent)

USING HIGGINS' MODEL WITH CORPORATE TAX
& STABLE PRICES

g* OF ACQUIRING COMPANY BEFORE MERGER	1.830692	:
g* OF ACQUIRED COMPANY BEFORE MERGER	6.596333	:
g* OF ACQUIRING COMPANY AFTER MERGER	12.746349	:

EXECUTIVE SUMMARY OF STATISTICS REGARDING MERGER

Using Higgins' Model With Corporate Tax & Stable Prices
(INSERT INFORMATION IN 'AS' COLUMN)

ACQUIRING COMPANY	AMERICAN CAN CO.	:
ACQUIRED COMPANY	VOYAGER GROUP	:
ANNOUNCEMENT DATE	JUNE 1, 1983	:
COMPLETION DATE	OCT. 19, 1983	:
PRICE PAID (IN MILLIONS)	44.1000	:
PREMIUM PAID (IN PERCENT)	-4.0000	:
BETA VALUE OF ACQUIRING COMPANY BEFORE MERGER	0.8500	:
BETA VALUE OF ACQUIRED COMPANY BEFORE MERGER		:
BETA VALUE OF ACQUIRING COMPANY AFTER MERGER	0.9000	:

TABLE OF g* VALUES (in percent)

USING HIGGINS' MODEL WITH CORPORATE TAX
& STABLE PRICES

g* OF ACQUIRING COMPANY BEFORE MERGER	-19.2723 :
g* OF ACQUIRED COMPANY BEFORE MERGER	0.546597 :
g* OF ACQUIRING COMPANY AFTER MERGER	4.386110 :

EXECUTIVE SUMMARY OF STATISTICS REGARDING MERGER

Using Higgins' Model With Corporate Tax & Stable Prices
(INSERT INFORMATION IN 'AS' COLUMN)

ACQUIRING COMPANY	PANTRY PRIDE, INC.	:
ACQUIRED COMPANY	ADAMS DRUG, INC.	:
ANNOUNCEMENT DATE	OCT. 3, 1984	:
COMPLETION DATE	DEC. 2, 1984	:
PRICE PAID (IN MILLIONS)	100.0000	:
PREMIUM PAID (IN PERCENT)	33.6000	:
BETA VALUE OF ACQUIRING COMPANY BEFORE MERGER	0.6500	: :
BETA VALUE OF ACQUIRED COMPANY BEFORE MERGER	0.9500	: :
BETA VALUE OF ACQUIRING COMPANY AFTER MERGER	0.7000	: :

TABLE OF g* VALUES (in percent)

USING HIGGINS' MODEL WITH CORPORATE TAX
& STABLE PRICES

g* OF ACQUIRING COMPANY BEFORE MERGER	30.261893 :
g* OF ACQUIRED COMPANY BEFORE MERGER	13.310155 :
g* OF ACQUIRING COMPANY AFTER MERGER	-3.901999 :

EXECUTIVE SUMMARY OF STATISTICS REGARDING MERGER

Using Higgins' Model With Corporate Tax & Stable Prices
(INSERT INFORMATION IN 'AS' COLUMN)

ACQUIRING COMPANY	MCDONNELL DOUGLAS, CORP.	:
ACQUIRED COMPANY	TYMSHARE, INC.	:
ANNOUNCEMENT DATE	FEB. 28, 1984	:
COMPLETION DATE	MAY 23, 1984	:
PRICE PAID (IN MILLIONS)	305.7000	:
PREMIUM PAID (IN PERCENT)	28.2000	:
BETA VALUE OF ACQUIRING COMPANY BEFORE MERGER	1.1000	: :
BETA VALUE OF ACQUIRED COMPANY BEFORE MERGER	1.2000	: :
BETA VALUE OF ACQUIRING COMPANY AFTER MERGER	1.1000	: :

TABLE OF g* VALUES (in percent)

USING HIGGINS' MODEL WITH CORPORATE TAX
& STABLE PRICES

g* OF ACQUIRING COMPANY BEFORE MERGER	6.507736	:
g* OF ACQUIRED COMPANY BEFORE MERGER	-0.900823	:
g* OF ACQUIRING COMPANY AFTER MERGER	11.488832	:

EXECUTIVE SUMMARY OF STATISTICS REGARDING MERGER

Using Higgins' Model With Corporate Tax & Stable Prices
(INSERT INFORMATION IN 'AS' COLUMN)

ACQUIRING COMPANY	OWENS-ILLINOIS, INC.	:
ACQUIRED COMPANY	HEALTH CARE RETIREMENT CORP. OF AMERICA	:
ANNOUNCEMENT DATE	SEPT. 5, 1984	:
COMPLETION DATE	DEC. 5, 1984	:
PRICE PAID (IN MILLIONS)	98.9000	:
PREMIUM PAID (IN PERCENT)	22.2000	:
BETA VALUE OF ACQUIRING COMPANY BEFORE MERGER	0.8500	:
BETA VALUE OF ACQUIRED COMPANY BEFORE MERGER		:
BETA VALUE OF ACQUIRING COMPANY AFTER MERGER	0.8000	:

TABLE OF g* VALUES (in percent)

USING HIGGINS' MODEL WITH CORPORATE TAX
& STABLE PRICES

g* OF ACQUIRING COMPANY BEFORE MERGER	1.639212	:
g* OF ACQUIRED COMPANY BEFORE MERGER	14.825147	:
g* OF ACQUIRING COMPANY AFTER MERGER	7.078360	:

EXECUTIVE SUMMARY OF STATISTICS REGARDING MERGER

Using Higgins' Model With Corporate Tax & Stable Prices
(INSERT INFORMATION IN 'AS' COLUMN)

ACQUIRING COMPANY	VF CORPORATION	:
ACQUIRED COMPANY	BASSET-WALKER, INC.	:
ANNOUNCEMENT DATE	OCT. 2, 1984	:
COMPLETION DATE	JAN. 8, 1985	:
PRICE PAID (IN MILLIONS)	290.0000	:
PREMIUM PAID (IN PERCENT)	19.6000	:
BETA VALUE OF ACQUIRING COMPANY BEFORE MERGER	0.8000	: :
BETA VALUE OF ACQUIRED COMPANY BEFORE MERGER		: :
BETA VALUE OF ACQUIRING COMPANY AFTER MERGER	0.9500	: :

TABLE OF g* VALUES (in percent)

USING HIGGINS' MODEL WITH CORPORATE TAX
& STABLE PRICES

g* OF ACQUIRING COMPANY BEFORE MERGER	20.51738	:
g* OF ACQUIRED COMPANY BEFORE MERGER	21.577657	:
g* OF ACQUIRING COMPANY AFTER MERGER	22.928770	:

EXECUTIVE SUMMARY OF STATISTICS REGARDING MERGER

Using Higgins' Model With Corporate Tax & Stable Prices
(INSERT INFORMATION IN 'AS' COLUMN)

ACQUIRING COMPANY	GULF WESTERN INDUSTRIES, INC.	:
ACQUIRED COMPANY	PRENTICE-HALL, INC.	:
ANNOUNCEMENT DATE	NOV. 6, 1984	:
COMPLETION DATE	DEC. 26, 1984	:
PRICE PAID (IN MILLIONS)	705.3000	:
PREMIUM PAID (IN PERCENT)	57.3000	:
BETA VALUE OF ACQUIRING COMPANY BEFORE MERGER	1.1000	: :
BETA VALUE OF ACQUIRED COMPANY BEFORE MERGER	0.8500	: :
BETA VALUE OF ACQUIRING COMPANY AFTER MERGER	1.1000	: :

TABLE OF $g*$ VALUES (in percent)

USING HIGGINS' MODEL WITH CORPORATE TAX
& STABLE PRICES

$g*$ OF ACQUIRING COMPANY BEFORE MERGER	-12.57532	:
$g*$ OF ACQUIRED COMPANY BEFORE MERGER	10.962634	:
$g*$ OF ACQUIRING COMPANY AFTER MERGER	9.050076	:

EXECUTIVE SUMMARY OF STATISTICS REGARDING MERGER

Using Higgins' Model With Corporate Tax & Stable Prices
(INSERT INFORMATION IN 'AS' COLUMN)

ACQUIRING COMPANY	U.S. GYPSUM CO.	:
ACQUIRED COMPANY	MASONITE CO.	:
ANNOUNCEMENT DATE	MAR. 27, 1984	:
COMPLETION DATE	MAY 16, 1984	:
PRICE PAID (IN MILLIONS)	377.9000	:
PREMIUM PAID (IN PERCENT)	17.8000	:
BETA VALUE OF ACQUIRING COMPANY BEFORE MERGER	0.9500	:
BETA VALUE OF ACQUIRED COMPANY BEFORE MERGER		:
BETA VALUE OF ACQUIRING COMPANY AFTER MERGER	0.9500	:

TABLE OF g* VALUES (in percent)

USING HIGGINS' MODEL WITH CORPORATE TAX
& STABLE PRICES

g* OF ACQUIRING COMPANY BEFORE MERGER	5.503033 :
g* OF ACQUIRED COMPANY BEFORE MERGER	5.031304 :
g* OF ACQUIRING COMPANY AFTER MERGER	20.515163 :

EXECUTIVE SUMMARY OF STATISTICS REGARDING MERGER

Using Higgins' Model With Corporate Tax & Stable Prices
(INSERT INFORMATION IN 'AS' COLUMN)

ACQUIRING COMPANY	DANA CORP.	:
ACQUIRED COMPANY	WARNER ELECTRIC BRAKE & CLUTCH:	
ANNOUNCEMENT DATE	DEC. 18, 1985	:
COMPLETION DATE	JAN. 25, 1985	:
PRICE PAID (IN MILLIONS)	156.7000	:
PREMIUM PAID (IN PERCENT)	15.4000	:
BETA VALUE OF ACQUIRING COMPANY BEFORE MERGER	0.8000	: :
BETA VALUE OF ACQUIRED COMPANY BEFORE MERGER		: :
BETA VALUE OF ACQUIRING COMPANY AFTER MERGER	1.0000	: :

TABLE OF g* VALUES (in percent)

USING HIGGINS' MODEL WITH CORPORATE TAX
& STABLE PRICES

g* OF ACQUIRING COMPANY BEFORE MERGER	4.969713 :
g* OF ACQUIRED COMPANY BEFORE MERGER	5.632328 :
g* OF ACQUIRING COMPANY AFTER MERGER	8.431287 :

EXECUTIVE SUMMARY OF STATISTICS REGARDING MERGER

Using Higgins' Model With Corporate Tax & Stable Prices
(INSERT INFORMATION IN 'AS' COLUMN)

ACQUIRING COMPANY	KANSAS POWER & LIGHT CO.	:
ACQUIRED COMPANY	GAS SERVICES CO.	:
ANNOUNCEMENT DATE	JULY 18, 1983	:
COMPLETION DATE	JAN. 10, 1984	:
PRICE PAID (IN MILLIONS)	68.4000	:
PREMIUM PAID (IN PERCENT)	52.4000	:
BETA VALUE OF ACQUIRING COMPANY BEFORE MERGER	0.6500	:
BETA VALUE OF ACQUIRED COMPANY BEFORE MERGER	0.6000	:
BETA VALUE OF ACQUIRING COMPANY AFTER MERGER	0.6500	:

TABLE OF g* VALUES (in percent)

USING HIGGINS' MODEL WITH CORPORATE TAX
& STABLE PRICES

g* OF ACQUIRING COMPANY BEFORE MERGER	3.902596 :
g* OF ACQUIRED COMPANY BEFORE MERGER	-2.456739 :
g* OF ACQUIRING COMPANY AFTER MERGER	5.991465 :

11

SUSTAINABLE GROWTH AND FIRM VALUATION

Growth is not a necessary or sufficient condition for an increase in shareholder value. Some firms with high growth have suffered financial distress. They have either been forced into bankruptcy or were acquired by another firm. Frequently these firms used excessive debt to support their growth. Their increased risk exposure led to distress when market forces shifted in a direction not suited to the firm. Some firms with high growth, however, have provided their shareholders with significant returns. These firms seem to have properly managed their growth and were able to take advantage of opportunities that existed in their markets or were able to expand into new markets.

Because it is possible for growth to lead to either increased or decreased value, it is important to focus on the factors that separate firms with balanced growth from those with unbalanced growth. Balanced growth results when the growth of the firm leads to an increase in shareholder value, whereas unbalanced growth results in the growth of the firm but not an increase in value.

The primary goal of the growth of the firm is the maximization of the market value of its stock. Effective management of the external and internal variables affecting growth that were discussed in the previous chapters should lead to stock maximization.

The external variables described in Chapter 1 that were related to the firm's growth included the growth of the markets in which the firm was operating and its market shares in these markets. The internal variables related to the firm's growth included its profit margin, retention ratio, ratio of assets to equity, and the ratio of sales to assets. Effective management of growth requires that the manager monitor the effects of the firm's growth on the value of these variables.

It is possible that the same growth rate may lead to increased or decreased shareholder value. The important issues that must be addressed are the effects of growth on the firm's market share and operating and financial performance measures, and not necessarily the growth rate per se. The purpose of this chapter is to develop a model that relates sales growth to the value of the firm. The model will integrate the external and internal variables affected by the firm's growth to the return earned by shareholders. Empirical evidence of the relations between growth and shareholder return will also be presented.

FIRM VALUATION: A STATIC ANALYSIS

It has frequently been asserted that the value of a firm is maximized at a growth rate that is less than the maximum growth it could attain. In a static analysis excessive growth leads to diminishing returns and exposes the firm to increased risk. Insufficient growth, on the other hand, results in foregone opportunities that may lead to increased risk in the long run.

Baumol (1962) and Herenden (1974) developed models that demonstrate that the growth that maximizes the value of the firm is less than the growth obtained by growth maximization. Although Baumol defines growth in terms of sales and Herenden focuses on asset growth, they both conclude that too much growth leads to reduced value.

The argument of these models is that the firm that attempts to maximize growth in a given period will experience diminishing returns. Beyond a certain point, further increases in growth will be accompanied by increasingly higher expenses. The proportionately higher expenses may be due to higher selling and administrative costs, overtime pay for labor, and additional waste as the firm approaches 100 percent fixed asset utilization. With expenses growing at a faster rate than revenues, a point will be reached where the firm's profits will be reduced as sales growth is increased.

Another expense that might increase with the growth of the firm is its interest payments. If the firm supports its growth with increased debt financing, its interest expense will increase. In Chapter 6 a model was developed that determined the firm's optimal sustainable growth. The optimal sustainable growth rate was defined as the sustainable growth that minimized the cost of capital and maximized the value of the firm. It was shown that the optimal sustainable growth occurred at a value less than the maximum possible sustainable growth.

As the firm increases its reliance on debt financing, its cost of capital initially falls, reaches a minimum, and then rises. Corresponding to its cost of capital, the value of the firm will initially rise, reach a maximum, and then eventually fall. However, the effect of additional leverage is to always increase the firm's sustainable growth. Consequently the cost of capital that maximizes the value of the firm is less than the cost of capital that maximizes its sustainable growth.

In sum, at a given point in time, the manager should not seek to maximize sales growth, since this will not lead to the maximum value of the firm. Proportionately higher operating expenses and higher leverage (risk) that will accompany too much growth will reduce the value of the firm to its shareholders.

FIRM VALUATION: A DYNAMIC ANALYSIS

From a strategic planning perspective, it might be more important to look at the long-term relation between growth and the value of the firm, which, through time, can be explained in terms of the external and internal variables affected by growth. The first step in depicting the relation between growth and value is to define the concept of the value of the firm. One measure of the value of the firm is the present value of the expected cash flows.

The firm's expected cash flows are typically defined as expected net income plus depreciation. Although this measure of cash flow does not include other cash flow components, such as the effects of changes in working capital, it will be used here because of its widespread acceptance and ease of measurement.

Finding the present value of the firm's expected cash flows entails discounting the flows by the shareholders' required rate of return. The shareholders' required rate of return is related to the perceived risk level of the firm as well as interest rates on other financial instruments. Assuming a constant discount rate for clarity of presentation, the value of the firm can be depicted by the following equation:

$$V_0 = \sum_{t=1}^{\infty} \{E[NI_t + DEP_t]\} / (1 + k)^t, \qquad (11.1)$$

where

$$V_0 = \text{value of the firm as of period 0;}$$

$$E[NI_t] = \text{expected net income for period } t;$$

$$E[DEP_t] = \text{depreciation expense for period } t; \text{ and}$$

$$k = \text{investor required rate of return.}$$

MARKET SHARE AND VALUE

It was demonstrated in Chapter 1 that the growth the firm attains during the planning period could be decomposed into the growth the markets were experiencing and the growth in market share. Because investors may not view these two effects in the same manner, it is possible that the same growth rate achieved by two firms may have different effects on the value of their stocks. It is important, therefore, to describe the effects of a firm's growth in terms of its effects on market share.

The sustainable growth models generally ignore the effects of growth on market share. It is implicitly assumed that the firm is not constrained by the external environment. For firms operating in perfectly competitive markets where there are a large number of buyers and sellers, each having a small portion of the industry output, this may be a reasonable assumption. However, for many firms that are operating in imperfectly competitive markets, the effects on market share of the firm's planned growth must be taken into consideration.

The effect of a change in market share on the value of the firm, as depicted by equation 11.1, will be to change the discount rate used to find the *present* value of the expected cash flows. A change in market share might signal to investors a change in the risk level of the firm; a different perceived risk associated with the expected cash flows will entail a revision in shareholders' required rate of return, k.

How the required rate of return changes will depend on the perceived probability of success of the firm's market share strategy. Buzzell, Gale, and Sultan (1975) classify market share strategies into three groups: building strategies, holding strategies, and harvesting strategies. Each strategy has implications for short- and long-term investment and profitability.

Bloom and Kotler (1975) claim that too high a market share can expose the firm to some unique risks: the target of complaints, demonstrations, and lawsuits from consumer and public interest organizations, and antitrust action from the government. They assert that risk is high for low market share firms, declines as market share increases, and increases again at a very high level. To the Buzzell, Gale, and Sultan strategies they add risk reduction for the firm with very large market shares. The risk reduction strategy includes public relations programs, competitive pacification, and diversification.

The recommended market share strategy—building, maintaining, or harvesting—is frequently described in terms of the expected growth of the markets in which the firm is operating. Four possibilities are presented in Exhibit 11.1: high market share–high growth (stars), high market share–low growth (cash cows), low market share–high growth (question

Exhibit 11.1
Traditional Growth Strategy

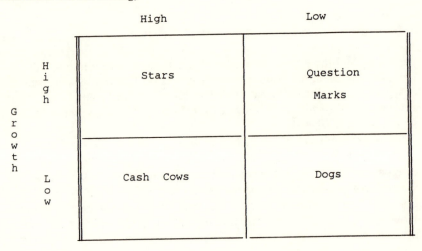

marks), and low market share–low growth (dogs). The traditional recommended strategy is to hold market share for the stars, harvest the cash cow, build the market share of the questions marks, and divest the dogs.

The maintenance strategy recommended for the stars assumes that the firm, if successful, will maintain the value of the firm, since the expected cash flows and required rate of return will probably remain constant. In terms of equation 11.1, since the expected cash flows, $E[NI_t + DEP_t]$, and required rate of return, K, are expected to remain constant, the value of the firm, V_0, will be maintained. The harvest strategy recommended for the cash cows assumes that the firm could invest the excess cash into different parts of the business or provide funds to engage in new businesses. If successfully invested, the diversification benefits would lower the required rate of return demanded by shareholders, k, thus raising the value of the firm, V_0. The strategy of building market share for the question marks assumes that the firm will be able to increase the expected cash flows, $E[NI_t + DEP_t]$, thus increasing the value of the firm. The strategy of divesting the dogs suggests that the value of the firm might be increased by diverting scarce firm resources to a potentially more profitable part of the business.

Unfortunately one cannot say that following the recommended market share strategy will always cause the value of the firm to increase. Malernee and Jaffe (1983), Govindarajan and Shank (1984), and Hax and Majluf (1983) point out that the recommended strategy ignores the financial consequences to the firm. There are numerous examples in which successful firms did not follow the recommended strategies because of the effects on the size and riskiness of their expected cash flows. These studies contend that the firm should integrate strategic and financial planning processes, since the market share strategies' implicit assumptions are not always appropriate.

EMPIRICAL RESEARCH ON MARKET SHARE

The empirical research focusing on market share has demonstrated that market share is positively related to profitability. Fruhan (1972) found that return on equity was positively related to market share for the domestic automobile manufacturers. In his study of the mainframe computer industry, he found that General Electric and RCA were unable to achieve their market share goals because the capital requirements exceeded their ability to generate funds. Thus, although they fell into the question mark category with respect to market share strategy, they did not follow the recommendation to build market share because of the prohibitive financial requirements.

Schoeffler, Buzzell, and Heany (1974) studied the effects of market share on return on investment, net income divided by equity, and long-term debt. They found that not only is return on investment positively related to market share, but also businesses with market shares greater than 36 percent averaged three times the return on investment of businesses with less than 7 percent market share.

Buzzell, Gale, and Sultan (1975) also found a positive relation between return on investment and market share. They offered three explanations for this result: economies of scale, exertion of market power, and quality management. Contrasting financial and operating ratios of firms with different market shares, they found four significant differences. First, profit margins increase sharply with increases in market share. Second, consistent with the argument of economies of scale and exerting market power, they found that the ratio of purchases to sales declines as market share increases. Third, and also consistent with the argument of economies of scale and exerting market power, is their result that the ratio of marketing costs to sales declines as market share rises. Fourth, businesses with high market shares were perceived to have products of a higher quality and tended to have higher prices for these products.

SUSTAINABLE GROWTH AND FIRM VALUATION

In Chapters 3 through 5 several sustainable growth models were presented that described the firm's growth in terms of financial and operating performance variables. Increases in these variables—profit margin, retention ratio, ratio of assets to equity, and the ratio of sales to assets—were shown to have a positive effect on the firm's sustainable growth. Although increases in each of these variables will cause an increase in the firm's growth, investors may not view increases in these variables in the same manner.

In Chapter 5 a sustainable growth model was presented in terms of operating and financial performance ratios. The model described is represented by equation 11.2. Because the model is used as a planning tool, the sustainable growth for any period t uses the values of the ratios as of the prior period.

$$g^*_t = P_{t-1}R_{t-1}A_{t-1}T_{t-1}/(1 - P_{t-1}R_{t-1}A_{t-1}T_{t-1}), \qquad (11.2)$$

where

g^*_t = sustainable growth for period t;

P_{t-1} = profit margin for period $t - 1$;

R_{t-1} = retention ratio = 1 − dividend payout;

A_{t-1} = assets divided by equity as of period $t - 1$; and

T_{t-1} = sales divided by assets as of period $t - 1$.

Using the data from Exhibits 11.2 and 11.3, the sustainable growth for My Ginger Baby, Inc., for 1987 will be equal to 11.11 percent.

Exhibit 11.2
My Ginger Baby, Inc., Consolidated Balance Sheet (Thousands of Dollars),
December 31, 1986

Assets		Claims	
Cash and Equivs.	$10000	Notes Payable	$30000
Accounts Receivable	20000	Accounts Payable	20000
Inventories	50000	Accruals	10000
Other Current Assets	10000	Total Current Liab.	$60000
Total Current Assets	$90000	Long Term Debt	50000
		Stockholders Equity	
		Paid in Common	30000
Net Fixed Assets	90000	Retained Earnings	105000
Other Assets	20000	Treasury Stock	-25000
		Cum. Translation Adj.	-20000
Total Assets	$200000	Total Claims	$200000

$$g^* = (.05)(.6)(2.222)(1.5)/[1 - (.05)(.6)(2.222)(1.5)]$$

$$= .09999/[1 - .09999]$$

$$= .1111 = 11.11\%$$

If the assumptions of the sustainable growth model are maintained, the firm's actual growth will be equal to 11.11 percent. Thus the firm's sustainable growth can be used as an estimate of its expected sales growth.

The sustainable growth for period t can be used to find the expected cash flow for period t. Expected net income can be determined by multiplying the firm's expected sales by its expected profit margin. Assuming the firm's sustainable growth measured with period $t-1$ data can be used as a proxy for expected growth during period t, the firm's expected sales for period t can be determined by multiplying the sales from period $t-1$ by $(1 + g^*_t)$. The firm's expected cash flows, therefore, can be defined in terms of equation 11.3, which states that the expected cash flow for any period t is based on the expected profit margin, the prior period's sales, sustainable growth, and depreciation.

Exhibit 11.3
My Ginger Baby, Inc., Consolidated Statement of Earnings (Thousand of Dollars), December 31, 1986

Net Sales	$300000
- Operating Expenses	-260000
- Depreciation	-5000
Net Operating Income	$35000
- Net Interest	-8000
Earnings Before Taxes	$27000
- Taxes	-12000
Net Income	$15000
- Dividends	-6000
Addition To Retained Earnings	$9000

profit margin	15000 / 300000	=	.05
dividend payout	6000 / 15000	=	.40
retention ratio	1 - .40	=	.60
assets / equity	200000 / 90000	=	2.22
sales / equity	300000 / 200000	=	1.50

$$E(CF_t) = E[(P_t)(S_{t-1}(1 + g^*_t)) + DEP_t] \qquad (11.3)$$

Thus the expected cash for period t as depicted by equation 11.3 can be substituted into equation 11.1, which described the value of the firm, V_0. The variables that affect the value of the firm include its expected profit margin, prior period's sales level, sustainable growth, expected depreciation, and the required rate of return demanded by investors.

The sustainable growth models assume that the expected profit margin for any period t is equal to the prior period's profit margin. The depreciation for any period t is related to the size of the fixed assets of the prior period and the fixed assets purchased during the period. Because the sustainable growth models assume that the ratio of sales to assets remains constant during the planning period, the expected depreciation can be related to the firm's sustainable growth. If the expected profit margin and depreciation are functionally related to sustainable growth, then the firm's expected cash flows for any period t can be described in terms of its sustainable growth, and thus the value of the firm.

The value of the firm as represented by equation 11.1 is somewhat cumbersome to use in practice. A more convenient measure of value for analytical purposes can be obtained by assuming that the firm will grow at a constant rate, g_e; that investors' required rate of return, k, is constant for all periods; and that k is greater than g_e. Given these assumptions, it can be shown that the value of the firm can be described by the following equation:

$$V_0 = \{E(NI_1 + DEP_1)\}/(k - g_e). \tag{11.4}$$

If the expected cash flow for period 1 can be defined in terms of the firm's sustainable growth, and if sustainable growth can be used as a proxy for expected growth, equation 11.4 can be redefined in terms of the following equation:

$$V_0 = [(P_0)(S_0) + DEP_0](1 + g^*)/(k - g^*). \tag{11.5}$$

Assuming that shareholders of My Ginger Baby, Inc., require a 15 percent rate of return, the value of the firm as of the end of 1986 is equal to $571260.

$$V_{1986} = [(.05)(300000) + (5000)](1 + .1111)/(.15 - .1111)$$

$$= 22222/.0389$$

$$= \$571260$$

If the firm's actual growth for period t is equal to its sustainable growth, the value of the firm will increase by the growth achieved by the firm. Exhibits 11.4 and 11.5 are constructed for My Ginger Baby, Inc., under the sustainable growth assumptions and the assumption that the firm's actual growth equals its sustainable growth. Using equation 11.5 we can find the value of the firm as of the end of 1987.

$$V_{1987} = [(.05)(333330) + (5555.5)](1.1111)/(.15 - .1111)$$

$$= 24690.864/.0389$$

$$= \$634727$$

Given the assumptions of our model, an equivalent way of finding the value of the firm for period t is to multiply the value of the firm as of period $t-1$ by $(1 + g^*)$. Using the data for My Ginger Baby, Inc., we obtain the same value of the firm for 1987 as above.

Exhibit 11.4
My Ginger Baby, Inc., Consolidated Balance Sheet (Thousands of Dollars),
December 31, 1987

Assets		CLAIMS	
Cash and Equivs.	$11111	Notes Payable	$33333
Accounts Receivable	22222	Accounts Payable	22222
Inventories	55555	Accruals	11111
Other Current Assets	11111	Total Current Liab.	$66666
Total Current Assets	$99999	Long Term Debt	55555
		Stockholders Equity	
		Paid in Common	30000
Net Fixed Assets	99999	Retained Earnings	114999
Other Assets	22222	Treasury Stock	-25000
		Cum. Translation Adj.	-20000
Total Assets	$222220	Total Claims	$222220

$$V_t = V_{t-1}(1 + g^*) \tag{11.6}$$

$$V_{1987} = V_{1986}(1 + g^*)$$

$$= (571260)(1.1111)$$

$$= \$634727$$

Exhibits 11.4 and 11.5 were based on the assumption that the firm would grow at its sustainable growth rate. And of course, it is implicitly assumed that the assumptions of the sustainable growth model are appropriate. Thus the value $634,727 can be viewed as an expected value of My Ginger Baby, Inc., for 1987, given information from 1986. For the actual value of My Ginger Baby, Inc., to be $634,727 requires that these assumptions be realized. If these assumptions are not realized, the actual value of the firm will not equal $634,727.

Suppose Exhibits 11.6 and 11.7 represented the actual balance sheet and income statements for My Ginger Baby, Inc., for 1987. Using equation 11.2 we can find the sustainable growth for 1988.

$$g^*_{1988} = (.053)(.6)(2.13)(1.47)/[1 - (.053)(.6)(2.13)(1.47)]$$

$$= .099569/(1 - .099569)$$

$$= .1106 = 11.06\%$$

Exhibit 11.5
My Ginger Baby, Inc., Consolidated Statement of Earnings (Thousands of Dollars), December 31, 1987

Net Sales	$333330
- Operating Expenses	-288886
- Depreciation	-5556
Net Operating Income	$38888
- Net Interest	-8889
Earnings Before Taxes	$29999
- Taxes	-13332
Net Income	$16667
- Dividends	-6668
Addition To Retained Earnings	$9999

profit margin	16667 / 333330	= .05
dividend payout	6668 / 16667	= .40
retention ratio	1 - .40	= .60
assets / equity	222220 / 99999	= 2.22
sales / assets	333330 / 222220	= 1.50

Substituting in the actual cash flow for 1987 and the new sustainable growth into equation 11.5, we can obtain a new value of the firm.

$$V_{1987} = [(.055)(339000) + 5556](1.11064)/(.15 - .1106)$$

$$= 24201(1.1106)/.0394$$

$$= \$682173$$

In this example the actual value of the firm at the end of 1987, $V_{1987} = \$682,173$, exceeded the expected value of the firm, $E(V_{1987}) = \$634,727$. The reason for the increase in value is that the firm was able to increase its profit margin while increasing its sales. The increase in the profit margin dominated the reduction in the use of leverage, as measured by the ratio of assets to equity, and the reduction in the total asset turnover, as measured by the ratio of sales to assets.

Exhibit 11.6
My Ginger Baby, Inc., Consolidated Balance Sheet (Thousands of Dollars),
December 31, 1987

Assets		Claims	
Cash and Equivs.	$15000	Notes Payable	$25000
Accounts Receivable	25000	Accounts Payable	30000
Inventories	58000	Accruals	20813
Other Current Assets	10000	Total Current Liab.	$75813
Total Current Assets	$108000	Long Term Debt	46000
		Stockholders Equity	
		Paid in Common	35000
Net Fixed Assets	102000	Retained Earnings	115780
Other Assets	20000	Treasury Stock	-25000
		Cum. Translation Adj	18000
Total Assets	$230000	Total Claims	$230000

Of course, the actual valuation of a firm is never quite as easy as any model might suggest. However, the examples point out several interesting aspects of the relation between growth and the value of the firm. The first is that the value of the firm could be expected to grow at the same rate as its sustainable growth if the assumptions of the model are realized and the actual growth equals the sustainable growth. Second, if the firm grows at a different rate than its sustainable growth or the assumptions of the model do not hold, the actual value of the firm would be different than the expected value.

At this point it might be useful to discuss the relation between actual growth and sustainable growth and actual firm value and expected value. A firm's actual growth, described in terms of operating and financial performance measures, can be represented by the following equation (see Appendix 11.1 for derivation):

$$g_t = [(P_t R_t A_t T'_t) + (e_{t-1}(y_t - y_{t-1}) + De_t(1 + y_t))T'_t/S_{t-1}]/$$

$$(1 - P_t R_t A_t T'_t), \tag{11.7}$$

where

g_t = actual growth for period t;

P_t = profit margin for period t;

A_t = assets/equity for period t;

Exhibit 11.7
My Ginger Baby, Inc., Consolidated Statement of Earnings (Thousands of Dollars), December 31, 1987

Net Sales	$339000
- Operating Expenses	-291728
- Depreciation	-5556
Net Operating Income	$41716
- Net Interest	-8300
Earnings Before Taxes	$33416
- Taxes	-15449
Net Income	$17967
- Dividends	-7187
Addition to Retained Earnings	$10780

profit margin	17967 / 339000	= .053
dividend payout	7458 / 18645	= .40
retention ratio	1 - .40	= .60
assets / equity	230000 / 108187	= 2.13
sales / assets	339000 / 230000	= 1.47

T'_t = change in sales/change in assets for period t;

e_{t-1} = the value of equity as of period $t - 1$;
y_t = total debt/equity for period t;

De_t = change in equity other than retained earnings during period t; and

S_{t-1} = sales for period $t - 1$.

Using the information for My Ginger Baby, Inc., presented in Exhibits 11.2, 11.3, 11.6, and 11.7, the actual growth in sales during 1987 is 13 percent.

$$g_{1987} = \{(.053)(.6)(2.13)(39000/30000) + \{(90000)[(122220/107780)$$

$$- (110000/90000)] + (7000)(1 + 122220/107780)\}((39000/30000))/$$

$$300000\}/[1 - (.053)(.6)(2.13)(39000/30000)]$$

$$g_{1987} = .13 = 13\%$$

As a check on the computation, we can find the growth in sales for 1987 by the following equation:

$$g_{1987} = (Sales_{1987} - Sales_{1986})/(Sales_{1986}) \tag{11.8}$$

$$= (339000 - 300000)/(300000)$$

$$= .13 = 13\%.$$

Although no one in his right mind would use equation 11.7 instead of equation 11.8 to compute the firm's actual growth in sales, equation 11.7 is useful to observe the effects of growth on the firm's operating and financial performance ratios. In particular, equation 11.7, which describes the firm's actual growth, can be contrasted to equation 11.2, which describes the firm's sustainable growth.

Common to both equations is the firm's profit margin, P. If profit margin increases as in the example, where it rose from .05 in 1986 to .053 in 1987, the firm's actual growth will exceed the sustainable growth. This will cause the actual cash flows to be greater than the expected cash flows and the actual value of the firm to be greater than the expected value of the firm.

Also common to both equations of growth is the firm's retention ratio, R. Because the retention ratio is equal to 1 minus the dividend payout ratio, a change in the retention ratio implies a change in the dividend payout. Although an increase in the retention ratio will result in actual growth exceeding sustainable growth, the effects of the value of the firm are subject to considerable debate.

Three positions have been postulated with respect to the relation between dividend policy (and implicitly the retention ratio) and the value of the firm: dividends do not affect the value of the firm; higher dividends (and thus a lower retention) will result in an increase in the value of the firm; and higher dividends will result in a lower value for the firm. Miller and Modigliani (1961), Fama and Miller (1972), and Black and Scholes (1974) support the irrelevancy of dividends argument. They argue that a higher dividend in the current period is offset by a lower dividend in a future period.

Gordon (1963) and Lintner (1962), however, argue that there is less risk associated with the receipt of a current dividend than the prospect of a higher future dividend. Investors, therefore, will prefer that the firm pay a higher dividend and that its value will be higher than those of other comparable firms with a lower dividend payment policy.

Litzenberger and Ramaswamy (1979) and Sharpe (1982) empirically investigated the relation between value and dividend policy. They found that high dividend yields are associated with high total yields after adjusting for risk, thus contradicting both the dividend irrelevance and bird-in-hand hypotheses. It appears that investors required a higher return from firms that paid a higher dividend. They speculated that since the tax rate on dividends is generally higher than the capital gains rate, investors required the higher return to offset the additional taxes.

Another variable common to both of the growth equations is the ratio of assets to equity, A. An increase in the value of A will cause actual growth to exceed sustainable growth and actual cash flows to exceed expected cash flows. The effect on the value of the firm, however, cannot be generalized, since an increase in A may also cause the discount rate used by investors to find the present value of the cash flows to change.

The discount rate, k, is related to the perceived risk level of the firm. One risk associated with the ownership of a firm is the risk of bankruptcy. Measures of this type of risk include the firm's ratio of assets to equity, A, and the ratio of total debt to equity, y.

A change in the ratio of total debt to equity is incorporated in the measure of actual growth as depicted by equation 11.7. Changes in this ratio are not included in the measure of sustainable growth described by equation 11.2, since it is assumed by the sustainable growth models that the debt-to-equity ratio would remain constant during the planning period. Because it can be shown that the ratio of assets to equity is equal to 1 plus the ratio of debt to equity, any change in the debt level can be represented by a change in A or y.

For low levels of debt, increases in A and y may be viewed favorably by investors, owing to the tax shield associated with debt, and the discount rate used may fall. Beyond a certain level, however, further increases in A and y may be viewed as increasing the probability of bankruptcy of the firm, and investors may require a higher return. Thus, although an increase in A and y will result in an increase in the cash flows of the firm, beyond a certain level further increases in A and y may cause investors to view the firm as being riskier and demand a higher return, k. In sum, we might expect that at low levels of debt, an increase in A and y will result in an increase in the value of the firm, since the cash flows will increase and the discount rate may decrease. At high levels of debt, however, the possible increase in the required rate demanded by investors may offset the increase in cash flow, thereby causing the value of the firm to decline.

Changes in the equity position of the firm other than retained earnings may also affect the discount rate used by investors. These changes include the issuance of new stock, purchase of treasury stock, and cumulative translation adjustments. Changes in these variables would be represented by the term De_t in equation 11.7. It should be noted the changes in these variables are not depicted in equation 11.2, since the sustainable growth models assume that they will not change during the planning period.

The issuance of new stock may decrease or increase the discount rate used by the original investors, depending on whether they expect the risk-return posture of the firm to be positively or negatively affected. If the issuance of new stock is viewed as reducing the risk posture of the firm, the required rate demanded by investors will decrease and the value of the firm increase. If the firm is not expected to earn a sufficient return with the proceeds, the issuance of new stock may be viewed as a dilution of the original wealth position of the shareholders. In this case the shareholders will impose a higher discount rate and the value of the firm will decline. The purchase of treasury stock may also change the discount rate, depending on the price paid by the firm to acquire the shares. The change in the cumulative translation adjustments account are equity adjustments for exchange rate movements of firms operating in international markets. For favorable exchange rate movements the investors of these firms might reduce their discount rate and increase the value of the firm.

The final variable to be considered is the ratio of sales to assets, T. The sustainable growth models assume that this ratio will remain constant throughout the planning period. If true, the term T' in equation 11.7, which is equal to the change in sales divided by the change in assets, will be equal to T. However, if the ratio of sales to assets changes during the planning period, T' will not equal T and actual growth will not equal sustainable growth. If the firm improves its asset turnover, $T' > T$, its actual cash flows will exceed its expected cash flow and the value of the firm will increase. Increases in asset turnover can be viewed as an improvement in the efficiency of the firm. The firm is deriving more sales per dollar invested in assets. One would expect that investors would view this event favorably and bid up the value of the firm.

Understanding the effect of growth on the value of the firm involves the determination of the actual growth rate and sustainable growth rate in terms of operating and financial performance measures. To this end we developed equations 11.7 and 11.2, respectively. A deviation between actual and sustainable growth is due to a change in one of the aforementioned operating or financial performance measures. We saw how changes in these measures might affect the value of the firm. To summarize, investors would prefer higher growth that was facilitated by an increase in the firm's profit margin, P_t, and the change in sales/change in assets, T_t'. Increases in these variables suggest improved operating efficiences and asset management. On the other hand, higher growth that was supported by an increase in the firm's relative amount of debt, as measured by A_t and Y_t, may not result in an increase in shareholder return. Beyond a certain level further increases in A_t and Y_t would result in increased risk.

The effects of the use of external equity, a component of DE_t, and higher retention ratios, R_t, to support the firm's growth may also be viewed negatively, at least in the short run, by investors. New equity may have the effect of diluting the wealth position of the original shareholders if the funds generated do not provide a sufficient return. Ghosh and Woolridge (1987) found that investors take a negative view, in the short run, of dividend reductions, and thus higher retention ratios, even when the stated objective is to finance growth.

FIRM VALUATION AND SHAREHOLDER RETURN

A difference between actual and expected value will result in a difference between actual and expected shareholder return. The expected return to a shareholder as of period 0 consists of an expected dividend yield and expected capital gain. The expected dividend and expected stock price are based on the value of the firm as of period 0, V_0, as determined by equation 11.1.

$$E(r_t) = [E(d_t) + E(p_t) - p_{t-1}]/p_{t-1}, \tag{11.9}$$

where

$E(r_t)$ = expected rate of return on the stock for period t;

$E(d_t)$ = expected dividend for period t;

$E(p_t)$ = expected stock price for period t; and

p_{t-1} = actual stock price for period t.

The actual return that the shareholder receives consists of the actual dividend yield and capital gain. The dividend and the ending stock price reflect the value of the firm as of period 1, V_1, as determined by equation 11.5.

$$r_t = [d_t + p_t - p_{t-1}]/p_{t-1}, \tag{11.10}$$

where

r_t = actual rate of return on the stock for period t;

d_t = actual dividend paid on the stock during period t; and

p_t = actual stock price value as of period t.

The relation between shareholder return and value is straightforward. Expected return is related to the expected value of the firm. The actual return earned by shareholders, however, is related to the actual value of the firm as of the end of the period. As with deviations between expected value and actual value, deviations between expected and actual return can be explained by changes in the variables affected by growth.

Two of the arguments of growth—the profit margin, P_t, and total asset turnover, T_t—were shown to positively affect growth and cash flows. An increase in these variables should lead to a higher than expected shareholder return. The other arguments of growth—the retention ratio, R_t, and the change in equity other than retained earnings, De_t—were also shown to be positively related to growth and cash flows. However, increases in these variables could also lead to increases in the discount rate used by investors. Thus increases in these variables may result in a lower than expected shareholder return if the increase in the discount rate more than offsets the increase in cash flow. It was also shown that the external effects of a firm's growth, a change in market share, might affect the discount rate of investors. An increase in market share, at least up to a certain level, could lead to a higher than expected shareholder return, owing to a decrease in the discount rate used by investors.

EMPIRICAL RESEARCH ON GROWTH AND SHAREHOLDER RETURN

The empirical research concerning sales growth generally focuses on the relation between growth and shareholder return. An early study by Nerlove (1968) found that the most important variables in explaining differences in rates of return over varying time periods were sales growth and earnings retention. A limitation of his study, however, was that no adjustment was made for risk.

The limitation was corrected by Stano (1976) in his study of growth versus return. He found shareholder return to be significantly related over varying time periods to sales and asset growth even when adjusting for risk. Elliot (1972), however, found no relation between shareholder return and sales growth using a three-way Analysis of Variance (ANOVA).

Consistent with Stano, Miedich and Melicher (1985) found in a cross-sectional study over various time periods a positive relation between return and sales growth. The study used models with and without beta as an explanatory variable. Miedich and Melicher assert that the evidence "contradicts the assumption that investors need not be concerned about the growth-return relationship in a risk-return framework, as held by Wood (1975) and others."

Miller (1987), however, argued that a firm's observed growth includes its anticipated and unanticipated growth. He states that "a problem with the Miedich and Melicher argument is that a correlation between returns and sales growth is to be expected if the returns are correlated with the amount of the unexpected growth. Thus, the Miedich and Melicher results are quite consistent with the capital asset pricing model." Although he asserts that their methodology is not appropriate for testing whether investors value growth more so than expected if the capital asset pricing model (CAPM) held, Miller contends that investors may indeed value past growth and overbid the price of growth stocks. In such a case the sign of growth in a modified CAPM would be negative.

In a study of the causal relation between unit sales volume and stock prices for the four domestic automobile firms, Edwards and Stansell (1983) found mixed results. The results were influenced by the measure used to test the causality (Haugh, Granger, or Sims) as well as the firm being tested.

Ghosh and Woolridge (1987) investigated the stock market reaction to growth-induced dividend cuts. They found that investors take a negative view of dividend cuts even if the stated purpose is to provide financing for future growth. The negative reaction continued for about six months, after which time the firms attaining growth outperformed the market by over 12 percent by the end of two years.

In sum, the present evidence between growth and shareholder return is mixed. The literature suggests that growth is either positively related to return or no relation exists between growth and return. For the studies that found a positive relation, it is possible that their samples consisted of firms that attained their growth by having higher profit margins or total asset turnovers. We saw that high values for these variables would lead to high return for the shareholders. For the studies that demonstrated no relation between growth and return, it is possible that their samples consisted of some firms that attained their growth at the expense of higher risk. The lower than expected return on these firms could have offset the higher than expected returns of firms that better managed their growth. Future research should focus on the components of the firm's growth that were described in this chapter to determine if we can separate firms that achieved high growth and high return from those that attained high growth but experienced a low return.

REFERENCES

Baumol, William. "On the Theory of Expansion of the Firm," *The American Economic Review*, December 1962, pp. 1078–1087.

Black, F., and M. Scholes. "The Effect of Dividend Yield and Dividend Policy on Common Stock Prices and Returns," *Journal of Financial Economics*, May 1974, pp. 1–22.

Bloom, P., and P. Kotler. "Strategies for High Market Share Companies," *Harvard Business Review*, November/December 1975, pp. 63–72.

Buzzell, R., B. Gale, and R. Sultan. "Market Share—A Key to Profitability." *Harvard Business Review*, January/Feburary 1975, pp. 97–106.

Edwards, C. E., and S. R. Stansell. "New Car Sales Data and Automobile Company Stock Prices: A Study of the Causal Relationships." *Business Economics*, May 1983, pp. 27–35.

Elliott, J. W. "Control, Size, Growth, and Financial Performance in the Firm." *Journal of Financial and Quantitative Analysis*, January 1972, pp. 1309–1320.

Fama, E., and M. Miller. *The Theory of Finance*. Hinsdale, Ill.: Dryden Press, 1972.

Fruhan, William E. "Pyrrhic Victories in Fight for Market Share," *Harvard Business Review*, September/October 1972, pp. 100–107.

Ghosh, C., and J.R. Woolridge. "Stock Market Reaction to Growth-induced Dividend Cuts: Are Investors Myopic?" presented at the 1987 annual meetings of the Eastern Finance Association.

Gordon, Myron. "Optimal Investment and Financing Policy." *Journal of Finance*, May 1963, pp. 264–272.

Govindarajan, V., and John K. Shank. "Cash Sufficiency: The Missing Link in Strategic Planning." *Corporate Accounting*, Winter 1984, pp. 23–31.

Hax, A. C., and N. S. Majluf. "The Use of the Growth-Share Matrix in Strategic Planning." *Interfaces*, February 1983, pp. 46–60.

Herenden, James B. "Alternative Models of the Corporate Enterprise: Growth Maximization and Value Maximization," *Quarterly Review of Economics and Business*, Winter 1974, pp. 59–75.

Lintner, John. "Dividends, Earnings, Leverage, Stock Prices, and the Supply of Capital to Corporations." *Review of Economics and Statistics*, August 1962, pp. 243–269.

Litzenberger, R., and K. Ramaswamy. "The Effect of Personal Taxes and Dividends on Capital Asset Prices." *Journal of Financial Economics*, June 1979, pp. 163–196.

Malernee, J. K., and G. Jaffe. "An Integrative Approach to Strategic and Financial Planning." *Managerial Planning*, January/February 1983, pp. 35–43.

Miedich, S. J., and R. W. Melicher. "Corporate Sales Growth Rates and Stockholder Returns: A Risk-Return Market Analysis." *Review of Business and Economic Research*. Spring 1985, pp. 35–43.

Miller, Edward. "Growth and Shareholder Returns: A Comment on Miedich and Melicher." *Review of Business and Economic Research*, Spring 1987, pp. 77–84.

Miller, M., and F. Modigliani. "Dividend Policy, Growth, and the Valuation of Shares." *Journal of Business*, October 1961, pp. 411–433.

Nerlove, Marc. "Factors Affecting Differences Among Rates of Return on Investments in Individual Common Stocks." *Review of Economics and Statistics*, August 1968, pp. 312–328.

Schoeffler, S., R. Buzzell, and D. Heany. "Impact of Strategic Planning on Profit Performance." *Harvard Business Review*, March/April 1974, pp. 137–145.

Sharpe, William. "Factors in New York Stock Exchange Security Returns, 1931–1979," *Journal of Portfolio Management*, Summer 1982, pp. 5–19.

Stano, Miron. "Monopoly Power, Ownership Control, and Corporate Performance." *Bell Journal of Economics*, Autumn 1976, pp. 672–679.

Wood, Adrian. *A Theory of Profits*. London: Cambridge Unviersity Press, 1975.

APPENDIX 11.1
DERIVATION OF ACTUAL GROWTH IN TERMS OF OPERATING AND FINANCIAL PERFORMANCE RATIOS

NOTATION

c_t = cash as of period t

r_t = accounts receivable as of period t

i_t = inventory as of period t

o_{ct} = other current assets as of period t

f_t = fixed assets as of period t

o_{ft} = other fixed assets as of period t

a_t = accounts payable as of period t

n_t = notes payable as of period t

o_{Lt} = other liabilities as of period t

L_t = long term debt as of period t

$e_{t-1} + De + P_t S_t(1 - d_t)$ = equity as of period t

e_{t-1} = equity as of period $t - 1$

De_t = change in equity other than retained earnings during period t

y_t = total debt$_t$/equity$_t$

y_{t-1} = total debt$_{t-1}$/equity$_{t-1}$

$G_{dt} = (y_t - y_{t-1})/y_{t-1}$ = growth in ratio of total debt to equity during period t

P_t = profit margin as of period t

d_t = dividend payout as of period t

$R_t = (1 - d_t)$ = retention ratio as of period t

$A_t = (1 + y_t)$ = (equity$_t$ + total debt$_t$)/equity$_t$ = assets$_t$/equity$_t$

T_t = sales$_t$/assets$_t$

T'_t = change in sales/change in total assets

S_{t-1} = sales as of period $t - 1$

S_t = sales as of period t

Ds_t = change in sales during period t

g_t = actual growth rate in sales during period t

g^*_t = sustainable growth rate for period t

By definition, the value of the assets as of period t must equal the value of the claims as of period t:

$$(c_t + r_t + i_t + o_{ct}) + (f_t + o_{ft}) = (a_t + n_t + o_{Lt}) + L_t + [e_{t-1} + De_t$$

$$+ P_t S_t(1 - d_t)]. \qquad (11.1A)$$

Assuming that the firm wants to achieve or maintain a target financial structure, y_t, equation 11.1A can be rewritten as

$$(c_t + r_t + i_t + o_{ct}) + (f_t + o_{ft}) = [e_{t-1} + De_t + P_t S_t(1 - d_t)](1 + y_t).$$

Solving for next period's sales, S_t, yields the following equation:

$$S_t = [(c_t + r_t + i_t + o_{ct} + f_t + o_{ft}) - (e_{t-1} + De_t)(1 + y_t)]/$$

$$P_t(1 - d_t)(1 + y_t). \qquad (11.2A)$$

A firm's growth in sales can be defined as

$$g_t = (S_t - S_{t-1})/S_{t-1} = (S_t/S_{t-1}) - 1. \qquad (11.3A)$$

Substituting equation 11.2A into equation 11.3A yields equation 11.4A, the firm's growth rate assuming a target capital structure.

$$g_t = \{[(c_t + r_t + i_t + o_{ct} + f_t + o_{ft}) - (e_{t-1} + De_t)(1 + y_t)]/$$

$$P_t(1 - d_t)(1 + y_t)S_{t-1}\} - 1 \qquad (11.4A)$$

Using the actual values of the variables of the right-hand side of equation 11.4A yields the firm's actual growth rate in sales. However, to define actual growth in terms of operating and financial performance ratios, equation 11.4A must be modified.

The expression $(e_{t-1} + De_t)(1 + y_t)$ from equation 11.4A refers to the equity as of period $t - 1$ and the change in equity other than retained earnings multiplied by 1 plus the ratio of total debt to equity as of period t. This expression can be restated in terms of the debt-equity ratio as of period $t - 1$.

$$(e_{t-1} + De_t)(1 + y_t) = (e_{t-1} + De_t)[1 + y_{t-1}(1 + G_{dt})]$$

$$= e_{t-1}(1 + y_{t-1}) + e_{t-1}y_{t-1}G_{dt} + De_t(1 + y_t)$$

$$= e_{t-1}(1 + y_{t-1}) + e_{t-1}(y_t - y_{t-1}) + De_t(1 + y_t) \qquad (11.5A)$$

The first expression on the right-hand side of equation 11.5A is equivalent to the size of the firm's assets as of period $t - 1$. Substituting equation 11.5A into equation 11.4A and rearranging terms yields equation 11.6A, which states that the change in assets must be equal to the change in claims.

$$[(c_t + r_t + i_t + o_{ct} + f_t + o_{ft}) - e_{t-1}(1 + y_{t-1})] =$$

$$[P_t(1 - d_t)(1 + y_t)]S_t + e_{t-1}(y_t - y_{t-1}) + De_t(1 + y_t) \quad \text{(11.6A)}$$

Redefining equation 11.6A in terms of operating and financial ratios and solving in terms of the change of sales yields the following equation:

$$Ds_t/T'_t = (P_t R_t A_t)(S_{t-1} + Ds_t)$$

$$+ e_{t-1}(y_t - y_{t-1}) + De_t(1 + y_t)$$

$$Ds_t = (P_t R_t A_t T'_t)(S_{t-1} + Ds_t) + [e_{t-1}(y_t - y_{t-1})$$

$$+ De_t(1 + y_t)]T'_t$$

$$Ds_t - (P_t R_t A_t T'_t)(DS_t) = (P_t R_t A_t T'_t)(S_{t-1}) + [e_{t-1}(y_t - y_{t-1})$$

$$+ De_t(1 + y_t)]T'_t$$

$$Ds_t(1 - P_t R_t A_t T'_t) = (P_t R_t A_t T'_t) S_{t-1} + [e_{t-1}(y_t - y_{t-1})$$

$$+ De_t(1 + y_t)] T'_t$$

$$Ds_t = [(P_t R_t A_t T'_t) S_{t-1} + (e_{t-1}(y_t - y_{t-1})$$

$$+ De_t(1 + y_t))T'_t]/(1 - P_t R_t A_t T'_t) \quad \text{(11.7A)}$$

Combining equations 11.3A and 11.7A yields equation 11.8A, which describes the firm's actual growth rate in sales in terms of operating and financial ratios. Equation 11.8A is equivalent to equation 11.7 in the chapter.

$$g_t = [(P_t R_t A_t T'_t) + (e_{t-1}(y_t - y_{t-1}) + De_t(1 + y_t))T'_t/S_{t-1}]/$$

$$(1 - P_t R_t A_t T'_t) \quad \text{(11.8A)}$$

INDEX

ABOUT THE AUTHORS

JOHN J. CLARK is Royal H. Gibson, Sr., Professor of Finance, and Director of Graduate Studies at Drexel University. His previous books include *Business Merger and Acquisition Strategies, Statistics for Managers,* and *The Lease-Buy Decision.*

THOMAS C. CHIANG is Associate Professor of Finance at Drexel University. His numerous articles in finance, business, and economics have appeared in such publications as *Journal of Money, Credit, and Banking, Quarterly Review of Economics and Business, Financial Review,* and *Journal of Financial Research.*

GERARD T. OLSON is Assistant Professor of Finance at Villanova University. He has consulted with many firms about the effective management of their growth.